DREAM
REVISIONARIES

DREAM REVISIONARIES

*Gender and Genre in
Women's Utopian Fiction*

1870–1920

Darby Lewes

THE UNIVERSITY OF ALABAMA PRESS

Tuscaloosa and London

Copyright © 1995

THE UNIVERSITY OF ALABAMA PRESS

Tuscaloosa, Alabama 35487-0380

All rights reserved

Manufactured in the

United States of America

DESIGNED BY ERIN T. BRADLEY

∞

The paper on which this book is printed

meets the minimum requirements

of American National Standard

for Information Science-Permanence of Paper

for Printed Library Materials,

ANSI Z39.48–1984.

Library of Congress Cataloging-in-Publication Data

Lewes, Darby, 1946–
Dream revisionaries: gender and genre in women's utopian fiction,
1870–1920 / Darby Lewes.
p. cm.
Includes bibliographical references (p.) and index.
ISBN 0-8173-0795-8 (alk. paper)
1. Fantastic fiction, English—Women authors—History and
criticism.   2. Utopias in literature.   3. Science fiction, English—
Women authors —History and criticism.   4. American fiction—Women
authors—History and criticism.   5. English fiction—19th century—
History and criticism.   6. English fiction—20th century—History
and criticism.   7. Sex role in literature.   8. Women and literature.
9. Literary form.   I. Title.
PR830.U7L4   1995
823'.0876609372—dc20   94-40947
                                                                 CIP

British Library Cataloguing-in-Publication Data available

FOR BOBBY, WHO BELIEVES

CONTENTS

ACKNOWLEDGMENTS

This project originated in James Chandler's and Elizabeth Helsinger's 1989 History and Culture workshop on "Utopia and Literature" at the University of Chicago. It was funded primarily by a Woodrow Wilson Foundation Charlotte A. Newcombe Dissertation Year Fellowship and was supplemented by an honorary Whiting Dissertation Year Fellowship (awarded by the University of Chicago) and a Lycoming College Loring B. Priest Research Grant. It was facilitated by the extraordinary patience, support, and guidance of my advisors, W. J. T. Mitchell and Elizabeth Helsinger. Tremendous support was also provided by utopian scholars, especially Marleen Barr, Lucy Friebert, Carol Farley Kessler, Lee Cullen Khanna, Carol Kolmerton, Vara Neverow, Kenneth Roemer, and Lyman Tower Sargent.

In any study of relatively obscure texts, libraries and librarians can make or break the project. I wish to acknowledge the assistance of the Bodleian Library, the British Library, the University of Illinois Special Collections, and the Newberry Library. I am also thankful for Arthur O. Lewis's magnificent collection of utopian literature, housed in the Pattee Library at Penn State University and tended by Charles Mann and Sandy Stelts. Many of the works in this study would have been impossible to locate and recover without the skill and tenacity of Sandy Appleton of the University of Chicago's Regenstein Library Interlibrary Loan. I will also forever be indebted to the bulldog persistence and detective work of Susan Beidler, Janet Hurlbert, and Marlene Neece of Lycoming College's Snowden Library.

The prose would have been far bumpier without the help of Bobby Stiklus, whose elegant editing always made my words come out right. Thanks also to the anonymous readers who reviewed the manuscript and made many useful suggestions. Several crucial texts were available for close analysis only because of the weeks Kimberley Lewes-Gray spent in front of photocopiers and microfilm duplication machines. My research assistant, Melanie Harris, helped shepherd the project (and me) through the final stages of revision. And my family has encouraged, rallied, bullied, cheered, and consoled me throughout this lengthy process; I will be forever grateful for their generosity, tolerance, hugs, and hot meals.

Finally, I wish to thank the following publishers for generously granting me permission to use extended quotations from their publications: excerpts from *Frontierswomen: The Iowa Experience* by Glenda Riley, copyright © 1981 by Iowa State University Press; excerpts from *A Sex Revolution* by Lois Waisbrooker, copyright © 1985 by New Society Publishers; excerpts from *Lest Ye Die* reprinted with the permission of Charles Scribner's Sons, an imprint of Macmillan Publishing Company from *Lest Ye Die* by Cicely Hamilton, copyright 1928 Charles Scribner's Sons; excerpts from Darby Lewes, "Nudes from Nowhere: Pornography, Empire, and Utopia," *Utopian Studies* 4, no. 2 (1993): 66–73, reproduced by permission of *Utopian Studies;* and excerpts from Darby Lewes, "Middle-Class Edens: Women's Nineteenth-Century Utopian Fiction and the Bourgeois Ideal," *Utopian Studies* 4, no. 1 (1993): 14–25, reproduced by permission of *Utopian Studies*; and excerpts from Darby Lewes, "Gynotopia: A Checklist of Nineteenth-Century Utopias by American Women," *Legacy* 6, no. 2:29–41, copyright 1989 by The Pennsylvania State University, reproduced by permission of The Pennsylvania State University Press.

DREAM
REVISIONARIES

Dream Revisionaries

In his celebrated essay "The Subjection of Women" (1869), John Stuart Mill argued that society places "too much faith in custom" and that "unnatural generally means only uncustomary" (441). If only, he lamented, "there had been a society of men and women in which the women were not under the control of the men, something might have been positively known about the mental and moral differences which may be inherent in the nature of each" (451). Yet, even as he wrote these words, "if-only" societies existed—if only in the hypothetical worlds of women's utopian fiction. Between 1869 and 1920, amid a general increase in women's writing, there was a sudden efflorescence of utopian narratives. More than a hundred texts of astonishing diversity appeared: profeminist and antifeminist,[1] socialist and capitalist; placed in Kentucky or London, at the North Pole, or on Mars; set in the past, present, future, or outside time altogether.

Although frequently witty and entertaining, these texts are not "great literature," at least not according to canonical criteria. The genre's mingled goals of storytelling and polemic have never been conducive to the production of acceptable "masterpieces," and even such celebrated utopian fictions as More's *Utopia* (1516) and Bellamy's *Looking Backward* (1888) are occasionally clogged with tedious debate and cramped by awkward phraseology, which, as Frances Bartowski (1989, 9) points out, "are just those aspects by which literary critics have often deemed it a marginal kind of fiction—a crossbreed of tract made palatable as literature through a poorly and hastily constructed romance." These generic handicaps are exacerbated in much of women's nineteenth-century texts: many are encumbered with laborious dialogue, episodic plot structure, and cardboard characters. Yet stylistic shortcomings do not inevitably affect literary worth; many critics have challenged the use of literariness as a reliable gauge of a text's intrinsic "value" (a term disturbingly linked to market exchange).[2] Certainly, the "value" of even the most painfully amateurish of these narratives is incalculable, for they provide insight into how a homogeneous group of women (sharing not only gender but language, race, and middle-class status as well)[3] at a particular historical moment imagined what men and women might be like in *un*customary societies. In doing so, these authors provide alternatives to the historically central male vision, probe a segment of the human condition not generally available to modern readers, and supply remarkably detailed insights as to what women like themselves felt their lives lacked. They articulate the yearnings and hopes of liminal outsiders, borderlined between the centrality of their race and class and the otherness of their gender, between the security of their homes and the peril of their enforced privatization, between centuries of a patriarchal past and tantalizing glimpses of an egalitarian future.

Yet, because these works do not conform to canonical notions of "great literature" and because their social agenda remains unfulfilled, they have been largely forgotten or ignored.[4] All are currently out of print, only a handful have been reprinted within the last two decades, and many survive today only as microfilmed curiosities.[5] Until quite recently, they have attracted virtually no critical notice. Frank and Fritzie Manuel's monumental *Utopian Thought in the Western World* makes no reference to any nineteenth-century utopia by a woman; indeed, the authors' only mention of a female utopist occurs in an assertion that Margaret Cavendish's "Blazing World" (1666) borders on schizophrenia and "has much in common with the delusions of Dr. Schreiber analyzed by Sigmund Freud in a famous paper" (Manuel 1979, 7).[6] Krishan Kumar devotes two full chapters of *Utopia and Anti-Utopia in Modern Times* (1987) to nineteenth-century utopian writing in Europe and America but makes no mention of any text by a woman. This critical disregard seems widespread: one can search for references to women's narratives in the work of such noted utopian scholars as Marie Louise Bernari, George Kateb, Karl Mannheim, Arthur Morgan, or Lewis Mumford to no avail.

Nineteenth-century women's utopian writing might have been lost altogether were it not for the efforts of recent feminist and utopian scholars. Reprints of several long-forgotten texts have helped generate curiosity about the remainder: Ann Lane's 1979 edition of Charlotte Perkins Gilman's *Herland* (1915), Carol Farley Kessler's *Daring to Dream* (1984), Pam McAllister's 1985 edition of Lois Waisbrooker's *A Sex Revolution* (1894), and Carol Kolmerten's 1991 edition of Alice Ilgenfritz Jones and Ella Merchant's *Unveiling a Parallel* (1893) have disentombed narratives that were unavailable for decades. Several useful bibliographies have also appeared: Carol Farley Kessler's "Notes toward a Bibliography: Women's Utopian Writing, 1836–1899" (1985) and "Bibliography of Utopian Fiction by United States Women, 1836–1988" (1990); Daphne Patai's "British and American Utopias by Women (1836–1979)" (1981); Kenneth M. Roemer's bibliographies in *The Obsolete Necessity: America in Utopian Writings, 1888–1900* (1976); and Lyman Tower Sargent's monumental *British and American Utopian Literature, 1516–1985* (1988).

Critical response to nineteenth-century women's utopias began to appear as early as 1977, when Carol Pearson's "Coming Home: Four Feminist Utopias and Patriarchal Experience" compared nineteenth- and twentieth-century utopias by women and discovered "surprisingly numerous areas of consensus," which she attributed to "the similar experiences and conditioning women share" (63). In 1981, Barbara Quissell's "The New World That Eve Made" examined eleven utopian texts by nineteenth-century American women, arguing that the views presented were "at once more fundamentally radical and more idiosyncratic than the issues debated by other nineteenth-century feminists" (149).[7] In 1983, Lucy Friebert examined *Herland* and three modern feminist utopias and discovered an "organicist structure" (59), a "systemic interdependence of the various fragments of the social structure," which "forms a basis for optimism" (50). Jean Pfaelzer's "A State of One's Own: Feminism as Ideology in American Utopias, 1880–1915" (1983, 311) argued that although utopian texts of the period "may have corrected the political and economic inequities of capitalism," they nonetheless "maintained the social and cultural assumptions which justified the inferior status of women." In 1988, Nan Bowman Albinski's "Utopia Reconsidered" examined the way in which many nineteenth-century women's fictional utopias responded to actual utopian experimental communities, and her *Women's Utopias in British and American Fiction* (1988) provided a comparative overview of the utopian responses of nineteenth- and twentieth-century British and American women. *Women's Utopias* examines how such narratives "relied on popular conceptions of their higher moral natures to determine their utopias, but within different frameworks" (4). The following year, Frances Bartowski's *Feminist Utopias* (1989, 5) compared one nineteenth- and several twentieth-century utopias by women to examine "the productive tensions and dialectics of feminist thought when it takes up forms of discursive strategies that are simultaneously fictional and profoundly theoretical," arguing that "the feminist utopian novel is a place where theories of power can be addressed through the construction of narratives that stretch the boundaries of power in its operational details."[8] In 1990, Albinski's "The Laws of Justice, of Nature, and of Right" examined a number of narrative approaches used by late nineteenth-century British women in their utopias.

This study builds on and expands the work of these and other scholars. Although it touches on several issues raised by Kessler and Albinski (most particularly, Albinski's assessment of the differences between American and British texts by women), it is narrower in scope and broader in detail. The central focus of the project is a body of work produced during a specific fifty-year period. This historical constraint, further limited by the use of representative focal texts, permits a level of close textual analysis that would be virtually impossible in a comprehensive overview. This not only allows the examination of a fairly wide range of issues in considerable detail but also an exploration of why and how many nineteenth-century English and American women used the genre to respond to texts by men, to address specific tensions within the feminist movement, and to confront forces determining and shaping larger political and social climates.

The work has six sections. "Pancakes, Preserves, and Patriarchy: Gender and Genre in Canonical Utopian Fiction" delineates the historical contours of mainstream utopian fiction, examines the place of women in these texts, and demonstrates how the utopian responses of seventeenth-, eighteenth-, and early nineteenth-century women paved the way for the late nineteenth-century texts in this study. "Genre and Herstory: Women's Nineteenth-Century Utopian Fiction in Context" observes how women's utopian fiction facilitated the creation of political and social manifestos that responded to the late nineteenth-century historical environment: written after the apparent failure of the British and American suffrage movements, the texts in this study proposed entire new worlds, in which reforms in voting, clothing, education, and employment resulted from a reformation of the social framework. "Worlds Apart: Contrasts in British and American Utopian Texts by Women" examines how nationality sometimes complicated and even overrode the authors' commonality of gender, race, language, heritage, class, and subject matter. "Dream Weaving" is divided into two parts: "Rationalism, Evangelicalism, and Vaticism" examines historically opposed feminist ideologies and early attempts to reconcile them; "Vaticism and Women's Utopian Fiction, 1870–1920" explores how many of the women in this study recognized the utopian perspectives implicit in feminism and then employed the genre to bind middle-class women of diverse political convictions through an appeal to their shared discontents. "Nightmares and Reawakenings: Post-1920 Women's Utopian Fiction" looks at women's subsequent utopian writing: narratives written between 1920 and 1960, when optimistic feminist utopias all but disappeared; and texts of the 1960s and 1970s, when there emerged a "new" type of women's utopian writing, which, despite its decidedly antibourgeois perspective, in many ways resembled that of a century earlier.

First, however, some lexicographical and biographical housekeeping is in order. Any study of utopian literature needs a few ground rules on definition, and any study of obscure writers should provide a bit of background information. This prefatory section will first offer a working definition of "utopia," sufficient to clarify the sense in which the study employs the term; then it will provide a brief introduction to the authors in this study, paying attention to the ways in which their narratives reflect their worldviews; and finally it will examine the particular attractions of the utopian genre for nineteenth-century women.

Defining "utopia" is not a simple matter. Specific denotation is difficult. Where, for example, does utopia end and science fiction or fantasy begin? Or, for that matter, when does a fictional utopia drift into the realm of pure polemic? Making matters even more complex is utopia's multiple identity: it can be an imaginary place or a concrete social experiment, a literary genre or a textual exercise in social intervention. The term is elusive and persists in doubling back on itself; indeed, one might define "utopia" (the literary genre) as a description of a "utopian" (ideal) society. This stubborn urge toward self-deconstruction stems perhaps from More's collapsing of both "*eu*topia" (good place) and "*ou*topia" (no place), for the equivalence he tacitly establishes between ideality and negation results in a paradoxical genre that is doubly fictive: a fictional, *nonexistent* society. A merely fictional community such as George Eliot's Middlemarch projects a sense of authenticity: it is a typically English landscape, populated by typically English men and women engaged in typically English activities. There is no likelihood that a bloomer-clad Dorothea Brooke will suddenly descend from the sky on a hang glider. Utopian fictions furnish no such guarantees. The impossible can for a time become the norm, preconceptions can be shaken loose, and boundaries can be redefined or eliminated altogether.

Defining utopia is thus an attempt to limit a genre that seems to defy limitation. The Manuels (1979, 4–5) suggest that one should not even attempt such a task, asserting that historically utopia has been "shrouded in ambiguity, and no latter-day scholars should presume to dispel the fog, polluting utopia's natural environment with an excess of clarity and definition." Yet while such literary ecology might be admirable, it is not particularly useful to this critical study. The utopian landscape is so vast and its terrain so complex that some guidelines must be established—if only to keep the utopian haze from fogging matters even further.

Lyman Tower Sargent (1988, xii), the undisputed champion of utopian taxonomy, defines utopia as "a non-existent society described in considerable detail." He then subdivides the genre into eutopia, a society that the author intended his readers to view as better than their own; dystopia, a society meant to be viewed as worse than the readers' own; and satirical utopia, a society intended as a criticism of contemporary society. Sargent is well aware of the problems involved in his definitions, particularly the question of authorial intent. His definition is founded on "the principle that we can still determine either the author's intent to produce a utopia or that a utopia has been written whatever the author's primary purpose was." Intentionality is essential to his classifications, for, as he points out, "authors [of utopias] write primarily for contemporary readers rather than for some ill-defined posterity and certainly not for scholars of utopias," and "works written as recently as the 1950s can be read as dystopias when the authors intended them to be eutopias."[9]

These difficulties notwithstanding, Sargent's criteria work well in the present study[10]: the texts under examination all present an imagined ideal society (or a fictional account of actual utopian experimental communities such as those of the Owenites, Shakers, or Rappites), offered as either a positive or negative exemplar to the reader. His definition also permits the use of "utopian fiction" to represent a fairly broad spectrum of texts: "realistic" fictions (including propaganda for or against "actual" utopias), dreams, visions, fantasy, satirical parodies of existing societies, and blueprints for better ones. Such a definition may seem overly broad and capacious, given this constrained histori-cal purview, yet breadth and capacity are essential to the study of how a specific situation fits into a larger problematic—how women in similar circumstances imagined widely differing utopian alternatives.

Who exactly were these women? The majority were forgotten until their rediscovery by utopian and feminist scholars. A few authors elude any attempt at biography and exist only as names on a page; some of these have been re-duced to initials sandwiched between a married title and a husband's name. Even the more prolific authors in this study are relatively unknown today; for instance, few readers will recognize Adelina Kingscote, despite her publication of nearly seventy books,[11] or Florence Young, who published more than sixty. The neglect of other authors is more understandable (and, it might be argued, more deserved), for they were amateurs, whose single texts are frequently the chief evidence of their authors' existence. Yet these forgotten women carried out memorable acts of subversion and construction; they appropriated a his-torically male genre and, in many cases, used it to attack the androcentric social model and construct an alternative.

They did so in a ladylike fashion, however, and with profound doubts about their own unladylike authority. The texts are characterized by an abundance of enigmatic authorship: roughly a third of these women used pseudonyms, while many others credited their texts to dream visions or to "automatic writing" dictated by spirits from beyond. One particularly reclusive writer, Mary Bradley Lane ([1880–81] 1889, vi), did not tell anyone in her social circle—not even her husband—that she had written and published a utopian novel. Even in works by clearly identifiable authors, there is frequently a dearth of authorial personality. Almost half the texts have male narrators, and although these men frequently find their opinions of women altered by the sturdy, competent fe-males they encounter, many authors still seemed to doubt that a woman's point of view could hold their readers' interest. Doubts about the importance of one's own voice can be alleviated by adopting an established genre; by employ-ing the utopian form, nineteenth-century women not only borrowed the pres-tige of such writers as Plato, Plutarch, More, and Bacon, but also used the genre's authority to sustain their own.

In addition, they used the genre to sustain their own middle-class world-views. At first glance, these women seem to be a diverse lot—professional authors and amateur scribblers, free-love advocates and ministers' wives, highly public women and faceless names on a page—yet the authors in this study shared not only language, heritage, and a staunch belief in bourgeois values, but also the conflict of the liminal outsider, torn between her desire for change and her unwillingness to give up the security afforded by existing ar-rangements. Hearteningly middle-class utopias afforded the wonders of trans-formation without the discomforts of remodeling: such texts were analogous to traveling in a house trailer and bringing along all the comfortable paraphernalia of home. Again and again, one discovers supposedly alien beings living in highly conventional nineteenth-century middle-class homes, decorated to reflect the owner's culture and taste and designed to accommodate his or her love of privacy; engaging in socially acceptable middle-class activities, which reflect the Victorian passion for educational and cultural self-improvement; and living sober, family-oriented, patriotic (or, in some cases, matriotic), and devout lives.

Cora Minnett's *The Day after Tomorrow* (1911, 127), for example, is set in 1975, but the homes of the future are reassuringly Victorian, relentlessly decorated in typical nineteenth-century fashion: not one square inch of wall, ceiling, or floor seems to have escaped embellishment. Rooms are

> luxurious to the highest point of man's ingenuity and woman's artistic taste. The polished floor was covered with a pale grounded carpet, in which gold ivy leaves, devised of real thread, glittered. The chairs were large and sumptuous—of a pale gold satin. The walls creamy tinted, with flights of birds painted in a realistic manner upon their smooth surface above the carved dado (an old fashion that had recently been revived). Curtains of rare lace shrouded the windows and lent a mellow tone. Across one corner a big circular couch was drawn, piled with silken cushions; across another a magnificent white and gold piano stood. Flowers were profusely arranged about the couch and the piano, and beautiful pictures hung on the low dado.

"Man's ingenuity" is not an essential component of such a dwelling, however; the all-female society of Mary Lane's *Mizora* ([1880–81] 1889, 67) boasts homes gorged with luxurious rugs, curtains, tapestries, statuary, and assorted objets d'art, including complex pieces of bric-a-brac that could appeal only to someone who relies on domestics to do the dusting. A coral vase, for example, contains "a large and perfect tiger lily, made of gold," which supports a tiny music box orchestra. Each stamen of the flower holds up "a tiny figure carved out of ivory, holding a musical instrument," and when the contraption is activated, each lilliputian musician actually plays, filling the room with tiny tunes. In Jones and Merchant's *Unveiling a Parallel* (1893, 20–21), the decor is similarly rococo: rooms are crammed with "exquisitely carved vessels of all descriptions, bronzes, marbles, royal paintings, precious minerals," along with "other objects equally beautiful."[12] Utopian homes, it would seem, are designed along the lines of museums or art galleries.

Utopian museums and art galleries, however, are designed more along the lines of academies, where students of history can learn never to repeat it: in Elizabeth Burgoyne Corbett's *New Amazonia* (1889, 44), museums feature exhibits such as an "instrument of torture . . . called a corset . . . one of the maddest and silliest fashions ever instituted"; in Lane's *Mizora* ([1880–81] 1889, 193), visitors to a portrait gallery lined with ancient paintings of men can study "the degradation of the human race" the portraits "force [one] to recall." Public buildings are devoted to the promulgation of useful lectures, uplifting music, and other decorous entertainments. Such diversions are fairly standard components of women's alternative communities, reflecting the nineteenth-century passion for self-improvement, cultural enlightenment, and social decorum—characteristics generally associated with women's ameliorative influence. In Lillie Devereux Blake's "A Divided Republic" ([1887] 1892), for example, women become disgusted with their inferior status and decide to live apart from males, whereupon society splits into a eutopian community of women and a dystopian community of men. The women continue to live according to their middle-class ideals, maintaining "absolute order" in "scrupulously tidy" (357) homes and devoting themselves to all branches of learning and culture. Since there is no need for policemen or jails, public monies are "spent in the construction of schoolhouses and other beautiful public buildings" (357). Schools headed by "feminine Boards of Education" are "brought to great perfection," and "free lectures [are] given on all branches of knowledge by scientific women" (358). The men's community, however, lacking the beneficial influence of women, immediately degenerates into a lower-class society of rabble and riffraff: saloons do "a roaring business," while barbershops are deserted and men go about "unshaven, and slouchy" (353). Homes become filthy, church services are no longer held, and houses of worship are turned into gambling parlors. An uncomfortable air of lawlessness and savagery predominates: the police force must be doubled (although it becomes harder and harder to find a sober constable); "brawling [is] incessant" (354); theaters feature "slugging matches . . . dog-fights and cocking-mains" (354); and a man is elected to Congress because he has "won distinction by catching five hundred live rats and putting them in a barrel in fifty minutes" (355). Despite this plethora of diversion, the men are not happy and long for a restoration of middle-class order and harmony; when one of their number proposes that the women be begged to return, the idea is "received with wild enthusiasm" (355).

For Blake, middle-class women are fundamentally necessary to civilized society; their industry and morality act as stabilizing influences that prevent the community from sinking into barbarism. Only middle-class women, after all, are in a position to reject both patrician and plebeian extremes—upper-class idleness and decadence, lower-class ignorance and depravity—in a staunch affirmation of their own class-based golden mean. Fairly typical of those in this study, Blake's ideal community is inhabited by industrious workers who consider idleness a vice and zealous devotion to home, family, country, and God the greatest of virtues.

Idleness is overcome by providing useful work for all, although utopian occupations are almost invariably of the white-collar variety: banking, engineering, architecture, and so forth. Dehumanizing menial toil is left to machines. In Annie Denton Cridge's *Man's Rights* (1870, 9), for example, one discovers "a wondrous machine that could cook, wash, and iron for hundreds of people at once." Lower-class employments that cannot be replaced by machinery are simply upgraded and absorbed into the middle class: a gifted cook is no longer dismissed as a convenient menial but is acclaimed as a creative genius; a nanny is now afforded the respect due any highly trained professional. At a Mizoran party (Lane [1880–81] 1889), a Russian visitor is horrified when "the cook, the chamber-maid, and in fact all the servants in the establishment, enter and join in the conversation and amusement" (70)—the cook is even called on to sing for the assembled company. Later, however, the visitor learns that domestic service is considered among the most dignified and honorable of professions: the musical cook "is one of the most distinguished chemists of this nation" (73); the maids are highly educated, skilled specialists in domestic management, whose duties demand "ladies of the highest culture and refinement" (74–75). Everyone lives and works in a climate of mutual respect and admiration; the universal work ethic has solved a wide spectrum of nineteenth-century problems in a reassuringly right-thinking manner. Industrious people will not suffer from disease, poverty, or hunger and are less likely to fall prey to such socially unacceptable evils as class unrest, drink, or prostitution.

Yet not all members of society can readily be absorbed into the middle class: some cannot; others will not. One of the more disturbing elements to be found in many of the texts in this study is a recurring elitism of race and class, as well as a distressing intolerance of those who cannot function within middle-class norms. Such prejudices emphasize liminal outsiders' need to distinguish and distance themselves from "true" outsiders, who lack the redeeming centrality of racial or social dominance: people of color, foreigners (even middle-class foreigners), lunatics, and "degenerates" are frequently lumped together as undesirables and are dealt with in ways ranging from merely unpleasant to absolutely horrifying. In Lane's *Mizora*, for example, there is a chilling racial hierarchy: the inhabitants of her utopia have eliminated not only all males from their society but all non-Aryans as well. The exclusively blue-eyed, blond females coolly assert that "the highest excellence of moral and mental character is alone attainable by a fair race. The elements of evil belong to the dark race" ([1880–81] 1889, 193). Mizoran women have learned to reproduce parthenogenetically, simply allowing those who do not conform to their ideal to die out. In some texts, elitism takes the form of xenophobia. Charlotte Perkins Gilman's *Moving the Mountain* ([1911] 1968), for example, treats foreigners as physical and social hazards who must have their foreignness scientifically extracted before they can be accepted into American society. Would-be immigrants must shed the alien filth of their homeland; they must "be antiseptically clean, they and all their belongings, before entering the ship" (53) that transports them. They are cleansed of their nasty alien customs as well, for "Compulsory Socialization" courses ensure that "no immigrant is turned loose on the community till he or she is up to a certain standard" (52).

Even those fortunate enough to be of an acceptable race and nationality, however, are not exempt from recurring "Final Solutions." Gilman's utopians freely admit that they have "killed many hopeless degenerates, insane . . . idiots, and real perverts, after trying our best powers of cure" (259). Those fortunate enough to survive the moral holocaust face grim alternatives. Drunkards are removed from society and placed in austere concentration camps, where they receive "hospital treatment and permanent restraint" (186). The morally weak face even bleaker futures: those oversexed unfortunates who cannot conform to the new model of marriages "on a much purer and more lasting plane" (102) are perceived as "cases for medical treatment, or even surgical" intervention (111), and must frequently be "incapacitated for parentage and placed where they [can] do no harm" (161). Not surprisingly, intemperance and promiscuity are not widespread in Gilman's utopia.

Such a society might seem distinctly dystopian to more modern readers, whose exposure to cultural relativism and penicillin have lessened fears of foreigners and venereal disease (although the homophobia and dread of casual sex brought on by the AIDS crisis are certainly analogous to Gilman's fears).[13] Yet, just as men had for centuries created ideal societies that were ideal for men, middle-class Anglo-Saxon women depicted utopian communities that protected the persons and affirmed the values of middle-class Anglo-Saxon women. The unwavering belief in the value of work for all appealed to women trapped in the enforced idleness of gentility; the promotion of education, self-improvement, science, and the arts fascinated women denied access to universities; the advancement of temperance, purity, and an unwavering faith in human goodness and Divine Providence cheered women frequently at the mercy of drunken, profligate, brutal males. For many women, middle-class virtues were ultimately as much a matter of physical survival as anything else.

Yet why did nineteenth-century women use the *utopian* genre to promote these virtues? It certainly was not the only textual outlet available to women, for the utopian boom took place during a general outpouring of women's writing. Rationalist yearnings for radically improved, imaginary elsewheres might have been more efficiently communicated by factual political treatises; accounts of women's oppression might have been more graphically presented in newspaper exposés. Champions of the domestic sphere might have limited themselves to the circulation of moral pamphlets while nurturing societal improvement within their families. Dreams of ideal societies might have remained just that, idle fancies conceived while rocking before the fire. Yet many nineteenth-century women, several of whom had never published anything else, felt compelled to *write down* these visions and fantasies. Why? What particular yearnings did the writing of utopian fiction satisfy?

Any answer to this question must address a complex blend of literary and social history and must examine essential elements of the genre. It must deal with the literary climate in which these authors wrote and must acknowledge not only the rise of the novel and its increasing potential as a source of income for women, but also the overwhelming sudden popularity (and resulting marketability) of the utopian novel after the publication of Edward Bellamy's *Looking Backward* in 1888. It must also examine the particular attraction of the genre's form and functions: its accessibility to an amateur; its unique correlation to nineteenth-century women's own alienated, ambiguous situation; its consolatory and cathartic qualities.

The novel had a number of decided attractions for middle-class women. First, it enabled them to earn money in a genteel fashion, in the security and privacy of their own homes. This was tremendously important in an age when female publicity was almost invariably linked with loss of status: a housewife secure in her own home was perceived as more genteel than a governess forced to support herself; a governess closeted with children was in turn more refined than a domestic forced to deal with tradesmen; the domestic was more respectable than that most public of women, the prostitute. Women who took up the craft of fiction could earn money from within the safety of the private sphere; they could arrange the production of a novel around their own domestic schedules, writing during the bits and pieces of their spare time. A literary career was relatively free of any sordid commercial taint, since, as Susan Coultrap-McQuin (1990) notes, "writing was [perceived as] an embellishment, a luxury, a pursuit for the leisured or for those with a lucrative career and time to spare" (13). This genteel cachet extended to the business of publishing as well: Coultrap-McQuin details the rise of "Gentleman Publishers," highly principled professionals who "professed beliefs in personal relationships, noncommercial aims, and moral guardianship" (28). Such a business associate would reassure all but the most delicate of women—and she could easily be spared any direct contact with a publisher, since even if one had no husband, brother, or father to negotiate contracts, virtually all details could be handled by mail. Second, there was the form of the novel itself. Since the genre was relatively new, it lacked the rules a long tradition might bring about. Its authors needed no classical education[14] and could frequently draw from journals, diaries, and letters—types of writing highly familiar to women. The novel's subject matter did not require a wide familiarity with the world; one could employ the characters of one's neighbors and friends and could use a local setting. Finally, women did not initially have to compete with men to be successful novelists. The novel sold well but was neither profitable enough nor of sufficient status to attract male competition—at least until relatively late in the nineteenth century, when "men of letters" finally expropriated the genre.[15]

All this held doubly true for the utopian novel: utopia is if anything the most private type of writing, since social dreaming is triggered by individual yearnings. Nor would these dreams be intimidated by monumental supertexts; despite such eminent progenitors as Plato and More, utopia remained a subgenre, a bastard child of fiction and polemic in which major authors dabbled for amusement—More's *Utopia* (1516) and Swift's *Gulliver's Travels* (1726) had been originally intended as elaborate practical jokes. The genre was not used for "serious" literature; it was little more than a site of experiment, and women could have less anxiety about comparison. Thus, the stakes were appropriate to an amateur. There was less distinction between the amateur and the professional—indeed, there was no requirement that the author *be* a professional.

Utopia also has certain characteristics that would have been particularly attractive to nineteenth-century women. The genre's popularity made it highly marketable; its formulaic structure made it extremely easy to write; and its fundamental story, an outsider struggling to survive in an alien world, bore a unique resemblance to women's own lives and gave the genre a consolatory function as well.

Utopian fiction was in great demand, particularly after the publication of Edward Bellamy's incredibly successful *Looking Backward*.[16] For the next three decades, utopias were quite the rage; Lyman Tower Sargent's bibliography (1988) lists an astounding 593 utopian texts written between 1889 and 1920 in England and America alone. Many of the texts in my study are clear replies to Bellamy[17]: Mary H. Ford's "A Feminine Iconoclast" (1889) criticizes the paternalism implied by his Nationalist sexual separatism; Pauline Carsten Curtis's "In the Year '26" (1890) argues that human nature will eventually undermine Bellamy's scheme; Mrs. C. H. Stone's *One of "Berrian's" Novels* (1890) purports to be a novel by the twenty-first-century author mentioned in *Looking Backward;* Ruth Ellis Freeman's "Tales of a Great-Grandmother" (1891) offers a twentieth-century retrospective focusing on how Nationalism benefits women; Frances Clarke's *The Co-opolitan: A Story of the Co-operative Commonwealth of Idaho* (1898) introduces a society based on Bellamy's (offering women the same limited roles in government and continuing to confine most "women's work" to the domestic sphere). *Looking Backward*'s popularity ensured a market for women's utopian writing and helped draw women to the genre.

Utopia's major appeal, however, probably lies in what a modern television producer would call its "high-concept" format. The genre itself supplies not only a prefabricated plot but conflicts as well[18]: a protagonist encounters a strange new world and is led through its political, social, and ethical complexities by a knowledgeable guide (and frequently comes to reevaluate his own society in the process). One can trace this formula back to the earliest utopias: Adam wakes to discover himself in Eden, where God explains the rules of the place[19]; Glaucon and Adeimantus are led through an imaginary republic by Socrates; Thomas More is given a panoramic view of Utopia by Raphael Hythloday. By the nineteenth century, hordes of protagonists had encountered myriad isolated worlds and had enjoyed countless extended dialogues with legions of highly vocal natives, who expounded at length on the social and political customs of their utopian/dystopian societies. The formula had become so customary that it was almost inextricably linked to the genre and had become a kind of "automatic writing" in its own right.

The hero-locale-guide model supplies more than plot and conflict, however. It also offers a comforting familiarity for the reader attempting authorship for the first time. The formula is a paradigm of the reading experience, for a reader is readily analogous to a utopian protagonist, and each text is a new world the reader must explore, guided by the author. In the nineteenth century, when women were expected to be spiritual guides in their own homes, and when prophesies of a "Woman Age" predicted that women would lead mankind into a new era of promise, the guide/author parallel made utopian authorship a comfortable step.

Utopia's popularity and uncomplicated format could help put bread on the table, yet the genre fed intellectual and emotional hungers as well. Women's utopian fiction is far more than an exploitation of a popular literary form: the mingled anger and hope that fill these works suggest that British and American women responded to the particular gratifications afforded by the genre itself.[20] Caught in the shadowy no-man's-land between centrality and exclusion, these women lived on the threshold of their own society: although they were members of the dominant class and race, their religion linked them with the fall of humankind, their political institutions considered them unfit to take any part in government, and their legal system relegated them to the status of property. It is no wonder that women sought the consolation of utopia, since the dialectical and ambiguous genre of lost outsiders in disorienting worlds mirrored women's own situation. Fictional utopias are projectively directed toward reality, and although a story may be set on Mars or a thousand years in the future, it nonetheless addresses problems afflicting the author's society.

Utopia's contrasting worlds offered an apt metaphor for the nineteenth-century middle-class woman's highly polarized society, in which the division between the public and private spheres frequently extended to the schizophrenic patriarchal perception of woman as both a public bawd (linked to fallen Eve, the treacherous seductress) and an inspirational household angel (associated with Mary, the new, and unfallen, Eve). Such contrasts are embodied in a genre that is founded on confrontation: the semiobligatory conversation between the uninformed visitor and the knowledgeable guide (for example, *Looking Backward*'s Julian West and Dr. Leete); the implicit dialogue between the world the fictional protagonist has left and the utopian society he encounters (Julian West's Boston of 1887 and Leete's Boston of 2000); the satirical confrontation between the author's real world and the fictional utopian society (Bellamy's America and the world of *Looking Backward*). Many of the authors in the present study used this inherent contrast to mirror the division inherent in their society. In *Man's Rights,* for example, Annie Denton Cridge (1870, 3) presents a world in which the poles have been reversed: pale and feeble "gentlemen housekeepers" are relegated to the domestic sphere, while women attend to public matters. Her sympathetic view of the men's plight points out that a polarized society, whether patriarchal or matriarchal, is unsatisfactory. Other authors dealt with opposition by exaggerating it. Lillie Blake's "A Divided Republic," with its utopian community of women and dystopian community of men, mocks the opposition of men's and women's separate spheres in nineteenth-century society. Still other writers responded to the polarization by presenting societies in which opposition cannot exist: Mary Lane's *Mizora* introduces a world in which men have been eliminated, leaving a eutopia free of war, poverty, ignorance, and disease.

Between opposing poles, however, lies the essential ambiguity of utopian fiction. Although Bellamy's ([1888] 1966) Julian West describes Boston past and present as "contrasting pictures side by side" (90), the two visions are more closely analogous to a gestalt illusion: just as the mind's eye shifts from two profiles to a single urn, past and present shift back and forth in Bellamy's text, eventually collapsing together when Julian is unable to distinguish between his nineteenth-century fiancée, Edith Bartlett, and her granddaughter, Edith Leete. The "two Ediths were blended in my thought," he marvels, "nor have they ever since been clearly distinguished" (181). Disorientation and confusion are hallmarks of the genre: people frequently have trouble understanding one another, not only because the differences between their worlds are too great, but also because the similarities are equally overwhelming.

Disorientation and confusion were also hallmarks of nineteenth-century women's position in society. The role of "belle-ideal" was fundamentally oxy-moronic: comporting oneself as the Angel in the House not only required im-possible levels of purity, meekness, and selflessness but assumed a profusion of doting papas and wealthy beaux as well—when in reality, there were simply not enough of these to go around. Additionally, many women argued that the role of household angel was an absurd function for a corporeal woman, requiring that she suppress her intellect in order to exist as a plaything for men, yet simultaneously exercise it sufficiently to manage the house and supervise the education of her daughters and young sons. The lives of middle-class women were simultaneously crowded and barren, an endless blur of shopping, visiting, domestic management, and social events, in which nothing of consequence ever seemed to get accomplished. Florence Nightingale remembered with hor-ror the monotony of her youth: "Oh, weary days—Oh evenings that seem never to end—for many years have I watched that drawing-room clock and thought it would never reach the ten!" (quoted in F. Fraser 1987, 141). Occupied yet idle, adult yet doomed to "incurable infancy" (141), women found their existence a paradigm of irreconcilability.

Many nineteenth-century women seized on utopia's ambiguous nature as a metaphor for their own condition, and their novels are frequently characterized by varying levels of disorientation. In Florence Dixie's *Gloriana* (1890), this takes the form of gender confusion: the lovely Gloriana de Lara conceals her gender and, as "Hector D'Estrange," attends Eton and Oxford, wins fistfights and horse races, and gains a seat in Parliament, escaping detection all the while. Utopian ambiguity may also take the form of social disorientation. In Blaze De Bury's *The Storm of London* (1904), all clothing disappears from England, and the resulting crowds of naked people are absolutely unable to recognize one another: archbishops are mistaken for ruffians, butlers are mistaken for lords, and even doting parents find it difficult to distinguish between their children and the domestic staff. Many texts use the mutual surprise afforded by the col-lision of two cultures not only to point out the differences between the two worlds but also to act as a metaphor for women's confusion about their own positions. In Jones and Merchant's *Unveiling a Parallel* (1893), the narrator and his guide hold several disjointed conversations in which neither has the faintest idea what the other is talking about, so dissimilar is their comprehension of such terms as "republic" and "citizenship." When Severnius, the Martian guide, learns that terrestrial women frequently work to support themselves and their families, he assumes that "they must receive princely wages—and of course they have no [domestic] responsibilities" (45). Disabused of this notion by the narrator, Severnius is "aghast" and unable to comprehend why earthly women would "submit to such conditions" (46) without revolting.

Revolution, however, requires a degree of fellowship and cooperation virtually unavailable to nineteenth-century middle-class women, whose position in society was one of isolation and vulnerability: alienated from society by the patriarchal insistence on female innocence and lack of worldly experience, alienated from others of their sex by the competitive need to secure the financial support of a rich husband,[21] alienated from themselves by the inherent absurdity of their position. It is no wonder that women were drawn to the utopian genre and claimed it for their own. There must have been some consolation in verbalizing their frustration with such oppressive and confusing social norms.

Utopian literature afforded consolation on a variety of levels, offering heartening visions to cheer author and reader alike. There was something for everyone: even the most realistic fictions provided a dizzying variety of alternatives to nineteenth-century society. For would-be communitarians, Marie Howland's *Papa's Own Girl* (1874) depicted the creation of a Fourierist cooperative stressing social reform, equitable relations between women and men, education, cultural enrichment, the dignity of work, economic independence, and full adult enfranchisement. For prospective entrepreneurs, Helen Campbell's *Miss Melinda's Opportunity* (1886) envisioned the establishment of a highly successful, cooperative Working-Women's Guild. For socialists, there was the solace of Jane Clapperton's *Margaret Dunmore* (1888), which detailed the history of a successful socialist commune extending the familial structure to the entire community. More devout feminists might be comforted by Eveleen Mason's *Hiero-Salem* novels (1889, 1898), which described the Eloiheem Commonwealth, a spiritual community devoted to abolishing inequities of sex, class, and race: female "father-mothers" are frequently family breadwinners, while male "mother-fathers" care for the home and children. Unhappy wives trapped in a perpetual round of childbearing could find hope in Rosa Graul's *Hilda's Home* (ca. 1897), the tale of a socialist community devoted to love, liberty, and learning, which gives women complete equality and frees them from the tyranny of wedlock and unwanted pregnancy. Such texts served as far more than polemic; they were fictions that enabled women of the present to escape the constrictions of their society as they savored reasonable alternatives, so realistic as to be believable.

Realistic utopias, however, have decided limitations: the author is bound by the laws of nature and society and must not only explain in some detail how such communities came to be (usually through a combination of good intentions and a large inheritance) but also must offer specific solutions to society's problems. Part of utopia's charm, after all, is its ability to criticize society without facing the dilemma of having to go out and *do* anything. The genre's chimerical nature made it an excellent surrogate for the real experience many nineteenth-century women found impossible to gain. Utopia is, by definition, unattainable—and therefore safe. Even the politically naive can have a voice in solving social problems, since one need only invent a place where the obstacles have been already overcome and then describe it, transcending the petty details of exactly how such an ideal society might be achieved. Many authors employed this shortcut to perfection, rejecting any pretense of reality and setting their fanciful utopias in a variety of far-flung, exotic locales. Anna Adolph's *Arqtiq* (1899) is a high-tech polar utopia inhabited by ideal people who enjoy complete gender equality. *Al-Modad* (1892) by M. Louise Moore depicts a society at the earth's core, deep beneath the North Pole, inhabited by a communal, technologically advanced society stressing education, sexual equality, and sexual freedom. Outer-space communities abound, reached by a variety of balloon vehicles and airplanes (along with spiritualist and wireless transmissions). The most popular planet is Mars, which appears in Annie Denton Cridge's *Man's Rights* (1870), Carra Depuy Henley's *A Man from Mars* (1891), Jones and Merchant's *Unveiling a Parallel* (1893), and Sara Weiss's *Journeys to the Planet Mars* (1903). The moon, Venus, and assorted other celestial bodies also provided the consolations and comforts terrestrial women were denied.

One such consolation was vindication: women in these narratives are assured of their innate worth and inherent right-mindedness. In Nettie Parrish Martin's *A Pilgrim's Progress in Other Worlds* (1908), the ne'er-do-well Ulysum Storries thoughtlessly abandons his wife and travels throughout the solar system, encountering worlds far more advanced than Earth in terms of spiritual development and relations between the sexes. His unsuccessful flirtations with a variety of extraterrestrial females open his eyes to his own failings; he finally returns to Earth, rejoins his ever-patient spouse, and lives as a good Christian and loyal husband. Vindication is also a standard feature in spiritualist texts, such as Mary Ann Fisher's *Among the Immortals, in the Land of Desire,* which envision equitable afterworlds offering a sharp contrast to mundane unfairness. Fisher's utopia (1916, 20) is set in heaven, where women are repaid for worldly suffering by a divine "law of compensation," a sort of "beatific welfare": those pockmarked on earth now have the best complexions, the deaf have the best hearing, and spurned wives may, if they choose, eternally spurn their eternally contrite husbands' eternal devotions. Serene faith in a utopian afterlife makes one more likely to forgive the imperfections of a temporal world.

The nineteenth-century utopian authors in this study had quite literally the best of both worlds: from their liminal perspective, they could enjoy a daydream endowed with the tactile reality of a text, a bound fantasy that not only mirrored women's own situation but also provided a tangible articulation of possible alternatives. Society had made it painfully clear that women—even women of the dominant race and class—were nonetheless outsiders; utopia at least provided a form in which these insider-outsiders might tell their own stories. Of more importance, they could tell it in their own ways. The reassuring conventions of the formulaic utopian model were so firmly in place that women could confidently re-form certain traditional features within the genre to suit their own purpose.

This purpose was most frequently the empowerment of women through the validation and amplification of the female voice: although male narrators are frequently employed, they are generally straw men whose androcentric worldviews are transformed by the powerful women they meet in their travels. Several authors risk a female point of view and allow brave, intelligent, and independent female narrators to replace their traditional male counterparts (indeed, a few texts exclude the male voice altogether). Nor are the words of these newly audible female voices drowned out by the Word of a male God, since androgynous or female gods frequently have unseated the patriarchal Father.

In Jones and Merchant's *Unveiling a Parallel* (1893), for example, the male visitor is a bumbling fool blinded by terrestrial prejudices and assumptions. He is adrift in an advanced society whose members treat him as they would a slightly backward child. The female characters in the novel are not relegated to the sidelines but instead are indispensable to the plot, active and articulate, and typically a central topic of discussion. The narrator and his male guide spend much of their time discussing Elodia, a typical "Martian" female who drinks, smokes, and enjoys her bachelor status; active politically, economically, and sexually, she votes, works as a financier, and has affairs (not to mention an out-of-wedlock daughter). Elodia herself is a visible and voluble participant in the text: in *Looking Backward* (Bellamy 1888), Edith Leete discreetly absents herself when the men enjoy their cigars, brandy, and serious conversation[22]; Elodia would settle down, light up, and join in. The narrator eventually becomes disenchanted with such worldliness and promptly falls in love with Ariadne, from the neighboring (and far more spiritually enlightened) state of Caskia. Yet, despite her piety and femininity, Ariadne is as active and articulate as Elodia: she is independently wealthy, holds a respected position as an educator, and is the central speaker during the final section of the book. Other texts repudiate the male voice altogether, presenting dialogues between brave female explorers and representatives of all-female societies: in Lane's *Mizora*, the heroic Vera Zarovitch survives a war, exile to Siberia, a shipwreck, abandonment, and a harsh winter spent living with "Esquimaux" ([1880–81] 1889, 16) and then strikes off alone across the Arctic Ocean in a rowboat. Finally, she is carried by a whirlpool to the center of the earth, where she discovers the all-female society. Irene Clyde's *Beatrice the Sixteenth* (1909) has as its narrator the intrepid scholar-scientist-explorer-MP Mary Hatherley, who travels through time to discover the Amazon culture of Armeria.

Such strong and central female characters responded to middle-class women's longing for power in a society that had rendered them helpless. This yearning for potency is also reflected in texts that feature androgynous or female gods and that replace male dominance with divine equilibrium. In Eveleen Mason's *Hiero-Salem* (1889) and *An Episode in the Doings of the Dualized* (1898), the members of the Eloiheem commonwealth worship an androgynous "Unified-Dual-Being" (1889, 153); the utopians of M. Louise Moore's *Al-Modad* (1892) venerate Lo, a divine hermaphrodite who inspires goodness, simplicity, and vegetarianism; the inhabitants of Janet Von Swartwout's (1895, 40) Olombia glorify a sexually ambiguous being, "the Father and Mother lost in androgynous oneness." Specifically female deities are worshiped by Lane's ([1880–81] 1889) androphobic Mizorans and Charlotte Gilman's (1915) matriotic Herlanders.

Concern for the female voice extends to questions of communication. Men's utopian writing is typically preoccupied with the language of the alien world: More created a Utopian alphabet and several lines of representative Utopian poetry; Swift's Gulliver spent countless hours mastering Lilliputian, Brobdingnagian, Laputian, and Houyhnhnm; Butler struggled manfully with Erewhonian. Language difficulties are infrequent in women's narratives, which tend instead to focus on semantics: in the rare cases when English is not the *lingua femina*, it is replaced by an eminently sensible tongue requiring little study. In Clyde's *Beatrice the Sixteenth* (1909, 55), Mary Hatherley readily understands the Armerians' mixture of Latin and Greek, spoken in a "stately, unhurried rate"; similarly, Gilman's (1915, 31) Herlander tongue is "not hard to speak, smooth and pleasant to the ear, and . . . easy to read and write." Other utopians communicate through thought transmissions and thus render language altogether superfluous: in the telepathic world of Bessie Story Rogers's *As It May Be* (1905, 64–65), people "have no secrets from each other," and thus "the whole universe feels towards each other as a very devoted family should feel with each other, every one working together." In texts such as these, communication difficulties are more likely to be a hermeneutic confusion, which echoes the feminist political rhetoric of the time. What, for example, is a "citizen"? Can a person indeed be a citizen without a right to vote? Unable to make their political voices heard, and frequently ignored or purposely misinterpreted by male political leaders, nineteenth-century women must have felt immense frustration—the nightmare of not being able to make themselves understood in their own language extended to their waking lives.

Not all utopian writing by nineteenth-century women was feminist, however. About one in ten of the texts under study view a truly egalitarian society as an overturning of the natural hierarchy of nature. Many of these texts argue that women are not natural leaders but are followers, meant to be dominated by men. In Mrs. J. Wood's *Pantaletta* (1882), for example, universal suffrage produces a society of effete, enslaved males and restless, dominant females who secretly hunger for the attentions of an old-fashioned, "manly" man. Similarly, class hierarchy is seen as natural: Bertha Thomas's satiric "A Vision of Communism" (1873) argues that human equality is impossible, since nature will overcome mankind's attempts at equality by producing the "intellectual millionaire" (304), granting a "large musical fortune" or an "enormous stock of beauty" (307) to fortunate individuals. To counter such natural inequalities, life must become "a handicap race" (305), wherein the mentally acute receive far less education than their duller fellows, the musically gifted play out-of-tune instruments, and the physically attractive wear unflattering clothing.

Although these antifeminist narratives are only tangentially touched on in this study, it is important to note that they demonstrate how women of antithetical ideological convictions responded to and sought out the same genre and how they used utopia not only to protest their oppressed status but to reaffirm it as well. Egalitarian, communitarian dream visions can be inverted: although the genre's chimerical and elusive qualities do not altogether exclude any possibility of a better world, antifeminist, antisocialist nightmares use utopia's impossible nature as a metaphor for the impossibility of re-forming what they perceive as a natural hierarchy. Feminists may use utopia to challenge the hierarchy, but antifeminists use the same genre to champion it: Annie Denton Cridge inverts society to show that a matriarchy is just as wrong as a patriarchy; Mrs. Wood inverts society to show that matriarchy turns the natural order topsy-turvy and results in chaos. Ultimately, it is change that is at issue: both eutopian and dystopian visions are revisions of reality, literary responses to the literal world.

Change is the focus of this study. John Stuart Mill deplored the tyranny of custom, and for centuries there had been a terrible sameness to women's existence—even in utopian fiction, which seemed to allow room for new social systems. There appeared to be no chance for change as long as it was customary for men to interpret woman's place in society. Women of the nineteenth century drew from their alarmingly small array of raw materials—a historically misogynistic genre, a new literary form, an emerging feminist tradition, and their own experiences—and forged them into an alternative vision, uncorrupted by the specter of male primacy, in which the ambiguous view of the liminal outsider became manifestly central. Their "if-only" societies became a kind of proof that, if only women's worth could be recognized by all and their values extended to society as a whole, then humankind in general would benefit dramatically from the change.

Hélène Cixous (1976, 879) defines writing as "the *very possibility of change*, the space that can serve as a springboard for subversive thought, the precursory movement of a transformation of social and cultural structures." Nineteenth-century middle-class women recognized and seized on this transformational possibility. Using their ambiguous status as a springboard, they developed parables of female experience written by those who had more at stake than had canonical authors—more to lose from stasis, more to gain from change. Their fictional utopias spurn the grim uniformity of woman's place in men's texts; as nineteenth-century women wrote their own utopias, the very possibility of change began to emerge. This study traces that emergence.

Pancakes, Preserves, and Patriarchy
Gender and Genre in Canonical Utopian Fiction

Like mundane real estate, fictional utopian landscapes have historically been the property of men. Ironically, the social group that might have benefited the most from a reworking of social structures—women—had very little say in the matter: as late as 1800, canonical utopian texts were historically *male* productions. To demonstrate the profound impact the male-dominated literary canon had upon women and their utopian writing, this chapter offers a brief overview of canonical narratives. It first shows how each new generation of texts responded to the particular tensions of its age; then it examines women's place within men's narratives; and finally, it demonstrates how the handful of utopian texts by women written before 1800 managed systematically to subvert the patriarchal vision even as they conformed to its conventions.

Utopian writing tends to reflect the culture that produces it. In prehistoric ages, when life was a ceaseless battle against weather, hunger, and exhaustion, retrospective utopias lamented lost golden ages and Edens in which the weather was always ideal, food abundant, and hard labor unnecessary. These early myths were produced by people who had been torn from their agricultural way of life by climatic changes, unwilling nomads who, J. W. Johnson (1968, 3) explains, were forced to roam "considerable distances from their subsistence-level homesites of the Stone Age. They must have been driven by despair and hope: despair for their lost way of life and hope of a new, better life someplace where food was plentiful and the ills and terrors of the nomadic life could be ended." It is no wonder they dreamed of the paradise lost, when people "lived as if they were gods, their hearts free from all sorrow . . . and without hard work or pain" (Hesiod 1959, 31). Nor is it surprising that they composed etiological myths to explain why this way of life no longer endured and why the Creator suddenly took such an intense personal dislike to His creations.[1] There was, after all, some small comfort in understanding *why* life was so harsh—and in having someone (almost invariably a woman) to blame for the loss of Eden or Arcadia.

With the rise of classical humanism, however, people began to rethink utopia. The golden age was lost to humanity, but could not the quality of one's life be considerably better nonetheless? There certainly seemed to be room for substantial improvement, after all, and as people began to settle the Mediterranean coasts of Italy, Greece, and Persia, city building began to evolve into city planning. Gradually, humanity became less reliant on the vagaries of divine favor and began to take utopia into its own hands. Cities proliferated at an amazing rate—Lewis Mumford (1941) notes that "Miletus is supposed to have begotten some three hundred cities, and many of its fellows were possibly not less fruitful" (29)—and old cities spawned not only new cities, but new ideas as well. Mumford reports that Phaleus, a fifth-century B.C.E. philosopher, designed an ideal state based on "a complete equality of property" (30), and that Hippodamus, an "architect, city planner, and sociologist" concerned himself not only with city design but also with "the more basic problem of social order" (30).

Not everyone agreed about the value of such planning; there was some disenchantment with what many perceived as the decadence of their urban communities and some longing for the Arcadian world of uncorrupted "natural" man. These yearnings for a simpler way of life are reflected in the work of classical historiographers such as Herodotus, who describes the wisdom and physical might of the Ethiopians, and Strabo, who recounts the virtue and cunning of the Scythians. Herodotus's (1942, 220) nobly savage Ethiopians are a robust and attractive people—"the tallest and handsomest men in the whole world"—who disdain the decadent comforts of civilization and thus retain a natural shrewdness and strength that elude effete city dwellers. When Cambyses, the acquisitive king of the Persians, decides to infiltrate, conquer, and enslave the Ethiopians, he sends spies pretending to be allies, bearing costly gifts. The native ruler, however, immediately sees through the deceitful stratagem and rebukes the agents: "Your king is not a just man—for were he so, he had not coveted a land which is not his own, nor brought slavery on a people who never did him any harm" (220). Strabo's (1924, 3:199) Scythians have been less fortunate, for the corruption of civilization has tainted a people once known as "the most straightforward of men and the least prone to mischief." Strabo laments that "our way of life has spread its change for the worse to almost all peoples, introducing among them luxury and sensual pleasures and, to satisfy these vices, base artifices that lead to innumerable acts of greed" (3:199). The natives' past glories, however, are still remembered, and Strabo lauds their celebrated proclivities for justice, temperance, and courage. These pseudohistorical[2] utopias mark an important shift in utopian thought, away from the lost paradises of the prehistoric period. The societies of the Ethiopians and Scythians might be extremely distant and might have lost a great deal of their former glory, yet they are not divinely created. They are instead the product of human beings in their natural state and exist in the historical, documented past. Ethiopia and Scythia were very much of this world, and, although certainly not immediately at hand for the average Greek, they were as real as Athens or Sparta.[3]

Such noble savages, however, offered proof positive that designing better cities was not the key to utopia: one needed to create better *people* as well. Only then could the benefits of urban planning combine with innate human nobility and culminate in the Hellenic ideal: a republic that eschewed the all too familiar vices of excess, indulgence, stupidity, and inequity, in favor of an exemplary pattern of moderation, temperance, courage, wisdom, and justice. Plato's *Republic* champions just such a model and offers a fairly detailed schematic for the good life. The work became a blueprint for subsequent utopias, setting out a number of characteristic confrontations and oft-used formulas: the dialogue structure, the call for an abolition of private property, and the creation of a three-part social order.

What Plato proposed was the elimination of extremes. His society would have neither great wealth nor dire poverty, neither gormandizing nor starvation. By eliminating excess, there would be enough for all. Of course, wealthy Greeks might find his scheme appallingly communitarian at first, but in the long run, even they would benefit from the stability of the resulting environment. Plato likened the body politic to the body human: a sore toe (that is, a discontented proletariat) may seem to have little impact on the stomach (feasting patricians), but, left untreated, it will eventually fester and infect and destroy the entire system. Moderation, Plato argued, was good for any body: physical excess resulted in a flabby and sick individual; civic excess, in a careless and weak republic. For both, intemperance could prove fatal.

Yet, since the requisite ideal people failed to materialize,[4] the ideal cities of the classical period came to nothing. The centuries-old civilization of the Greeks fell before the tempered might of the Roman army; the Roman Empire fell in turn, corrupted by a plethora of sore toes and bad stomachs. By the fifth century, utopia seemed farther from humankind's reach than ever. Surely, if the military might, cultural prosperity, and philosophical wealth of the greatest empire in history could not ensure an ideal society, there must be no real point in trying to create an earthly utopia. Fallible human beings could never achieve perfection. It was as simple as that. Or was it?

For European Christians, at least, matters were a bit more complex. Christ's sacrifice in 33 C.E. had supposedly redeemed Eve's sin and Adam's gullibility. Paradise was no longer lost but was waiting in heaven—once again the sole province of God, but for the first time available to humankind in general. Admittedly, there were two decided drawbacks: not only did one have to live a spotlessly pure existence on earth—no gluttony, lust, sloth, or any of the other qualities that make life bearable—but death was also a requirement for admittance.[5] Yet since one was bound to die anyway, why not try to spend eternity in the blissful surroundings described by Saint John's revelations: a holy city with "the glory of God, its radiance like a most rare jewel, like a jasper, clear as crystal" (Rev. 21:9), its "river of the water of life, bright as crystal," and "on either side of the river, the tree of life with its twelve kinds of fruit" (Rev. 22:1–2). The alternative, described in alarming detail by the prophet Isaiah, was certainly unattractive: a dystopian nightmare-vision of eternal Armageddon, a land "soaked with blood" (Isa. 34:7) in which streams were "turned into pitch" and "soil into brimstone" (Isa. 34:9), a place of "nettles and thistles," the "haunt of jackals" (Isa. 34:13).

This was uncomfortably reminiscent of home, after all. Most medieval Europeans (particularly the poorest and meekest, who, according to the New Testament, were the likeliest to gain entry to heaven) had suffered everything from the ravages of interminable wars to the horrors of the black plague. With all four apocalyptic horsemen tramping back and forth through one's front yard at regular intervals, it was difficult to disagree with Saint Augustine's assessment (1945, 2:388) of temporal existence as a "tempest of cares, sorrows, repinings, fears, mad exultations, discords, altercations, wars, treasons, furies, hates, deceits, flatteries, thefts, rapines, perjuries, pride, ambition, envy, murder, parricide, cruelty, villainy, luxury, impudence, unchastity, fornications, adulteries, incests, several sorts of sins against nature (filthy even to be named), sacrilege, heresy, blasphemy, oppression, calumnies, circumventions, cozenages, false witnesses, false judgements, violence, robberies, and suchlike."[6] It was a long list, but a fairly accurate representation of medieval life.

Augustine's City of God was a state of mind, and the devastating impact of mundane afflictions could be overcome by shifting one's attention to the glory of the everlasting world to come. Contemplating paradise made earthly woes seem positively trivial—and dangerously distracting, since preparing oneself to be worthy of heaven was a full-time job. Resisting vice, sin, and the grosser demands of the flesh required constant vigilance. One should not waste one's energies on the petty consolations of corporeal pleasures but instead should devote oneself to seeking out virtue, performing good deeds, and remembering Christ's promise of eternal bliss. That way, one would simply overlook the miseries of the world—"cold, heat, storms, showers, deluges, lightning, thunder, earthquakes, falls of houses, fury of beasts, poisons of airs, waters, plants, and beasts of a thousand sorts, stinging of serpents, biting of mad dogs," Augustine (1945, 2:389) continues helpfully—and, by making the best of things, live a relatively happy life, if not in paradise proper, at least in a not-too-distant suburb.[7]

A thousand years of suburbia was too much for Renaissance humanists, however, who reembraced the classical certainty that paradise on earth was within the control of humanity. After the fall of Constantinople in 1450, renewed interest in classical cultures led to a rediscovery of texts such as the *Republic*, and to a reawakened fascination with the possibility of utopia brought about by a Neoplatonic balance of reason and virtue. The Arcadian tradition, which reappeared in texts such as Spenser's *Faerie Queene* (1590, 1596) and Sidney's *Arcadia* (1590), revalued a simple, pastoral life; histories celebrating the triumphs of the Roman Empire seemed like evidence for a past utopia. Just as important was the discovery of the New World, sparking hope of a new route to the exotic East, the fantastic wealth and luxury of which made it something of a utopia in its own right. When Europeans discovered that they had instead stumbled on a previously unknown continent, new wonders came hard on one another—indeed, it became almost impossible to differentiate fact from fancy. Mayans and Utopians and Incas and New Atlantians, El Dorado and Florida and Mexico and the Fountain of Youth—all were jumbled together in a wonderful olio of marvels.

Renaissance writers used the new worlds to promote classical ideas. Thomas More drew from Plato's *Republic*, the work of Roman satirists, medieval monasticism, and the wondrous tales of the New World and fused them into a parable of pagans who are somehow more Christian than Christians[8]; Francis Bacon blended the Platonic spirit with science to create an island peopled by devoutly religious utilitarians; Michel de Montaigne wrote of bloodthirsty cannibals whose ethical system was superior to that of Europeans; and Thomas Campanella designed a classless meritocracy, in which all social institutions had been re-formed in order to benefit humankind in general. Collective happiness became a reasonable construct: certainly, if all the members of a society work to improve it, if all are adequately fed, clothed, and housed, and if all adhere to principles of virtue and self-improvement, then utopia will be a very real possibility. Scores of utopian texts began to appear throughout Europe, offering a bewildering variety of stratagems for earthly paradise, but one common factor infused them all: utopia was within the reach of humankind, if only people would strive to make themselves worthy of it.

But that, of course, had been the stumbling block all along. The hope for an earthly paradise might have been reborn in the Renaissance, but humankind's apparent aversion to a simple, egalitarian existence based on moderation in all things had never died. Throughout the sixteenth and seventeenth centuries, the wealthy continued to enjoy such mundane pleasures as magnificent estates, glorious (if gaudy) clothing, and marvelous feasts, while the poor continued to be in no position to complain. Models for ideal human behavior were sadly lacking: certainly one could not look to religion, given the bloodshed and butchery brought on by the Reformation and Counter-Reformation; neither could one follow the example of international brotherhood, given the savage nationalism of France and Sweden during the Thirty Years' War—or, for that matter, the vicious international commercial rivalries. Even national unity did not amount to much. England, for example, spent a good part of the seventeenth century immersed in varying levels of fierce civil war.

It is little wonder that, by the eighteenth century, writers again held the idea of an earthly paradise in fairly low regard. "Little odious vermin" (Swift

[1726] 1970, 108) were unlikely candidates for utopia. Humankind was basically depraved, and utopian schemes were little more than escapist fantasies. There was no escape in the temporal universe, for no matter what its size or shape, base humanity was fallen and imperfectible: Swift's Gulliver, for example, repelled by the pettiness of the Lilliputians, the physical grossness of the Brobdingnagians, and the intellectual pretensions of the Laputans, discovers a rational utopia in Houyhnhnmland but cannot partake in this society because his own human frailties condemn him forever to Yahoo-hood.

Because of utopia's perceived impossibility, many eighteenth-century writers rejected the genre as a positive model. Instead, they employed the utopian paradigm as a negative exemplar, which enabled them not only to level direct satirical attacks at their society and contemporaries (while eluding the harsh penalties of libel laws) but also to make moral points. Samuel Johnson's *Rasselas* (1759), for example, demonstrates the futility of seeking happiness in earthly pleasure. Prince Rasselas lives in almost Cokaygne-like luxury, yet all he wishes to do is escape. When he does, he explores every avenue of life available to humankind, yet all eventually lead to boredom or distress. The only place utopia can be achieved is in the afterlife, and thus any search for happiness in a fallen world is futile. One must be patient and virtuous and wait for the everlasting joy of heaven. That, if nothing else, was incontrovertible.

After the tumultuous final quarter of the eighteenth century, however, nothing seemed absolutely certain any more. Society had undergone a tremendous upheaval, as three revolutions—the American, French, and industrial—profoundly changed social, economic, and political relationships and made utopia seem a real possibility once again. The American Declaration of Independence asserted that mankind had an "unalienable right" to pursue happiness, granted not by church or state but by "Nature and Nature's God." Of more importance, it argued that humankind must take steps to secure its own happiness; the oppressed must seek to overthrow their oppressors, for to do so was not only "their Right," but "their Duty" as well. The French Revolution emphasized even more strongly the ideals of human rights and equality (although, as the next chapter will demonstrate, much of this equality was perceived as an exclusively male prerogative). In addition, new technologies seemed to guarantee enough for all—surely, if factories could mass produce furniture and clothing, no one would lack a seat or a shirt. An earthly paradise seemed so nearly within humanity's grasp that the production of purely fictional utopias declined in the first half of the nineteenth century, replaced by actual "scientific" utopian experiments.

The earliest of these experiments were sectarian communities, religious groups such as the Shakers, the Ephrata Cloister, the Moravian Brethren, the Rappites, and the Oneida Perfectionists, many of which developed in Europe in the eighteenth century and later emigrated to America. The nineteenth century saw not only the continuation of these religious groups, but the development of reform communities and economic cooperatives as well. In 1808, for example, Charles Fourier proposed breaking society into cooperative agricultural communities that would concern themselves with the welfare of the individual. Society, he argued, should adapt itself to the needs of the individual, rather than vice versa, and outmoded, wasteful systems such as capitalism should be abandoned. His plans sounded so reasonable that people decided to try them out, and for the first time "no place" became some place with an actual address, as Fourierist experimental communities were established in France and America.[9] In 1813, Robert Owen, a Welsh manufacturer who had greatly improved the lives of his employees in the factory community of New Lanark, published two essays that argued that human character was largely a product of environment. Social amelioration, he asserted, was simply a matter of proper influence and education. New Lanark was a success, and Owen decided to expand his experiment. America was proving highly fertile soil for the cultivation of utopias, and he founded the New Harmony community in Indiana. His 1831 pamphlet, *Outline of the Rational System of Society,* lays out the fundamental principles of his utopian scheme. Today, such projects seem impossibly, well, *utopian,* but in the exhilarating atmosphere of the *début de siècle,* anything—even utopia—must have seemed possible.

This sense of an imminent earthly paradise was reinforced in the course of the nineteenth century by the combined impact of Darwinism, Marxism, and Freudian theory. Darwin's work implied that humanity, far from being doomed by the sin of Eve, was constantly evolving into a higher form. Indeed, the story of Genesis might not be historically accurate, given all those unexplained fossils lying about. If the world had not come into being in quite the fashion that the Bible described, then it was reasonable to question the whole concept of fallen humankind and original sin. If humanity had indeed descended from bits of prehistoric flotsam and jetsam, then it could be quite proud of its accomplishments and anticipate further progress. For many, the work of Karl Marx seemed to expound just that kind of progress. Various forms of communitarianism had been components of utopia since Plato, after all, and the nineteenth century seemed as economically far removed from the golden mean as the classical period. No one could deny that wealth and poverty were still rather unevenly distributed, what with gentlefolk in frock coats doing no work and living quite nicely, while the poor worked extremely hard and starved. One could not even blame one's misery on the divine order of things, since Freud's work indicated that humankind's unhappiness was the result not of divine rancor but of predictable crises within the individual psyche—and that the unhappiness could be eased through psychoanalysis.

The concepts of evolution, communism, and psychoanalytic theory had a profound effect on the utopian fiction of the late nineteenth century: the boundary between "literary" and "real-world" utopias became blurred, as fictional utopias began to inspire actual communities. Cooperative commonwealths were modeled on Lawrence Gronlund's 1884 book of the same name; Altruria colonies were based on the ideas put forth in William Dean Howells's

A Traveler from Altruria (1894); and nationalist colonies were modeled on the most influential utopian text of the age, Edward Bellamy's *Looking Backward* (1888).

It is difficult to comprehend the full impact of *Looking Backward* on its society. It inspired a host of imitators: in the eleven years that preceded its publication, about eighty works of utopian fiction had been published in Britain and America; in the eleven years following, that number more than tripled.[10] The work was translated into more than twenty languages. By 1890, only two years after its publication, more than 150 Bellamy clubs had been organized throughout America. When, in 1935, Charles Beard, John Dewey, and Edward Weeks independently made lists of the most influential books of the preceding fifty years, each listed Karl Marx's *Das Kapital* first and *Looking Backward* second.

Part of the reason for the book's success might have been the manner in which it reflected the tensions of America in the 1880s. Bellamy's readers were painfully familiar with what must have seemed to be social, political, and moral chaos: their society was a bewildering composite of Molly Maguires, Haymarket riots, "ten thousand strikes," astonishing political corruption, colossal monopolistic wealth, and dire sweatshop poverty. His metaphor of society as a huge coach in which the rich ride on the toil of the poor was a powerful reminder that his age was not golden but merely gilded. The grace, refinement, and elegance that seemed to characterize late nineteenth-century society was no more than an exquisite veneer, built on a substructure of misery.

Bellamy, a lifelong advocate of social change, Christian principles, and human solidarity, used the future perfect to illustrate the deficiencies of his present imperfect. He attempted to answer the question that had plagued utopian writers since Plato: why on earth would anyone in his right mind give up a single comfort (let alone a seat atop the coach) in order to benefit the rest of humankind? With the images of the American Civil War still relatively fresh in the national consciousness, Bellamy sought an answer in the army: heroic soldiers, after all, perform brave deeds for which no amount of financial recompense would be sufficient reward. How much money would induce an unwilling individual to lead a cavalry charge up a hill into a barrage of waiting cannon fire? A soldier's only reward is the *honor* awarded him by a grateful citizenry. So Bellamy created a future society whose currency is noble action and whose people work as diligently to accumulate honor as nineteenth-century humankind strove to accumulate wealth. In addition, Bellamy worked into his utopia the new industries that were cropping up throughout Europe and America. Factories need not be dehumanizing monsters, feeding on the powerless. Technology could be a benign, humane force, which, when properly utilized, could manufacture enough for all. Mass produce everything, Bellamy reasoned, and retail it through a single government-run company, and all merchandise could be produced and marketed at the lowest possible price. It was the bugaboo of pecuniary competition that prevented people from having what they needed. Of course, factory work, even when done for the good of the nation, can be dull and monotonous, even dangerous. To ensure that there would be a sufficient labor force, Bellamy devised an equitable work schedule in which dreary, tedious, or physically demanding occupations would require fewer hours of employment; stimulating, exciting activities would entail more. Evenhanded policies such as these were the key to a successful society and would produce a nation that was a sort of factory itself, turning out a host of happy, prosperous citizens.

Such a scheme, however, would require an impossibly bureaucratic, highly centralized government, administered by efficiency experts whose primary concern would be to see that things ran smoothly. Mass-produced items must have mass appeal; they must please the lowest common denominator of society. Bellamy's technocratic vision seemed long on Yankee ingenuity but short on art, craftsmanship, and beauty. In the nineteenth century, this was quite an oversight, considering that both America and Britain were profoundly influenced by aestheticians such as John Ruskin, who asserted that "great nations write their autobiographies in three manuscripts;—the book of their deeds, the book of their words, and the book of their art . . . of the three, the only quite trustworthy one is the last" (cited in Clark 1964, 196).

For the British political radical-artist-poet-craftsman William Morris, *Looking Backward* was anathema. Bellamy's centralized government directly opposed the socialist quest for a *de*centralized existence—what would amount to a nongovernment, by nineteenth-century (or, for that matter, twentieth-century) standards. Bellamy's mass-produced textiles, furniture, and other items for daily use contradicted Morris's valuation of individual craftsmanship. The concept of a shortened workday and increased leisure as compensation for distasteful work must have seemed nonsensical to an artisan who, Paul Thompson (1967, 255) notes, believed that "the aim of progress should not be more leisure, more gadgets, with everyday work remaining equally monotonous: for leisure to those who did not find satisfaction in their work would always be empty."

Morris responded to Bellamy's vision with a counterutopia. In *News from Nowhere; or, An Epoch of Rest* ([1890] 1920) the nineteenth century seems to have been followed hard on by the twelfth: in the future world of 1952, England is a Renaissance Faire run amok, everyone is his own artisan, and handcrafted articles of singular beauty are in abundance. Despite the industrious population (people are constantly on the lookout for employment of any sort), the age is truly an "epoch of rest," since work is seen as not only recreational but also re-creational: people are intellectually renewed and physically invigorated by their labor. News of a haying that needs workers draws hundreds of men and women, who journey by boat or carriage or on foot to reach the crop site. Beautiful women and handsome men, gaily dressed and richly adorned, work side by side in good fellowship, sharing one another's sorrows (which are few), joys, and goods. The Picadilly market is full of shops displaying gorgeous merchandise, but the merchants are "ignorant of the arts of buying and selling" (44) and gladly give away their stock to anyone who fancies it. Morris's time-traveling Guest learns that the socialist revolution that brought this happy state of things was originally triggered by the Bloody Sunday riots of 1887[11]—although, in 1952, few people remember such things. There is no concern for the past or its memorials: Westminster Abbey has been stripped "of the beastly monuments to fools and knaves, which once blocked it up" (42); the Houses of Parliament are now used to store manure. "The last harvest, the last baby, the last knot of carving in the market-place, is history enough" for people "assured of peace and continuous plenty" (69). The citizens of this future world live in an eternal, everlasting now, savoring each moment as it passes.

As the twentieth century approached, utopian literature had spanned over two millennia. In prehistoric myth, classical historiography and political theory, medieval biblical analysis, Renaissance humanism, Enlightenment skepticism, and nineteenth-century enthusiasm, men had sought either to palliate, ameliorate, or just explain the condition of humankind. There is a distinct irony, however, in the fact that these views were presented by those whose lives were in no particular need of palliation or amelioration, and who indeed had the most to gain from maintaining the status quo: literate males with the leisure to engage in creative endeavor. Plato was a well-born adviser to kings; More, a lawyer and chancellor of England; Bellamy, a lawyer and editor. These financially secure, politically sophisticated males engaged in a sort of literary noblesse oblige. Their largesse did not extend to women, however. From prehistoric myth to nineteenth-century polemic, the place of women in utopia underwent virtually no change. Overwhelmingly, men's utopias remained just that—utopias for men—and, as Elaine Hoffman Baruch (1984, 209) notes, "with few exceptions, women are no better off there than they are any place else."

The misogyny of prehistoric myths, for example, is integral to their plot structure, since the original paradise, whether that of Eden or of the golden age, is inevitably lost as a result of the frailty of a woman. In Genesis, Eve "saw that the tree was good for food, and that it was a delight to the eyes," and that it was "to be desired to make one wise" (Gen. 3:6): in other words, it satisfied her monstrous carnal appetites—physical, sensual, and cerebral—while paying no heed to spiritual hunger. The Greek myth of the lost golden age is no less misogynistic: in Hesiod's *Works and Days* (1959), Pandora is a gorgeous artifact, created by Jupiter in heaven and presented to Epimetheus (who, aided by his brother, Prometheus, had given fire to mankind). Epimetheus gladly accepts such an enchanting gift but discovers too late that she is actually "a sorrow to all men who eat bread" (27), sent to punish the brothers for their theft and mankind for receiving stolen goods. The modern version of the tale is relatively mild: alone in her new master's household, Pandora gives way to curiosity, opens the box containing the miseries of the world, and looses them upon mankind; only hope remains. In Hesiod's version, however, Pandora is not merely overcurious but is an "evil thing," from whom "originates the breed of female women" (158). In the *Theogony,* his description of Pandora's creation rapidly deteriorates into a misogynistic diatribe: women, the daughters of Pandora, "live with mortal men, and are a great sorrow to them . . . hateful poverty they will not share, but only luxury" (158). Females are like drone bees, Hesiod asserts, who "garner the hard work of others into their own bellies" (158); they are "for mortal men an evil thing, and they are accomplished in bringing hard labors" (159).

This is hardly a character recommendation and reflects the continuation of misogyny into the classical period. Classical utopias generally exclude women: Herodotus's tale of the Ethiopians, for example, is concerned with male members of the tribe; females are never mentioned. Strabo (1924, 3:179) discusses the place of women in his description of Scythian life, but they might have better gone unnoticed: he cites the geographer Poseidonus's assertion that the most virtuous Scythian men avoid female contamination by living "apart from woman-kind." Celibate men are held in great honor; they "have been dedicated to the gods and live with freedom from every fear" (179). Other historians, Strabo notes, are in disagreement with Poseidonus and report that the tribe practices polygyny,[12] with some men having "twelve or more" (183) wives; still others assert that the Scythians hold their wives and children in common. In any case, none of these options seem particularly attractive for the women: they are treated either as corrupting forces or as property.

As classical utopian writers go—and, indeed, as utopian writers of any age go—Plato is among the least misogynistic. Yet the *Republic* (1955) cannot be considered feminist, at least by twentieth-century standards. After explaining that the citizens of his model state will perform the work for which they are best qualified, Socrates asserts that the only pursuits of humankind in which women excel are "weaving, and the management of pancakes and preserves" (176). It is a sad fact, he remarks, that although "all the pursuits of men are the pursuits of women . . . in all of them a woman is inferior to a man" (176). A young male must be prevented from imitating a female, whose activities are frequently disruptive and sometimes even heretical: "quarrelling with her husband, or striving and vaunting against the gods in conceit of her happiness" (96). Baruch (1984, 211) notes that Plato's "plan has nothing to do with the individual and everything to do with the state; it is predicated on a communalization of wives, children, and property, to say nothing of a controlled system of eugenics which turns out to be a characteristic of twentieth-century dystopias."

Women were discounted in the medieval period as well. Although the New Testament did offer a positive model for women—Mary, the New Eve—traditional negative stereotypes persisted throughout the essentially misogynistic Bible. Paul gives a particularly explicit analysis of woman's inferior status, arguing that "the head of every man is Christ; and the head of a woman is her husband; and the head of Christ is God" (1 Cor. 11:3), and asserting that "a man ought not to cover his head, since he is the image and glory of God; but woman is the glory of man. (For man was not made from woman, but woman from man)" (1 Cor. 11:9–10). Augustine's view of women is similarly patriarchal: in the *City of God,* he argues that caretakers (that is, males) should command, while those who are cared for (that is, females) must obey. The male-female relationship is likened to that between parent and child, or master and servant. "And this is so much in accordance with the natural order, that the head of the household [is traditionally] called 'the father of the family' " (*paterfamilias*), who is free to correct "with strokes, or some other convenient punishment" (1945, 254) any misdeeds committed by his wife, children, and servants.

Renaissance texts continued to support this patriarchal hierarchy. More's utopians have firmly established men as the head of the legislative, judicial, religious, and familial structures. Utopian women are absolutely subject to the will of their spouses: women have the same relationship to their husbands that children have to their parents. During Lent, for example, women are expected to "kneel before their husbands . . . to confess their various failures and negligences, and beg forgiveness for their offenses" ([1516] 1975, 86). There seems to be no corresponding shrift for husbands; as editor Robert M. Adams points out in a note to this passage, "It is not specific that husbands have anything to confess or anywhere to confess it" (n., 86).[13] This preoccupation with female submission to male rule is typical of Renaissance utopias by men: in Thomas Lupton's *Siuqila* (1580), for example, a representative from the country of Mauqsun brags to a visitor that "there are no wives on the earth more obedient to their husbands than ours be" (37)[14] and explains that to maintain women's purity, females "very seldom go out of their houses, unless to the Church or Market. And when they go abroad, their faces are covered, and all their whole bodies with a linen mantle down to the ground, and all one fashion" (60).

In addition, there is a decided devaluation of women's contribution to society: More's *Utopia* demonstrates a blissful inattentiveness to household responsibility, which persists for the next four centuries in utopias written by men. More ([1516] 1975, 42) posits full-time employment for women as an efficient way to bolster the economy, noting that in Europe, "hardly any of the women, who are a full half of the population, work." He ignores the probability that women of the period were far too busy to work, having frittered away their time shopping, cooking, serving, washing, sewing, cleaning, and caring for children. As editor Adams notes, "If this doesn't constitute 'work,' that word must have a very special meaning" (n., 42). At any rate, More's relegation of women to the domestic sphere is just warmed-over Plato: women's preeminence is still limited to the management of pancakes and preserves.

The link between misogyny and utopia persists in varying degrees throughout seventeenth-century texts. Thomas Campanella's *The City of the Sun* ([1623] 1981) is perhaps the most enlightened narrative of the period, yet even he notes a female tendency to "idleness" (63), which must be overcome to avoid unattractive feminine pallor and feebleness. The healthy life of Solarian women (along with some eugenic breeding) almost guarantees that they are physically attractive and tall—yet unfortunates who must deceitfully wear makeup or high heels to camouflage a lack of comeliness or height are summarily executed (an uncomfortable precursor of Julia's punishment for wearing makeup and high heels in Orwell's *1984*). Since there is no corresponding provision made for similar deceits on the part of men, one must assume that either all males are perfect specimens or that physical appearance is of less importance in their case. Certainly an androcentric bias is present: males are permitted to "indulge in sexual intercourse with sterile or pregnant women or with women of scant worth" (57), but a sterile woman is not granted the same privileges as women who bear children, lest she purposely sterilize herself "in order to become a wanton" (59). Given the deceitful and immoral natures of some Solarian women, it is no wonder that the city is liberally furnished with "fine statues of illustrious men that the women gaze upon" (55) to "improve their offspring" (107), although statues of illustrious women, which might provide more direct inspiration, are never mentioned. Women in Francis Bacon's *The New Atlantis* are largely invisible, devoted to housekeeping and childbearing. On feast days, the family patriarch is enthroned in the place of honor before his family; the mother sits unseen, closeted behind him. The father is served exclusively by his male offspring; "women only stand about him" ([1627] 1966, 282). Montaigne's "Des Cannibales" ([1580] 1965, 212–13) explains that the New World savages are polygynous, and since a man gains more honor as he gains more wives, his loyal spouses devote themselves to procuring additional wives for their husband to increase his standing in the community. Montaigne notes with wonder that women are "more careful for their husbands' honor than of anything else, and they strive to secure as many fellow wives as they can, since it is a testimony to their husbands' virtue" (author's translation).[15]

Many texts of the period are more frankly misogynistic. Bishop Joseph Hall's *The Discovery of a New World* ([1605] 1937) introduces the woman-run state of Shee-Land, a place of noisy chaos, obsessive vanity, and ruthless brutality. A woman who treats her husband kindly has her head shaven and is pilloried; to atone fully, she must "bring a cudgel into the Court, all dyed with the fresh blood of her husband's broken pate" (74).[16] Hall views women's rule as against nature: in his topsy-turvy world, even "the very stones seem to beg to be at man's dispose, and to abhor the ordering of womankind" (75). Richard Brome's satirical farce, *The Antipodes* (1640), portrays a mentally ill young man jolted back to sanity by the alarming spectacle of an antiworld in which women rule. In 1686, Thomas D'Urfey's *A Common-Wealth of Women* depicted a community of bored, man-hungry Amazons, who joyfully relinquish their independence when a group of sailors lands on their island; indeed, the Amazons passively permit themselves to be raffled off to the men, and each promptly falls in love with whatever sailor is her lot.

Eighteenth-century utopists might have thought little of mankind's potential for perfectibility, but their views of womankind were frequently even more critical. The enormous size of Swift's ([1726] 1970) Brobdingnagians, for example, makes even the most well-favored among them seem grotesque, but the women are depicted in particularly repulsive terms. Gulliver describes in great detail a female breast "so varified with Spots, Pimples and Freckles, that nothing could appear more nauseous" (71) and female complexions "so coarse and uneven, so variously colored . . . with a Mole here and there as broad as a Trencher, and Hairs hanging from it thicker than Pack-threads . . . " (95). The women's morals are no more attractive than their appearance: in sections that border on the pornographic, Gulliver describes a roomful of huge naked women, who strip him and thrust him between their breasts; one, he asserts, "would sometimes set me astride upon one of her Nipples; with many other Tricks, wherein the Reader will excuse me for not being over particular" (94).

This pornographic impulse continues in works such as "Samuel Cock's" *A Voyage to Lethe* (1741). Cock's sexual metaphors are at times a bit confused but are consistently obscene: in a section that relates the sale and subsequent deflowering of an eager young woman, the narrator relates how he takes possession of "the charming Sally," a vessel "of an admirable Dimension," with "a most beautiful Slope from stem to stern; the one pleasing with an agreeable Jut, and the other striking the Eye with all the awful Sweetness of Majesty; her Port Holes were all of due Aperture" (10). Sixteen years of age, she is launched from "Herman Swivius's Wet Dock" (10) and delivered into the hands of the narrator, who immediately boards her. This delights the onlookers, of whom "all who knew any thing of a ship, was ambitious of sailing in her" (11). Her new owner is loath to lend her out, however, and instead sails for such remarkable places as the "Pillars of Diana," "Buttock-Land," and "the Gulph of Venus" (27–28). After navigating the Gulph, he encounters Voluptuaria, who congratulates him on "mounting up so high as the Palace," assuring him that "Admiralty Barges have much ado to come within the Gulph . . . neither do the Royal Yatchs [*sic*] quite reach up" (30).[17] Captain Cock explores the area thoroughly, then, finding nothing else of particular interest, leaves in search of new *terrae feminae*. A similar text, Thomas Stretzer's *A New Description of Merryland* (1741), described the female body with an even more alarming economy, reducing it to genitals and breasts. "A pleasant Mount called MNSVNRS . . . overlooks the whole country; and . . . round the Borders of Merryland is a spacious Forest which . . . seems to have been preserved for the Pleasure of Variety, and Diversion of Hunting" (17). The only other topographical features worth noting are two mountains known as BBY, "which tho' at some Distance from Merryland, have great Affinity with that Country, and are properly reckoned as an appendage to it" (28). The land is guarded by "two forts called LBA," fortifications that "are not very strong" and are "never known to hold out long against a close and vigorous Attack" (15). Beyond lies the canal, a "Place of great Traffick" (12), although the most highly prized lands are those that "have never been broke up, nor had Spade or Plough in them" (10–11). Indeed, "so fond are People of having the first Tilling of a fresh Spot, that I have known some Hundreds of Pounds given to obtain that Pleasure" (11). Men are the invaders who seize control of this land; the natives are its male children, "who, the Moment they come into the world . . . leave the particular Spot they were born in, and never after return to it but wander about till they are 14 or 15 years old, at which Age they generally look out for some other Spot of Merryland, and take Possession of it [at] the first opportunity" (20). Stretzer's narrative is meant to be humorous, yet it offers a grim assessment of woman's place in the world: she is a nameless hole, a property whose primary purpose is to provide males with pleasure and whose secondary function is to generate more male children—and more disembodied female vulvas and breasts to satisfy them.[18]

Of course, most eighteenth-century utopias were not obscene; indeed, among the best known is Dr. Johnson's *Rasselas* ([1759] 1977), which aims for a considerably higher moral tone. Yet *Rasselas*'s essential structure remains consistently androcentric, and the text frequently exhibits a misogynistic impulse. The Happy Valley that Rasselas detests is a Cokaygne pleasure palace, designed to keep royal offspring, primarily male offspring, from usurping their father's throne. Women are peripheral elements: it is Rasselas who decides to escape; his sister Nekayah, an unusually intelligent and courageous female specimen, follows. Her exposure to male company makes women unbearable to her: she deems their conversation "childish levity and prattle which [has] no meaning"; their desires "low, and their merriment often artificial"; their pleasures "embittered by petty competitions and worthless emulation" (111). Rasselas investigates the public world of men and is for a while amused; Nekayah, however, finds no similar distraction in her study of the domestic sphere—the traditional site of women's power—and finds it "more gloomy than solitude" (114). Although Nekayah is presented sympathetically, women in general are portrayed as vastly inferior to men, in many cases unfit to serve even in their biblically designated capacity as helpmeet.

The actual utopian experiments of the nineteenth century attempted to blow apart outmoded social systems and thus might have seemed to offer women a new kind of life as well. Yet the patriarchal hierarchy remained intact, and women continued to provide what Carol Kolmerten (*Women*, 1990, 2) describes as "a permanent class of secondary citizens created, as it were, to serve men by guaranteeing that all the bothersome, endlessly trivial work will get done without question." Jill Harsin (1968) notes that Owenite women, despite the Eleventh Law of the Universal Code (which stated that "both sexes shall have equal education, rights, privileges, and personal liberty" [75]), were given the entire responsibility for child care, gardening, factory work, making clothing, and cooking. This work was accomplished communally, in the interest of saving time—time, Harsin asserts, that "would leave women free to clean their homes" (82). She argues that Owen's utopian communities " 'freed' women from the drudgery of domesticity by adding outside labor to their unpaid household duties" (82). Rappite women faced an identical situation, for they were encouraged to work in the fields with the men during daylight hours and yet were expected to tend to household duties as well. Amana women were under the absolute control of the male hierarchy and were excluded from any community policy decisions. Mormon women's position was equally subordinate: Brigham Young once asserted that "all [women's] council & wisdom (although there are many good women) don't weigh as much with me as the weight of a Fly Tird. . . . It is not a woman's place to council her Husband & the moment a man follows a woman he is led astray & will go down to Hell unless he retracts his stepts [*sic*]" (cited in Lee 1955, 1:7).

This attitude toward women and women's work continued into the later nineteenth century, when utopian thinking was dominated by Bellamy's *Looking Backward*. Bellamy asserts that the women of the future are equal to men in all things. Yet they do not have equal political opportunity: the president and his cabinet are all males, with the exception of one woman who represents the entire female half of the population. Neither are women equal in terms of employment, for "under no circumstances is a woman permitted to follow any employment not perfectly adapted, both as to kind and degree of labor, to her sex" ([1888] 1966, 155). Actually, she is fortunate that she has any employment at all, save childbearing and rearing, for it is only because "the men of this day so well appreciate that they owe to the beauty and grace of women [no mention is made of intelligence] the chief zest of their lives and their main incentive to effort, that they *permit* them to work" (155, emphasis added).

Bellamy's beautiful and graceful Edith Leete, apparently meant to be the model of twenty-first-century womanhood, is really little more than a transplanted Victorian "belle-ideal": highly decorative, reassuringly ignorant about the world, and decidedly "feminine," that is, blushing and weeping at the slightest provocation. Julian West's initial response is to her beauty. He is bewitched by her "deep blue eyes, delicately tinted complexion, and perfect features," "the faultless luxuriance of her figure," and her "feminine softness and delicacy" (26). He makes no pretense of being drawn to her intellect and even admits that her "absorbed intensity" affects him "as it would not have done had she been less beautiful" (27). His lack of interest in her mind is actually rather fortunate, given that Edith is something of a dim bulb. Her greatest passion seems to center on shopping in gargantuan department stores[19]; although she professes to be a devotée of music and literature, she is a passive auditor of symphonies who neither plays an instrument nor sings, and although she claims to have read all of Dickens's works, she is constantly amazed at Julian West's accounts of nineteenth-century life. Although sympathetic to a fault, she seems to have no real idea of what goes on in the world; with a vapidity worthy of the coyest southern belle, she assures Julian that "even to fancy myself in your place makes my head swim" (105). Julian is finally enraptured, however, by her devotion to him: he realizes he loves her not only for her physical charms but also for her "sympathy" (177), her "womanly compassion" (179), and her "beauty and goodness" (179). He is also probably taken by her Victorian devotion to her home, for when she is not tending to his needs (or shopping), her life seems to consist mainly of arranging flowers. For the most part, she serves only as Julian's love interest and is otherwise nonessential to the book; with the exception of conversations about cultural matters (and shopping), Julian's discussions about the future world are invariably held with Dr. Leete—after dinner and over cigars, when Edith and her mother (who barely speaks a word throughout the book) have discreetly absented themselves.

Close attention to the text might reveal just where the women are during these absences. Dr. Leete, after all, has explained that housework is no longer necessary, since all laundry is sent out and the evening meal taken in a public hall. With a carelessness reminiscent of Thomas More's, however, he fails to clarify just who shops, cooks, and cleans up after breakfast and lunch and who makes the beds, dusts, and cleans the bathrooms. Either a great deal of drudgery has been disregarded, or twenty-first-century Americans bolt down one meal a day and have alarmingly lax standards of hygiene. Nineteenth-century women would have known only too well who would be expected to pick up the slack: the image of Edith Leete armed with scrub bucket and mop may be absurd, but it is certainly far more plausible (and has substantially more precedent) than that of Dr. Leete similarly outfitted.[20]

Even in William Morris's *News from Nowhere* ([1890] 1920), written in opposition to Bellamy's proposals for the future, the position of women is virtually the same. Graceful, attractive, and scantily clad young women scatter sweet-smelling herbs, arrange flowers, pick strawberries, bake bread, sweep floors, prepare meals, serve food, and mind the children. Housework dulls neither their spirits nor their physical charms, however, for they sing and smile as they work.[21] The narrator is quite taken by the charms of a woman of forty-two who looks twenty; she has "skin as smooth as ivory . . . cheeks full and round . . . lips as red as the roses she had brought in," and "beautiful arms, which she had bared for her work" (29). They are as decorative as a Morris tapestry, and nearly as discreet: when the conversation shifts to politics and history, the women grow bored and drift away, allowing the traditional utopian dialogue between males to take place without the distraction of their feminine charms. Women have little to do with the plot; they merely form an attractive backdrop for the action, a chorus of lightly clad, barefoot young women "flitting to and fro" (23). All are "at least comely," "kind and happy-looking in expression of face . . . shapely and well-knit of body, and thoroughly healthy-looking and strong" (23).[22] In addition, all are available; they realize that "a child born from the natural and healthy love between a man and a woman, even if it is transient, is likely to turn out better in all ways . . . than the birth of the respectable commercial marriage bed. . . . Pleasure begets pleasure" (79). One such pleasure must be child rearing, since the women are expected to assume full responsibility for the offspring of such casual unions. Morris's females, vigorous young creatures whose only duties are to serve and please men, typify utopian womanhood in men's texts. Despite the span of centuries, they would require only minor modification to fit comfortably into Plato's republic, More's Utopia, or

Bellamy's futuristic Boston. Decorative and useful, they are man's hushed and docile helpmeets.

Yet female voices, while muffled, had not been absolutely still during this time. Many women realized that they had no true place in men's utopian texts; there was nowhere that females could function as equals, independent of male control. They sought to create such a place in their own narratives. After all, the well-intentioned schemes of well-educated, financially sound, politically connected males with fairly abundant leisure time had little to say to poorly educated, economically disenfranchised, politically anonymous women whose days were crammed full managing a house.[23] Men's utopian writing was the result of a surplus of education, money, position, and time; women's utopias grew out of deficiency.

This deficiency, of course, extended to literary models, and female utopian writers have historically been forced to draw from men's texts. Mary Wroth's *Urania* (1621), for example, was written in response to her uncle Philip Sidney's *Arcadia* (1590). Yet there are numerous subtle differences, as Wroth quietly modifies the genre for her own use. Sidney's prose romance detailed the adventures of young men. Wroth's protagonists are females, yet they are as bold and valiant as men: despite cruel fathers, faithless lovers, and brutal husbands, the women enjoy a relatively unfettered existence (at least by seventeenth-century standards), engaging in such masculine pursuits as writing poetry, hunting, fishing, and even fighting. Wroth's text adheres strictly to the conventions of her age—her heroines are virtuous, pious, and faithful to their men—yet it is quietly subversive as well, valorizing united sisterhood as a force that can withstand patriarchal might.

Equally subversive was Margaret Cavendish's "The Blazing World" (1666), the first true utopian work by a woman.[24] The narrative, which will be examined at some length in the fifth chapter, draws not only from utopian literature but also from fantastic travel fantasies such as Francis Godwin's *Man in the Moone* (1638). "The Blazing World" recounts the exploits of a shrewd, courageous, and highly intelligent young woman, who discovers the Lost Eden and marries its emperor. In the majority of Renaissance texts, a woman's adventures would end with her marriage; for Cavendish's protagonist, however, they have only begun. Her boundless intellectual curiosity permits her to escape the confines of gender through a series of out-of-body excursions; her courage and resourcefulness enable her to compete successfully in two traditionally male arenas, the courtroom and the battlefield. Cavendish's text uses utopia to undermine the entire androcentric structure of her society by presenting a revolutionary vision of free women and detailing the heights to which they might ascend.

Yet Cavendish, like male utopian writers, did not support herself by her pen and could afford to be a bit outrageous. A commercial writer such as Aphra Behn had to use the utopian genre far more conventionally. Two of her texts make use of utopia: her brief comic farce *The Emperor of the Moon* (1687), which uses it only as a peripheral element (in an attempt to distract his beloved's possessive father, a rogue assumes the guise of a cabalist from Eutopia and expounds on the supposed nature of the Moon-World to the gullible philosopher), and *Oroonoko* (1688, 147), which offers a brief description of a West Indian society, whose inhabitants seem "an absolute idea of the first state of innocence, before man knew how to sin." The naturally modest natives live happily without religion, laws, or clothes and enjoy the full bounty of nature in their prelapsarian Eden. Even in this West Indian Eden, however, women live in a decidedly postlapsarian state: they are little more than slaves, and their responsibilities are limited to housework, procreation, and the gratification of male desire. The latter duties are apparently the most consequential. The society is polygynous, and older and presumably less sexually attractive wives do the majority of domestic chores, freeing the younger and more appealing women for amorous activity.

In the eighteenth century, women's narratives mimicked the undercurrents of scandal and obscenity so prevalent in men's texts. In Mary de la Rivière Manley's *Secret Memoirs and Morals of Several Persons of Quality of Both Sexes* (1709), the "New Atalantis" is England; the "memoirs" are thinly disguised contemporary scandals. Yet, like Wroth and Cavendish, Manley replaces the conventional dialogue between men with a dialogue between women. The utopian visitor is the impeccably virtuous Astraea, the goddess of justice, innocence, and purity, who, having long since abandoned the world, revisits it to determine whether humankind is still "defective." Her guide is her own mother, the bedraggled and neglected Virtue, who describes society's deplorable state. Although the text points out the foibles of men and women alike, the fact that humankind is being judged by *women* skews the androcentric order of things somewhat.[25]

One eighteenth-century text offered a direct response—and something of a challenge—to a male narrative. Ellis Cornelia Knight's *Dinarbas* (1790) refutes both the misogyny and pessimism of Dr. Johnson's *Rasselas*. In Knight's text, the world-weary prince returns to war-torn Abyssinia and eventually reassesses his gloomy view of life, discovering that life offers more pleasure than pain, that God is a support during periods of trial, and that marriage can offer a great deal of happiness. In a valorization of the domestic, Rasselas and his sister both meet suitable mates and achieve happiness through wedded bliss, and although neither wife would presume to interfere in public matters, both are nonetheless free to establish charities and patronize the arts.

The eighteenth century also saw the emergence of the first true "gynotopia"—a place for women, free of male oppression. Sarah Robinson Scott's *A Description of Millenium Hall* (1762), which will also be discussed at some length in the fifth chapter, describes a pastoral country estate in Cornwall inhabited by a group of energetic, artistic, and highly virtuous celibate women, who have retreated from the corruption of the world to spend their lives in study, prayer, and good deeds. From the conventlike atmosphere of their sheltered community, they keep the world of men at bay; their pleasures are simple, wholesome, and Christian; their sisterhood sustains them.

Christian principles and communal living were carried over into the new century, as women, like men, began to attempt actual utopian experiments. The most familiar of these is probably the United Society of Believers in Christ's Second Appearing, more commonly known as the Shakers. The movement was founded by Mother Ann Lee, an illiterate Manchester factory worker who argued that woman was not inherently subordinate to man: Eve's inequality was a consequence of her sexual relationship with Adam, and those who lived in celibacy could reattain an unfallen state.[26] Mother Ann claimed to be the new messiah, who would lead her disciples back to paradise—in the form of a Shaker community in America. By the 1850s, thousands of members populated fifty-eight Shaker villages in ten states, governed by men and women alike, in an imitation of the dual nature of the bisexual deity they worshiped. Ruby Rohrlich (1984, 5) points out that the governing body included both "elders and 'eldresses,' deacons and 'deaconesses,' " and "foremen and forewomen." Yet women were relegated to essentially the same roles they filled in the outside world: as Charles Nordhoff (1875, 166) explains, "They very sensibly hold that in general life the woman's work is in the house, the man's out of doors; and there is no offer to confuse the two." Admittedly, child rearing was not a problem, since celibacy was so central to the movement; cooking and cleaning, however, remained women's work.[27] The management of pancakes and preserves was still woman's domain.

An entirely different sort of community was established by the dauntless Frances Wright, a highly public and outspoken champion of such radical concepts as absolute sexual equality, "amalgamation of the races" (Perkins and Wolfson 1939, 193), and free love. Although she was almost universally castigated for what critics considered her outrageous beliefs and highly unorthodox lifestyle, Wright nonetheless persisted in her rationalist crusade by inaugurating the ill-fated experimental utopian community of Nashoba: amid two thousand acres of mosquito-infested Tennessee swampland, during the worst outbreak of malaria in a century, Wright sought to establish a scrupulously egalitarian society in which the concepts of public and private spheres would eventually cease to exist. Her philosophy diametrically opposed conventional notions: the sanctity of marriage, for example, was for Wright the "servitude of matrimony"—an institution "of no force," since "no woman can forfeit her individual rights or independent existence, and no man assert over her any rights or power whatsoever beyond what he may exercise over her free and voluntary affection" (193). Women in the community were vigorous and active, if not healthy (the swampland took its toll on everyone), and, clad in comfortable coats and pantaloons, actively participated both in government and physical labor. Education was compulsory, coeducational, free, and open to all races. Religion, however, was not part of the curriculum—an innovation that horrified the pious. Although the community's children received training in ethical behavior, they had no "belief in [or] homage to a Being or Beings not cognizable by the senses of man" (194).

Perhaps the most successful nineteenth-century utopian experiment by women is the least well known today: the Woman's Commonwealth, a Texas community that A. Harriette Andreadis (1968, 91) describes as "a model for successful religious, economic, sexual, and emotional self determination." The community originated in 1866 as a middle-class women's Bible study group held at the house of Martha McWhirter. Eventually, its twenty-four members began to explore fairly radical ideas regarding sexual and economic authority: when they decided to practice celibacy, a disgruntled Mr. McWhirter moved out of his home. His place was taken by a number of women who left their husbands, families, and servants and began to establish an independent economy by selling wood they chopped, butter they churned, and eggs they raised. Other women worked as domestics for outside employers and turned their wages over to the commune. Eventually, the members were able to purchase additional land and build the highly profitable Central Hotel. The communal wealth generated by this venture enabled them to travel the world, study professions such as dentistry and blacksmithing, and purchase a second hotel. Their utopian enterprise continued until 1906; it had been moved to the District of Columbia in 1898 and failed to attract new members there.

Yet few nineteenth-century women could gain the economic backing to fund an experimental community, and few had the fortitude necessary to withstand the negative opinion such an undertaking invariably engendered. Men had a long-standing tradition of ideal male-dominated societies and could readily put their ideas into place; women, however, had no real place in these worlds and, lacking corresponding female paradises of their own, might have had less confidence in actual utopian movements. Most of the early nineteenth-century writers in this study preferred to quest after utopia in the less demanding climate of fictional landscapes—in the idyllic past, in the technological paradise to come, or in dream fancies that circumvented the confines of time and space altogether.

In 1822, two years before her ill-fated Nashoba experiment, Frances Wright wrote *A Few Days in Athens,* set in the third century B.C.E. Her narrative, ostensibly about the young Stoic Theon and his prejudice against the supposedly debauched Epicureans, introduces the brilliant Leontium, a beautiful, intelligent, and highly articulate young woman who studies and lives (virtuously) with Epicurus. Her dilemma mirrors Wright's own: a brilliant woman, trapped in a society that devalues female intellect, seeks out a more sympathetic environment. She does this in spite of negative public opinion; like Wright, Leontium is mislabeled a prostitute by unenlightened outsiders. Within the security of her new community, however, her worth is recognized and her aspirations encouraged. Many nineteenth-century women, unable to acquire any sort of higher education, must have found Leontium a combination of kindred spirit and inspiration.

Leontium's Epicurean paradise was ancient history, however. In the progressive atmosphere of the midcentury, utopias by women were generally set well in the future. Wright's text contrasts sharply, for example, with Jane Webb Loudon's *The Mummy!* (1827), which offers a vision of twenty-second-century England. Although the plot of Loudon's novel follows the conventions of gothic romance and is primarily concerned with the affairs of men, women and their concerns are certainly not relegated to the sidelines: the central conflict focuses on which of two *queens* shall rule England, and the story features a brave princess who disguises herself in male attire to follow the man she loves. In addition, Webb suggests that a technologically advanced society might greatly ease women's burdens: moving houses glide along the road, saving housewives the trouble of packing for a trip; kitchen automaton-organs summon domestic assistants from throughout the home when a single chord is struck; and modern conveniences, such as chemical fire, folding drinking cups of malleable glass, inflatable air mattresses, and feather fan vents to recycle the air, offer some relief from the backbreaking labor of housework.

A slightly more feminist futuristic utopia is Mary Griffith's "Three Hundred Years Hence" (1836), a dream vision anticipating Bellamy's *Looking Backward* in form: the narrator fancies himself buried alive by an avalanche and awakened in the year 2135. He encounters a United States dramatically improved by technology and morality, in which trains, ships, and farm machinery are powered by an unspecified but unlimited energy source; a passage to India is accomplished in only twenty days; and war, capital punishment, monopolies, child abuse, and slavery have been abolished. These changes have come about not through political agitation but through the domestic influence of women (although *how* change has been effected is never specifically addressed). Although they have achieved social and legal equality, Griffith's women are by choice politically subordinate. They are "now equal to men in all that they ever considered as their rights" (125), but "the proper distinction [is] rigidly observed between the sexes," and women keep "within the limits assigned them by the Creator" (125). The authority they seek is moral and private, not legislative and public. "As soon as women had more power in their hands," the narrator is informed by his utopian guide, "they became more enlightened as they rose higher in the scale, and instead of encroaching on [man's] privileges . . . women shrunk farther and farther from all approach to men's pursuits and occupations" (99–100); that is, they refused to abdicate the power afforded them by the domestic sphere. Women sought no "independent power of their own" (100), wishing only to use their influence to guide humanity away from war, crime, and poverty, toward a blissful future of peaceful harmony—the joys of the family hearth extended to the world in general.

Yet many women found the joys of their individual family hearths falling far short of Griffith's ideal. For them, dreams of the future were far too distant; for them, fantasy utopias offered consolation and compensation. Elizabeth Barrett Browning's "An Island" ([1838] 1900), for example, is a dream vision of a sheltered, cloistered, alternative world, apparently free from worldly male interference. Her island is a feminine, fertile, pagan landscape: the land, undulating in luxurious disorder, is a hidden place, "full of hills and dells, / All rumpled and uneven" (2:37), bursting with fruit and blossoms. The hidden world draws its light not from a God's heaven, but from Mother Earth and her fecundity. "Pleiades of flowers" illuminate the island and "star her over" with their glow: in a process that owes more to poesy than physics, "the rays of their unnumbered hues" are "all refracted by the dews" (2:39) and bathe the place with their brilliance. Animals and humans (a group of female poets) wander at will, equals with nothing to fear from one another: island sheep roam "unruled by shepherds" (2:40); island poets are equally free of interference, divine or temporal. The community has exchanged "man's voice and use, / For Nature's way and tone" (2:41). Nature mistresses them as the moon mistresses the ocean—there is no domination, only a harmonious communion, "like a harp of many lays, / moving its master while he plays" (2:42).

In the mid-nineteenth century, women began to write about utopian experimental communities. Their initial responses indicated not only a great deal of reserve but also a concern that women's existence in such places was, if anything, more dismal than mainstream life. Rebecca Harding Davis's "The Harmonists" (1866), for example, offers a dystopian view of a Rappite colony in Economy, Pennsylvania. The stern idealism of this celibate religious communal group has degenerated into hopeless repression and materialism: lonely withered women are virtual slaves, whose only creative outlet is cooking for gross male masters obsessed with obtaining capital.[28]

By 1870, men had been writing utopian fiction for more than twenty-four centuries. Yet, despite the myriad settings of their narratives—past, present, or future; in gardens, islands, valleys, polar circles, inner earth, outer space, or heaven—women's position was generally the same throughout: inferior. Women had written only a handful of texts, and these, crafted largely from *within* the dominant male perspective, had adhered to the conventions of a patriarchal society. Yet women had already begun to use the genre to articulate their own philosophies and agendas, to make a small place for females in an androcentric society. In 1870, this gynotopic impulse finally emerged full-blown, as women commandeered a historically male genre and used it to blend feminist and historical perspectives into entirely new forms of social interaction and gender relationships. In short, they transformed the genre from a literature *about* outsiders into a literature *by* outsiders. Why and how they did so will be examined in the following chapters.

THREE

Genre and Herstory
Women's Nineteenth-Century Utopian Fiction in Context

Prior to 1869, women's utopian writing was rather scarce and, at least by current feminist standards, somewhat tame. During the seventeenth, eighteenth, and early nineteenth centuries, women produced only a handful of utopian texts; and although many of these proposed increased personal autonomy for women, not one openly defied society's androcentric structure, not one envisioned a truly egalitarian society in which women could overcome their biblically ordained subjugation. In Margaret Cavendish's "Blazing World" (1666), for example, the protagonist is an empress who rules an entire world—yet her sovereignty is granted by her emperor husband, and she does not govern actual *men*, since her subjects are animal-human amalgamations. Sarah Scott's *Millenium Hall* (1762) and Frances Wright's *A Few Days in Athens* (1822) both envision utopias where noble women can retreat from the dissolute world of men, yet such a retreat is in itself a testimony to male preeminence. The women of Mary Griffith's "Three Hundred Years Hence" (1836) submissively accept divinely ordained limits, and the dream author of Elizabeth Barrett Browning's "An Island" (1838) abandons her feminist paradise to return dutifully to the patriarchal God. Even Jane Appleton's "Sequel to 'The Vision of Bangor in the Twentieth Century'" (1848), which attempts to free women from the second-class status imposed by the Genesis myth, ultimately defers to the might of the patriarchy, for her women reject enfranchisement; although at one time they had been "obliged to take part in government" (260) because man's greed had turned society "topsy-turvy" (261), once women had restored "order and beauty," they had "no wish" (258) to participate further in affairs of state.

It was not until 1869 that a very different kind of utopian text emerged, one that redefined women's role in society and questioned the very foundations of the social structure—no longer was male dominance perceived as inevitable. Although these texts built on much of what had come before (they continued to champion women's intellectual and moral capacities, for example), their central focus was innovative; they challenged the presumed superiority of males, castigated the unfairness inherent in male rule, and advocated universal suffrage. Elizabeth Corbett's "My Visit to Utopia" (1869) advocates a nonhierarchical society in which male-female relationships are based on kindness, courtesy, and mutual respect. Women enjoy equality in both public and private spheres: universal suffrage is the rule, and women are active politically; "obeying" is omitted from the marriage service; and men share both household chores and child-rearing duties. Annie Denton Cridge's *Man's Rights* (1870) presents a complete inversion of the existing order: on Mars, traditional sexual roles and stereotypes are reversed, as pale, feeble "gentlemen-housekeepers" (3), either overworked and nervous or vain and lazy, must stay at home, while stately, dignified women rule. The basis for women's autonomy is the Martian Bible, which tells how "*Adam* was tempted by the serpent, and gave the forbidden fruit to his wife; for which reason it was said to the man that 'she (the woman) shall rule over thee,' and 'in sorrow thou (the man) shalt attend the children' " (42). Cridge does not suggest that her Martian society is better or fairer than that of Earth; indeed, her dystopia acts as a negative exemplar, demonstrating that any hierarchical society is inherently unjust. Yet, while exposing this unfairness, she offers a tantalizing vision of politically empowered womanhood. These texts were succeeded by a steadily increasing number of narratives exploring alternate social models, all written by English and American women—there was no similar outpouring anywhere else. Clearly, something particular to late nineteenth-century Britain and America caused so many women to seek out the utopian genre and to use it in such new ways. A close reading of the texts in question suggests that women's experiences with contemporary politics, fashion, health, education, and employment triggered their production of this new kind of utopian narrative.

Part of this efflorescence, after all, was a response to an intellectual climate highly conducive to radical ideas. Both England and America had felt the combined impact of the Enlightenment, the American and French revolutions, technological breakthroughs, scientific innovations, and the rise of socialism. Additional revolutionary notions had been contributed by all branches of feminism—belief in women's natural equality, a heightened consciousness of women's sphere, and concern for women's legal rights. Nevertheless, as Frances Bartowski (1989, 7) has argued, specific "ruptures in Western social history, those times when utopian desires/projective longings are driven by hope and fear, those times particularly marked by anticipation and anxiety," seem to provoke increased interest in utopian literature. The specific "rupture" that acted as a catalyst for the outpouring of women's utopian fiction was most probably a political one: middle-class women's overwhelming frustration during the late 1860s with the apparent failure of the suffrage movement.

A half-century of debates on "the woman question" and various campaigns for suffrage had advanced with agonizing slowness, and all progress seemed to come to a grinding halt with the passage of the Second Reform Bill in England

(1867) and the Fifteenth Amendment in America (1870). Robert Fulford (1957, 75–76) describes the English struggle for enfranchisement as a "huge vehicle which . . . advanced steadily toward the summit of a hill"; yet by 1869, suffrage machinery was at a standstill: "in vain the enthusiasts crowded round to push, to advise, or to suggest alterations or strategy but the only result of their efforts was a shudder, a scuffling of dust, a sense of disturbance. There was no forward movement." To a lesser extent, American suffrage hopes saw a similar slowdown: although women had enjoyed local successes in the territories of Wyoming (1869) and Utah (1870), these were not only outweighed by the specific exclusion of women in two constitutional amendments but were also undermined by dissension within the woman's movement. In Britain and America, women were baffled and angry as they contemplated what appeared to be the collapse of their hopes.

The English suffrage movement had begun quietly, growing out of feminist organizations concerned with women's education, employment opportunities, and property rights. As early as 1825, William Thompson's *Appeal of One Half the Human Race* (rpt. 1983, 196) exhorted women: "demand with mild but unshrinking firmness, perfect equality with men: demand equal civil and criminal laws, an equal system of morals, and, as indispensable to these, equal political laws, to afford you an equal chance of happiness with men." In 1832, after the First Reform Bill enfranchised large numbers of men, the radical "Orator" Hunt presented a petition before the House of Commons proposing that "every unmarried female, possessing the necessary pecuniary qualification, should be allowed to vote" (Fulford 1957, 33). In 1847, the Quaker Anne Knight published the first pamphlet in support of female suffrage; in 1851, the Sheffield Association for Female Suffrage was formed. Barbara Bodichon and Bessie Rayner Smith, who would both become deeply involved in the cause of feminine enfranchisement, had worked together since 1856, when they collected petitions supporting the Married Women's Property Bill.

Support for suffrage gradually increased in the 1860s, and there was a flurry of enfranchisement activity between 1866 and 1868. Enthusiasm was generated both by the democratic climate surrounding debate on the Second Reform Bill and by women's acquisition of a champion in Parliament, John Stuart Mill. In June of 1866, Mill presented to the House of Commons a suffrage petition drafted by Barbara Bodichon and signed by 1,499 female property owners; in May of 1867, as Parliament considered a reform act that would nearly double the exclusively male electorate, Mill proposed an amendment to omit the word "man" and insert "person" in its place. Enfranchisement seemed a very real possibility—a matter of simple justice—and middle-class women awaited the outcome of the debate with eager anticipation. These hopes were short-lived, however; the amendment was soundly defeated, 196 to 73. Samuel Laing spoke for the majority, arguing that "between the two sexes it was abundantly evident that Nature had drawn clear lines of distinction," one of these being that "the contests of political life" were not "suited to the nature of woman" (Helsinger,

Sheets, and Veeder 1983, 2:45–46). Women's only hope seemed to lie in a legal technicality. Lord Brougham's Act (1859) stated that "in all Acts words importing the masculine gender shall be deemed and taken to include females unless the contrary . . . is specifically provided" (Helsinger, Sheets, and Veeder 1983, 2:48). Since the Reform Bill used the word "man," perhaps the term might be given this liberal interpretation. Using this rationale, a group of 5,346 Manchester women registered to vote in 1868; when their names were later removed from the rolls, they retained an attorney and took the matter to court. Once again, they were disappointed: not only did one of the judges suggest that "removing the name of a woman from the voters' roll was like removing the name of a dog or a horse" (Sachs and Wilson 1978, 24), but in a subsequent trial, it was ruled that "man" meant "a member of the male sex" (Helsinger, Sheets, and Veeder 1983, 2:49) and that usage had invalidated whatever claim to enfranchisement women might have once had.[1] With no further avenues left to explore, Englishwomen settled unhappily into what Lady Frances Balfour called "the doldrum years" (Tickner 1988, 4).

Meanwhile, the American suffrage movement was plagued with similar setbacks. Early attempts at voting reform were linked closely with abolitionism, and when emancipation engendered new enfranchisement legislation, many women assumed that the gains made by blacks would extend to white middle-class women as well. However, the first test of this assumption, an 1867 Kansas referendum on women's suffrage, was a dismal failure. The next test was the controversy surrounding the Fourteenth Amendment, which provided full rights of citizenship to "all persons born or naturalized in the United States." The debate centered on the legal interpretation of the word "person," a point similar to the use of the word "man" in England's Second Reform Bill. By inserting the word "male" directly into the Constitution, however, Congress avoided legal dispute over the amendment, ratified in 1868. In 1869, feminists' enfranchisement hopes were raised once more by the proposed Fifteenth Amendment's assertion that race should offer no bar to voting rights. Women campaigned vigorously to modify the amendment to read "race or sex," but despite their efforts, debate on the matter had ended by the close of 1869, and the amendment was ratified in early 1870. Majority opinion was distressingly similar to that of the Second Reform Bill: Senator Frelinghuysen of New Jersey asserted that women's "milder, gentler nature . . . disqualifies them for the turmoil and battle of public life" (Flexner 1971, 151); Senator Williams of Oregon argued that a woman "who undertakes by the use of some independent political power to contend and fight against man, displays a spirit which would, if able, convert all the now harmonious elements of society into a state of war, and make every home a hell on earth" (151). As Eleanor Flexner points out, "for fifty years to come, no rational appeal to fact was able to make a dent in either of these two arguments of the anti-suffrage arsenal" (152).

Despite decades of debate and agitation, change had failed to materialize, and women in both countries felt as if they were back at square one. Indeed,

American women had actually *lost* ground. Prior to the Fourteenth Amendment, Flexner (1971, 143) notes, "the question of whether or not [women] might vote had been regarded as a state matter. . . . In the early years after the American Revolution they had voted in some parts of Virginia and New Jersey, and their *right* to vote had been specifically denied only with the adoption of constitutions in the several states which limited suffrage to white male voters in certain property categories." The adoption of the Fourteenth Amendment meant that women's unequal status was no longer merely custom but law[2] and that yet another amendment would be required to grant women federal suffrage. To make matters even worse, many of women's efforts on the behalf of suffrage had introduced elements of divisiveness into their organizational structure. The specter of racism had emerged when some argued that Anglo-Saxon women should be enfranchised because they were more competent to vote than blacks; in the February 1869 issue of the radical feminist publication the *Revolution,* Elizabeth Cady Stanton derided "Sambo," swore she would "cut off this right arm of mine before I will ever work for or demand the ballot for the Negro and not the woman," and denounced the enfranchisement of the "Africans, Chinese, and all the ignorant foreigners the moment they touch our shores" (Flexner 1971, 143). Yet another schism occurred when women disagreed on whether to focus their attention on the single issue of suffrage or to continue to include concerns such as free love, labor conditions, and education. By the fall of 1869, the major women's suffrage organization, the American Equal Rights Association, was disbanded, its members split into smaller, dissenting factions. This division would persist throughout the remainder of the century: American women, it seems, had their own version of the British "doldrum years."

As English and American women helplessly watched the collapse of all the hopes embodied in enfranchisement legislation, they were forced to confront the glaring proof of their own inequality—a devastating blow for women who had not merely glimpsed the promised land but had carefully mapped its topography. One of their responses to the loss of the land of promise was the production of a series of utopian dream visions—and re-visions—that emphasized the tension between women's legally reenforced isolation and their desire to participate in public matters. It is not the most hopelessly oppressed who dream of freedom, after all, but those who have their expectations raised and then frustrated. The lost utopian alien wandering in strange realms, the quintessential outsider, must have been an oddly familiar and hence comfortable and consolatory figure to women who felt like strangers in their own society, ill-equipped travelers "wandering in the wilderness of prejudice and ridicule" (Anthony and Harper 1902, 4:134), through a complex, perplexing world. They were moral exemplars who were linked to the fall of humankind, household managers who were considered incapable of participating in government, and domestic goddesses who had the legal status of furniture. After struggling so long for a world in which they might be welcomed as equals, they now realized their vision had been snatched from them, causing their repressed condition to seem even more so.

These outsiders wrote utopias that engaged the central issues confronting their society and challenged fundamental societal assumptions—although frequently in unexpected ways. One might anticipate, for example, that oppressed women would comfort themselves with gynocentric inversions of an androcentric society. Yet this is not the case. Unless the intention of the author is specifically ironic (as in Cridge's text), women's nineteenth-century utopias replace patriarchies not with matriarchies, but with scrupulously egalitarian communities offering men and women equal opportunities to manage the community and to nurture children.[3] Similarly, one might expect the misogynistic Old Testament God to be dethroned by a devouring, revengeful goddess; instead, one discovers gentle, nonjudgmental deities, more frequently androgynous than female. Matriotism rejects such patriotic concepts as empire and manifest destiny (although the utopians in this study are invariably Anglo-Saxon and usually middle class) and stresses harmony and mutual respect in most aspects of life.

Such harmonious new worlds make possible a new type of heroine, a powerful and valued member of society, characterized by nobility, dignity, radiant good health, and immense intellectual power. She forms a sharp contrast to the nineteenth-century middle-class "belle-ideal": docile and submissive; preoccupied with frivolities and fashion; given to "vapors," migraines, and hysteria; poorly educated; and weighed down by legal, social, and physical restrictions on her person. Yet the utopian heroine was not inherently stronger or brighter: her sound body and mind sprang from an environment that encouraged her to reach her full human potential.

Such heroines reflected the frustration of middle-class women who, denied the vote, looked at other ways to ameliorate their lives—and to further their chances at eventually gaining enfranchisement. Reforms in health care (particularly dress reform) and education seemed most immediate and referred to suffrage, since sickly women or frivolous belles would lack both the energy and creditability to carry on an enfranchisement campaign, while poorly educated women would lack the credentials and experience. Health and educational reforms were frequently addressed in nineteenth-century utopias by women whose heroines have escaped the snares of fashion and ignorance: free women are not smothered in awkward, restrictive clothing but stride boldly in sensible garb that allows them to breathe and run and become physically strong; free women are not trapped in ignorance but are given the higher education and professional training that allow them to compete and develop and become intellectually powerful.

Clothing, which might seem at first to be a rather trivial matter, was a profoundly serious concern for nineteenth-century middle-class women. Dress was, after all, a cultural signifier: an 1893 article in *Godey's Lady's Book* asserted that "nothing is so true an index to a woman's character as her clothes" (Kin-

nard 1986, 305). Certainly clothing provided an index to her financial and social status: long, trailing skirts were the mark of a wealthy woman who lived
in an insulated world of carpets and carriages; tight corsets and thin-soled,
fragile shoes indicated an inactive woman with no need to bend or walk, since
servants would attend to her every need. The latest French designs signified
that the wearer had both the leisure to keep up with constantly changing fashions and the wealth to purchase the new and discard the old. Yet feminists de-
cried the ridiculous figure cut by a fashion-mad female obsessed with the latest
gaudy ruffle or frill, reading nothing more stimulating than *Godey's*, and devoting her life to self-decoration. How could such a woman, they lamented,
ever be taken seriously? Of more importance, health professionals condemned
the pathetic figure of a stylish woman imprisoned in restrictive feminine clothing that hampered breathing, made exercise an impossibility, and, by deform-
ing women's internal organs, was frequently life threatening. How could such
a woman function as a useful member of her society? The authors examined
in this study offer alternatives to the tyranny of fashion, frequently drawing
on historical dress-reform movements to clothe their heroines in a dignified yet
unconstrained manner. Women in Owenite communities wore pantalets and
coats buttoned to the knees; "rational dress," consisting of a short jacket, a
knee-length skirt, and loose trousers, was proposed by Amelia Jenks Bloomer
in 1850. In 1874, Abba Gould Woolson espoused simple, graceful clothes, most
frequently designed along the Grecian model, which complemented women's
natural dignity and permitted freedom of movement. In the 1880s, the English
Rational Dress Society advocated a divided skirt, and in 1911, Paul Poiret's
"harem pants," draped trousers worn under a midcalf skirt and knee-length
tunic, enjoyed some limited popularity.

Annie Denton Cridge (1870) devotes more than half of *Man's Rights* to fashion and demonstrates that making oneself a living objet d'art is essentially an
exercise in self-abasement. In her inverted society, however, it is men who,
trapped in their foolish clothing, "lack dignity" (25) and have lost any vestige
of human nobility: "tricked off in finery," half-smothered in "little flounces
. . . and fringe down the front, round the sleeves, and round the coat-tails," a
fashionable man is ridiculous, "a monkey standing on two feet" (34). Everything about male fashions is infantile, "little," designed to reduce the status of
the wearer: "little ruffles . . . round the bottom of the pants," "rows of small
ruffles" on the vest, "little flat hats" with childish "ribbon streamers" (13).
"Master Willie" (or "Sammie" or "Johnnie"—men's names are infantilized as
well) wears a "little green velvet cap" and carries a "tiny porte-monnaie" decorated with "little chains" (35). Cridge is far less specific about the clothes of
her women, who are too concerned with serious matters to devote much attention to fashionable trumpery. Girls wear "substantial over-garments, and thick
shoes" (26); "noble-looking, stately women" (18) are dressed in "plain, substantial clothing" (16), "plain flowing robes" (17). These clothes are quiet, sober, utilitarian, and free of ornament. Frivolous clothing, after all, suggests a

frivolous mind, and an obsession with frills and furbelows seems to preclude more serious thought. "Willie," his feminine observers remark, "had better take off his fashionable gear before he pretends to talk about the dignity of men" (35).

The dangers of fashionable dress, however, threatened far more than personal dignity; many nineteenth-century fashion trends were hazardous to women's physical health as well. Stays had been in vogue throughout the century. C. Willett Cunnington ([1937] 1990), citing a contemporary reference, points out that even under the relatively relaxed "Empire" silhouettes of 1800–1820, women relied on highly restrictive undergarments to "compass into form the chaos of the flesh" (72). No one was exempt: expectant mothers employed "Pregnant Stays . . . to compress and reduce to the shape desired the natural prominence of the female figure in a state of fruitfulness" (73); nursing corsets were available for "ladies fulfilling the dearest offices of maternity" (205), and children's corsets molded the emerging figures of the next generation into acceptable contours. By midcentury, skirts had increased to alarming dimensions: a walking skirt was commonly four to five yards in circumference, and a ball gown was a huge tentlike structure,[4] so large that a careless woman might lose track of its whereabouts, catch her hem in a fireplace, and go up in flames.[5] The upper half of the figure, however, was still compressed, in an interminable quest for an eighteen-inch waist. Many women who wore tight stays discovered that they could "not sit upright without them" and were "compelled to wear night stays when in bed" (127). Another complaint was a marked increase in the size of the right shoulder, and a corresponding decrease in the left: "the former, being stronger and more frequently in motion somewhat frees itself, and acquires by this means an increase of which the left side is deprived by being feebler and subjected to continuous pressure" (127). By the close of the century, skirt dimensions were reduced considerably, replaced by huge bustles and long trains, which gradually receded over the years. Bodices, however, were more tightly fitted than ever (sleeves were so narrow that a fashionable woman could not lift her arms), and sixteen-inch waists were "not uncommon" (379). The fin-de-siècle woman endured such an "extreme degree of tight-lacing" that even "so eminent a physician as Professor [Thomas Henry] Huxley believed that women, unlike men, did not use the diaphragm in breathing. In his day they could not" (369).

It is no wonder that the pursuit of a modish silhouette eventually took its toll on women's health. The most common side effect of corseting and tight lacing was a prolapsed uterus—indeed, this occurred so frequently that a common middle-class fashion accessory during the latter half of the century was a supporter worn in the vagina to prevent uterine sagging or collapse. Harvey Green (1983) reports that "between 1850 and 1885, at least twenty-six [varieties of uterine supporters] were patented" (123). These contraptions were worn throughout the day and frequently at night as well; Green notes that at least one model had the advantage of not interfering with sexual intercourse (124).

Other remedies included "sponges forced into the vagina, injections of alum and water, the application of faradic electricity (which was thought to strengthen abdominal muscles), tonics, enemas [and] hip baths" (122). Stylish clothing also restricted breathing and movement in general: a modish female, bustled, tightly corseted and smothered in up to thirty pounds of voluminous petticoats, half-crippled by high heels one or two sizes too small,[6] was a pathetic figure, a far cry from the long-striding, deep-breathing heroines of utopian fiction.

The seven-foot-tall women of Elizabeth Corbett's *New Amazonia* (1889, 44), for example, wear graceful knee-length divided skirts, sensible laced boots, and tunics; a corset now exists only as a horrific museum display, a reminder of the unfortunate Victorian woman who, by wearing it, "deliberately forced her ribs out of their proper places, and prepared an early grave for herself, in order that she would meet with the favour of some idiot of the other sex, who preferred fashion and doctor's bills to health and happiness." Similarly, in Mary Bradley Lane's *Mizora* ([1880–81] 1889), the Mizorans reject the idea that nature can be improved on by "crowding your lungs and digestive organs into a smaller space than she, the maker of them, intended them to occupy" (222), and they believe that "disregarding nature's laws, or trying to thwart her intentions" results in "coarse features and complexions, stoop shoulders and deformity" (223). Mizoran clothes are made of simple, light fabrics—even ceremonial gowns are relaxed and loose fitting—and the resulting freedom permits women to expand to their natural contours. Their waists, for example, are never "less than thirty inches in diameter, and it [is] rare to meet with one that small" (37). A tapering waist is seen as a "disgusting deformity," while "a large waist [is] a mark of beauty" because it permits "a greater capacity of lung power" (38). The narrator asserts that she saw "one little lady, not above five feet in height . . . draw into her lungs two hundred and twenty-five cubic inches of air, and smile proudly when she accomplished it" (38). Such physical freedom must have appealed to many nineteenth-century women, gasping in their corsets.[7]

But women wished to do far more than breathe, and texts such as Lillie Devereux Blake's "A Divided Republic" ([1887] 1892, 358) foresee throngs of competent, professional women, all sensibly clad. In Blake's short story, there has been "a complete revolution in dress": not only have "compressed waists" given way to "loose garments," but "blouse waists, short skirts and long boots" are "all the fashion." Self-reliant female architects, contractors, and plumbers cannot be burdened with cumbersome garments, nor will they sacrifice comfort for fashion: at home, they wear "graceful and flowing robes of Grecian design." The true emblems of sartorial freedom, "common-sense shoes," are "universal."

Some utopias do without gender-specific clothing altogether,[8] opting instead for unisex garb. In Louise Moore's *Al-Modad* (1892), the Lost Eden's inhabitants share "perfect similarity in form, stature, dress and deportment as well as features" (72); there is "little difference in the kind or quality [of their clothes] to indicate the sex of the wearer" (76). Similarly, the utopians in Alice Ilgenfritz Jones and Ella Merchant's *Unveiling a Parallel* (1893) wear soft, "womanish" (16) garments, hanging in "elegant folds . . . from the shoulders and the waist" (17). There is almost no difference between men's and women's clothing: "the women's stuffs are of a little finer quality ordinarily, but . . . not usually so elaborately trimmed as the men's garb" (18). Neither gender is given to extravagant personal adornment, however, for "both sexes wear white, or a soft cream," made of "a sort of fine linen, or a mixture of silk and wool" (18). Since shoes are sensible proto-sneakers made "of white canvas" (19), women can walk "swiftly, with long, free steps" (29). Charlotte Perkins Gilman's *Herland* ([1915] 1979, 26) offers women and men what must have seemed to be the ultimate in comfort and utility. Herlander clothing is "simple in the extreme, and absolutely comfortable, physically." A "one-piece cotton undergarment, thin and soft," reaches "over the knees and shoulders . . . and a kind of half-hose" reaches "to just under the knee" and is supported by "elastic tops." There is "a thicker variety of union suit . . . of varying weights and somewhat sturdier material," as well as "tunics, knee-length, and some long robes."

Yet while utilitarian, these garments are never dowdy. Nineteenth-century middle-class women did not wish to appear frumpy or drab, and the utopian authors take considerable pains to make their clothing as attractive as possible. In Bessie Rogers's *As It May Be* (1905), for example, decency requires that women wear bloomer dresses, since the preferred means of transportation is a form of hang gliding. To offset the possible objections of readers who found such garments unattractive (Mrs. Bloomer's proposals had, after all, been mocked and largely rejected[9]), Rogers reassures her readers that these outfits are "much prettier" (37) than the average bloomer suit. "It really [is] a pretty gown" (37), available "in the most elaborate styles" (38). Similarly, although the "big, vigorous, fresh-colored, free-stepping women" of Charlotte Perkins Gilman's *Moving the Mountain* ([1911] 1968, 117) wear "whatever kind of clothing their work demands" (26), generally a "trim short skirt" (66), they also assume more traditionally "feminine" apparel: "a sort of Florentine gown, long and richly damasked" perhaps, or "a Grecian flow of drapery" (66). Utopian clothing may be simple and dignified, but the authors in this study generally include a detailed description of at least one costume of incredible richness and beauty. At a professorial inauguration, for instance, a Mizoran candidate wears "a sea-velvet robe with a voluminous train . . . adorned with a wreath or band of water lilies, embroidered in seed pearls" and covered by a "white lace overdress of filmiest texture," which falls "over the velvet, almost touching the wreath of lilies, and [looks] as though it were made of sea foam"; the costume is enhanced by "a girdle of large pink pearls . . . at the waist" (Lane [1880–81] 1889, 175). Such lavish elegance would have appealed to even the most devoted followers of *Godey's*.

Yet the purpose of dress reform was not to make clothes even more luxurious, but to enable women to function on an equal footing with men. Unhealthy clothing restricted far more than a woman's physical person; it also acted as the initial link in a patriarchal chain of reasoning that effectively prevented women from entering public life. Restrictive, injurious clothing *made* women frail, which was terrible enough. But even worse was the manner in which this frailty was used to restrict them to the domestic sphere: frail women were unable to withstand the rigors of intellectual study (an "unnatural" and hence debilitating activity for even the heartiest of females). The ramifications of female frailty extended even further, however, for uneducated women could not enter the professions.

Garments that encouraged physical activity weakened this chain by promoting an image of woman as healthy and vital.[10] Such an image was tremendously important in an age when Edward H. Clarke, one of the most highly respected physicians of his era, asserted that education was highly hazardous to women's health and caused "neuralgia, uterine disease [including atrophy of the uterus], hysteria, and other derangements of the nervous system" (cited in Kinnard 1986, 228). Females were limited by their biology to certain specific activities— all centered around marriage, for, as Harriet Martineau ([1837] 1966, 2:47) noted, "the sum and substance of female education in America, as in England, is training women to consider marriage as the sole object in life." Wifely duties consisted of the domestic chores that women had been performing successfully for centuries: cooking (shopping, baking, canning, preserving, dressing slaughtered meat, gardening, churning butter, making cheese), laundering (sorting, carrying buckets of hot water, scrubbing clothing on a washboard, ironing), cleaning (sweeping, beating rugs, dusting, washing dishes, making beds, washing windows, scrubbing floors), and sewing (making clothing and undergarments, knitting scarves and socks, mending). In addition, women were responsible for nursing invalids, which, as Janet Horowitz Murray (1982, 80) points out, was generally "emotionally draining, physically exhausting, and tragically frustrating"—and, because of the possibility of contagion, was frequently dangerous as well. Finally, nineteenth-century women were expected to rear—and, to a certain extent, educate—their children. These activities were physically grueling[11] yet were perceived as beneficial to women because they were natural, womanly occupations.

The root of the problem, it seemed, was that women were now attempting to engage in *un*natural activities, such as formal education, which would in turn lead to even more unnatural activities, such as making money and taking part in political action. Male doctors were quick to point out that such attempts were doomed from the start, since female biology incapacitated women for intellectual activity. Women could not engage in intellectual exertion, D. G. Porter explained, because of the different physical textures of the male and female brain: man's brain, which is firm and tough, "grows stronger and firmer by exercise," while woman's becomes "irritated and enfeebled by the same process" (cited in Kinnard 1986, 229). Many women agreed with his assessment. Miss M. A. Hardaker, for example, pointed out in 1882 that females are substandard "in brain, body, food assimilation, and power. Man can do more thinking in an hour because his brain gets more blood." Thus, she concludes helpfully, "the necessary outcome of absolute equality of the sexes would be the extinction of the human race" (cited in Kinnard 1986, 256). Eliza Lynn Linton argued that higher education for women was morally and physically harmful: it not only made women "arrogant, pretentious, [and] vain" but "ruin[ed] them for pregnancy, lactation, and child rearing" (cited in Kinnard 1986, 232). Clearly, women should be satisfied with the education that satisfied their foremothers.

That education had been firmly rooted in the domestic sphere. Women had long been trained in music, ornamental arts, and domestic management; even early feminists such as Mary Wollstonecraft, Maria Edgeworth, and Harriet Martineau, who suggested that women's minds should be developed, were careful to point out that better-educated women would make better mothers and wives.[12] Women had also been free to work—lower-class women as seamstresses, factory workers, and domestic help and middle- and upper-class women as household managers—but they were denied access to the lucrative or politically empowering occupations that required extended and highly specialized training. Lucy Stone observed that as a girl, she "seemed to be shut out of everything I wanted to do. I might teach school . . . I might go out dressmaking or tailoring, or trim bonnets, or I might work in a factory or go out to domestic service; there the mights ended and the might nots began" (cited in Rothman 1978, 43). Nineteenth-century "careers" for women were almost invariably poorly paying affairs that offered no chance for advancement.

By 1869, the only true professions open to women were nursing and teaching, and both of these had some decided drawbacks from a feminist standpoint. Both professions were extensions of the domestic sphere: since women had long been accepted as nurses in a family setting (as well as in certain religious orders), the move to an acceptance of women ministering to patients outside the family circle was not particularly revolutionary[13]; the progression from mothers teaching their own children, to governesses teaching others' children, to women as professional educators at the elementary level, seemed similarly conventional. Additionally, both careers became available largely because men gradually abandoned them in favor of more lucrative work elsewhere, and both were devalued in status and salary as women entered the professions. Finally, males were still very much in charge of both professions: nurses worked under the direction of male physicians, and schoolteachers were answerable to male administrators and school boards.

Later in the century, the invention of the typewriter and the development of department stores seemed to offer women an opportunity to enter the business world. There was a real need for secretaries and sales help, which could not be satisfied by lower-class males: secretaries, after all, had to be literate; salespeople had to be genteel. Middle-class women were ideally suited to such occupations. Thousands of young women suddenly acquired the opportunity to become respectable white-collar semiprofessionals. Yet, as Sheila Rothman (1978, 47) points out, "no matter what the job, women remained at the lower end of the ladder. In the public schools, they were the classroom teachers, not the principals or superintendents; in offices, they made up the ranks of typists and stenographers, not the executives; in the retail stores, they were the clerks and cashiers, not the floorwalkers or managers. In other words, the job that a woman first assumed was generally the one she kept as long as she worked."

The education that would prepare women to compete equally with men for the most profitable occupations was virtually unobtainable, and the legal system did its utmost to maintain that situation. In 1869, a group of women led by Sophia Jex-Blake initiated a case against the University of Edinburgh Medical School, asking to be permitted to attend classes, take examinations, and graduate; the court decided, however, that the university "had been founded for the education of male students only" (Sachs and Wilson 1978, 14). Women were similarly restricted in law, business, and politics. The situation in America was correspondingly limiting: although educational institutions for women did exist (Troy Seminary was established in 1821, the Ipswitch Female Seminary in 1828, coeducational Oberlin College in 1833, and Mount Holyoke College in 1837), these schools were not intended to provide preprofessional education, except to train teachers of women and children.[14]

Vassar College, founded in 1865, was the first institution to attempt to provide women with an education fully equal to a man's. To do this, however, the school had to circumnavigate contemporary ideas about women's physical and mental ability to survive such a rigorous intellectual ordeal. Physical health was stressed to such an extent that, as Rothman (1978, 28) asserts, "the daily routine of the students seemed closer to the ways that medical asylum administered institutions to cure the insane. Vassar's trustees assumed that they were dealing not only with a class of young women who needed maternal supervision and moral guidance but who were prone to insanity as well." Classes in physical education and hygiene were mandatory, as were the traditional regimen of popular and ornamental coursework: domestic management, music, art, and so forth. Such a program helped calm the fears of medical professionals. Yet it restricted the amount of attention that students could devote to more intellectual pursuits; students were forced to spend so much time and energy learning to be "True Women" that their purely scholarly endeavors were secondary. That seemed to be an appropriate ordering. After all, concern for her husband and children was expected to take precedence over a woman's purely intellectual endeavors. There was no need to train Vassar women in law or political science. Indeed, college president John Raymond was "more than doubtful" that women had "a vocation to either" and assured graduates that they would "not need to handle the ballot, or mount the hustings, or mingle in the debates of Congress, in order to make [their] influence felt in moulding and purifying politics and ennobling the national character and life" (cited in Rothman 1978, 38). Even after the best education available to women of the time, their influence would still be limited to hearth and home.

To take their place as man's true equal, women needed readily available training in the professions and sciences; but such training, it seemed, was the stuff of utopian dreams. No wonder a consistent theme of feminist utopian fiction is education and its link to economic and political equality. In Cridge's *Man's Rights* (1870), for example, a young man busily engaged in sewing ruffles on his trousers complains that "men can not earn money as well as women" and longs "to learn a business" (15). His father assures him that a boy's business "is to get married"; he must "learn to be a good housekeeper . . . that is enough business for any man" (15). Cridge's stately, educated women contrast sharply with "the vain, silly, half-educated men who staid [*sic*] at home" (16), men who are "degraded . . . without a motive in life, limited in education and culture, shut out of every path to honor and emolument, and reduced to the condition of paupers on the bounty of the opposite sex" (19). Mary Lane's *Mizora* ([1880–81] 1889) is possibly the most extreme example of this preoccupation with knowledge; her all-female society is an immense academy, where everyone is involved in some sort of teaching or learning process. Mizorans study from the cradle to the grave: from "infant schools" (61) to a national college, which functions as the center of social, judicial, legislative, and cultural activity. Scholars receive the adulation that twentieth-century society usually reserves for motion picture stars and sports heroes. Teaching is the most highly respected and rewarded profession, and brilliant educators are treated as demigods. This "aristocracy of intellect" (75) enjoys all the rewards society can afford it: teachers live in magnificent homes, surrounded by luxury. Universal education is seen as the solution to all problems: it is "the great destroyer of castes . . . the conqueror of poverty and the foundation of patriotism," which "purifies and strengthens national, as well as individual character. . . . The nation is wise that will educate all its children" (149).[15]

Given the opportunity, these authors assert, women will prove to be as talented and productive as men. Lillie Blake's all-female "Divided Republic" ([1887] 1892, 357–58) allows its women to discover their "natural talents," and, because male repression has been eliminated, female architects, contractors, plumbers, and so forth create a "scrupulously tidy" community that emphasizes education. Public moneys are spent on "the construction of schoolhouses and other beautiful public buildings," and the schools, "under the care of feminine Boards of Education," are "brought to great perfection": music is taught, and women, "undismayed by men," write "operas and oratorios"; "free lectures" are presented "on all branches of knowledge by scientific women . . . supported by the State, and debating societies [meet] nightly for the discussion of questions of public policy."

Indeed, education is so important in these texts that some authors carry the need for learning beyond the grave: even death, it seems, need not end the educational process. Mary Shelhamer's *Life and Labor in the Spirit World* (1885, 54–55) examines the importance of scholarship in heaven, where "Wisdom schools" can be found throughout the spirit world, and students, "young and old, and of both sexes," throng the celestial halls to hear distinguished speakers lecture eternally on chemistry, metaphysics, literature, and music. The need for education never ends—even such a distinguished scientist as the late Michael Faraday is a member of the student body (if that term can be used for so noncorporeal a group), straining eagerly to catch each of the lecturer's words.

These utopian worlds, products of what Lyman Tower Sargent calls "social dreaming," offer glimpses of healthy, educated, powerful, free women, central figures in their communities. Yet real-world nineteenth-century British and American women were marginalized in a society where "the contests of political life were not suitable to the nature of women," where "removing a woman from the voters' roll was like removing the name of a dog or a horse," where a political woman would "make every home a hell on earth," and where women's nature "disqualifie[d] them for the turmoil and battle of public life." Their marginalization was historically, legally, and divinely sanctioned; it was sensible, orderly, and logical. It is no wonder that women were drawn to the irrational realm of social dreaming to develop a model of empowered womanhood. In hypothetical worlds, where all difficulties had already been overcome, the historical outsider could at last become an insider.

Michel Foucault (1970, xviii) asserts that "utopias afford consolation: although they have no real locality there is nevertheless a fantastic, untroubled region in which they are able to unfold; they open up all cities with vast avenues, superbly planted gardens, countries where life is easy, even though the road to them is chimerical." Utopias afforded nineteenth-century women the consolation of the quiet contemplation of a better world, certainly. But the genre also offered them a great deal more: the cathartic relief furnished by a scathing critique of one's own community, the distraction provided by the creation of alternative societies, the amusement generated by a defamiliarization of existing arrangements, and the sense of power derived from the creation and control of entire worlds. Indeed, the genre provided a "fantastic, untroubled region" in which female equality (or superiority) was the norm and male dominance was no longer perceived as inevitable. Bitterly disillusioned by antisuffrage legislation, women wrote utopian literature because it freed them to redefine their role in society, to translate their frustration with a constricted environment into the literature of dissatisfaction. Their impatience with political exclusion resulted in a reworking of past and present into a historical perspective drawn from the future: a revisionary pretelling of history.

Worlds Apart

Contrasts in British and American Utopian Texts by Women

Despite the homogeneity of the authors in this study—their commonality of gender, race, language, heritage, class, and subject matter—nationality sometimes complicates and even overrides these similarities. One can isolate distinctly British or American arguments about the appropriate site and time for utopian change, as well as the nature of the utopienne(s) who will help the process along. British texts tend to reject contemporary frontier settings, preferring a future, high-tech London, where women eschew the domestic sphere and opt instead for a public life, whereas American narratives are most often rural and contemporary, featuring heroines who extend the benefits of the hearth and home to the community as a whole. This dichotomy reflects fundamental differences in middle-class British and American women's perceptions of their respective frontiers (that is, the colonial empire versus the western territories), the prospect of immediate change, and potential sources of female empowerment.

Ever since Thomas More coined the term, utopian narratives have commonly employed exotic foreign landscapes, the "nowheres" of his bimodal pun, as settings for their ideal societies. Nineteenth-century British and American women each had a frontier *out*opia from which to draw, yet the British women in this study tend to reject the imperial frontier[1] as a site for their ideal societies, preferring instead to situate their utopias in London. They do not employ contemporary London, however, dismissing it as an inhospitable climate for social dreaming. Instead, they seek out a future metropolis, where women have managed to infiltrate and control existing political structures. American authors, on the other hand, tend to view their western frontier far more optimistically, seeing it as an embryonic paradise, the potential of which might be unlocked by any reasonably industrious present-day visionary. In reality, the two frontiers offered women quite similar experiences—diaries of both British and American pioneer women are filled with comparably bleak accounts of killing work, incredible physical danger, widespread disease, and unremitting loneliness. Yet the British and American women who remained at home and wrote utopias had decidedly differing perceptions of their respective frontiers, perceptions derived from opposing symbolic, physical, moral, and political considerations.

The imperial project was an inherently *manly* undertaking, aggressive during war and paternalistic during peace. Contemporary rhetoric repeatedly stressed that femininity and empire were contradictory: Indian viceroy George Curzon asserted that "for the discharge of great dependencies of the Empire in distant parts you want the qualities not of the feminine but of the masculine mind" (B. Harrison 1978, 75); parliamentary discussions asserted that imperial policy "should be directed in [a] masculine, virile way"; indeed, since the empire was "built by the mental and physical capacity of men, and maintained, as it always must be maintained, by the physical and mental capacity of masterly natures," one member was led to ask, "Is there a place for women [in the colonies]?" (Rover 1967, 46). Certainly women would not be considered for any position of power because the empire employed male hierarchies—institutions such as the army, police, judiciary, and civil services—as models for colonial rule. The colonial landscape was a prospect, a scenic overlook, a field for the imposition of male power—an incongruous site for women's utopias. If anything, the imperial frontier seemed to stress the more depressing aspects of the way things were run at home; there were, after all, grim parallels between international colonialism and the cultural colonialism practiced in London. British feminists were already chafing under what A. P. Thornton (1965, 16) terms "the empire of men over both women and their property," an empire "as old as the record of men themselves." The colonial arrangement extended and exaggerated this paternalism: it encompassed not merely women but also the native population in general. Expatriate females on the British frontier were apparently more in need of male protection than ever. The empire that seemed a potential utopia for men—and which had been used by everyone from More to Samuel Butler—held no similar promise for women. They were more alien there than at home.

The British frontier also posed tremendous social and physical hazards. The empire was a site of exile, a social purgatory too harsh for any but the most distressed and desperate gentlewomen. A. James Hammerton (1979, 83) maintains that the middle class "regarded the very need for emigration as a confession of social decline," while Susan F. Bailey (1983, 69) suggests that, at best, emigration was seen as the "least of several evils." There was a tremendous surplus of unemployed, unmarried middle-class women in England. Joanna Trollope (1983, 23) points out that, partly because of the tremendous demand for young men to serve and colonize imperial territories, "by the middle of the century over 35 per cent of [English] women between twenty and forty-four were single." One would think that the promise of high wages and eager bachelors waiting in Australia, New Zealand, and Natal would generate a corresponding female exodus, yet this was not the case—at least not for respectable middle-class women.[2] In the first place, there was no real demand for them. As William Rathbone Greg explained in 1862, "The *class* of women who are redundant here is not exactly the class that is wanted in the colonies, or that is adapted for colonial life. The women most largely wanted there would be found among the working classes, and in the lower ranks of the middle classes: the women who are mostly redundant . . . in England, are chiefly to be found in the upper and educated sections of society" (cited in Murray 1982, 52). The best-known relocation organization for such women, Maria Rye's Female Middle Class Emigration Society, settled barely three hundred women in the colonies in more than twenty-three years (Trollope 1983, 64). Greg's prediction that they were not "adapted for colonial life" certainly seemed to be accurate. After all, how could decent, well-bred, genteelly reared women be expected to live in a remote, alien place, separated from England by thousands of miles and multiple oceans, teeming with fevers, diarrhea, dysentery, and cholera, and inhabited by savage natives, wild beasts, and exiled felons? Canada had been declared "not a fit country for white women" (Bailey 1983, 28); India was the site of not only filth and famine, but mutiny and revolution as well (the horrors of the Sepoy Revolt in 1857, for example, were circulated throughout the drawing rooms of England); Asia was a nightmare of "God-forsaken loneliness," "soul shattering monotony and . . . utter dreariness" (Bailey 1983, 28); Australia was a penal colony.[3] Africa was simply out of the question; Trollope (1983, 118) notes that the entire continent "remained almost without white women until the turn of the century, for the climate was known to be a killer." An outlandish world filled with social pariahs, loneliness, and disease hardly fit the utopian paradigm: a visitor stumbling on such a place would find no typically ideal paragons of virtue and wisdom to emulate, no exemplary models for social amelioration to follow, no technological marvels at which to wonder—egalitarian social arrangements were clearly out of the question. Savages and social outcasts grubbing out a violent existence in a hostile patriarchal environment? This was the stuff of *dys*topia.[4]

There was also a distasteful atmosphere of mingled egotism, waste, and oppression associated with empire. The imperial project, some suspected, was at least partially grounded in Queen Victoria's personal vanity: her son-in-law was soon to be emperor of Germany, and, Trollope (1983, 18) suggests, many of her subjects believed that "her wish to be Empress was no more than a ruse to give her children precedence over those at the German court." Despite jingoistic rhetoric extolling a passionate commitment to British influence overseas, many people questioned the value and virtue of such an endeavor. Even the supposedly humanitarian justification for the imperial project—the need to assume "the white man's burden"—could not entirely efface the terrible cost of such a load: during the final third of the century, South Africa alone claimed the lives of hundreds of thousands of British soldiers (Trollope 1983, 22).[5] There was also the distasteful fact that Britain was profiting greatly at the expense of native peoples; the view of appropriately dominant whites governing happily submissive people of color did not hold up under close scrutiny. This queasy ethical construction not only raised moral questions but also once again offered women a bleak parallel to the situation at home: childlike natives were "protected" against their uncivilized ways yet were frequently worked nearly to death in a most uncivilized manner; child-women were "protected" from the difficulties of public life yet were frequently expected to support themselves (and families) in a hostile public environment. In both cases, their protector/oppressor smugly justified his actions as working to the common good, despite the unhappy realities that belied this assertion.

He could ignore these realities with impunity, for the colonies' inferior political status limited their inhabitants' access to power. Ultimately, the British frontier was a collection of displaced places, outlands whose central purpose was providing fodder for England's voracious factories. Disraeli noted perceptively that "the best mode of preserving wealth is power" (Trollope 1983, 20); imperial London retained absolute control over both. Colonists were simply too far away from the center of things to be significantly involved yet were too valuable a resource to be permitted autonomy. This simultaneous exclusion/incorporation provided yet another alarming metaphor for the middle-class women who wrote utopias. After the Second Reform Bill's failure to enfranchise them, many British women viewed themselves as similarly displaced persons, human colonies whose central purpose was providing raw material (that is, children) for England's imperial enterprise, while men retained control of all wealth and power. Colonial women were thus doubly displaced: they represented an unprecedented marginalization of an already marginal gender. From the perspective of the authors examined in this study, an emigrant woman would be an exile, banished to a place where she would not only be unable to play the game but would no longer even be able to *see* it. Why on earth set a utopia there?

Better to dig in and hold one's ground; if London is the seat of power, then London will be the seat of change as well. If a plot requires an initial rural setting, fine—but the action must move to London before real change can occur. Mary Ann Hearn's *Nineteen Hundred?* (1892), for example, details how a group of young Christian activists forms a model factory community in rural Wales but then sets about to acquire enough popular support to head a majority in the House of Commons. British women's utopias might occasionally stray as far afield as Ireland, Scotland, or Wales, but never to Africa or New Zealand; texts may be set on Mars or the moon, but only if the Martian or lunar society closely resembles that of London. Everything is reassuringly familiar, including the mechanics of power: the British authors in this study rarely propose new political frameworks but opt instead to work within (and frequently take over) conventional political structures such as Parliament. Victorian women had witnessed firsthand the tremendous power of Parliament over their lives. It seemed far more reasonable to appropriate this power than to set up new systems doomed to crumble before the established might of the old.

Similarly, futuristic settings seemed far more receptive to new ideas than did their staid and static contemporary world. Nineteenth-century London did not seem ripe for utopian change: British suffrage efforts, for example, appeared doomed, a mishmash of too little and too late. Although the British movement was much more militant than its American counterpart, it involved far fewer women[6] and began considerably later. Britain also had a long-standing tradition of antifeminist legal decisions,[7] which Parliament's exclusion of women in the Second Reform Bill only reinforced. Although many British territories would extend suffrage to females—the Isle of Man in 1881, New Zealand and South Australia in 1893, Western Australia in 1899, the Commonwealth of Australia and New South Wales in 1902, Tasmania in 1903, Queensland in 1905, and Victoria in 1909—things remained discouragingly orthodox in London, the perceived seat of power. Women were still confined to the tremendously limiting sphere of home and church—a place where education was nearly impossible to obtain and where intellectual acuteness and political savvy were considered "unfeminine" liabilities. Motherhood, the symbol of woman's generative power, could also be the emblem of her repression—nineteenth-century antisuffrage literature and posters characteristically depicted abandoned, unhappy children, crying for absent mamas who were engaging in political activity.[8] British feminists lacked not only political and economic power, but also the means by which to achieve this power: as Lisa Tickner (1988, 7) points out, "They had no forum in which to formulate demands, and no means of compelling attention that did not 'unsex' them."

Thus, the majority of British authors in this study looked to the future, to a high-tech twenty-first- or twenty-third- or twenty-sixth-century London. There, the Victorian political doldrums would be a memory, and Victorian suffragists mocked in their own age would be celebrated as heroines. Nineteenth-century scientific breakthroughs would bring about social amelioration: since evolution ensures that the animal kingdom moves toward perfection, why not society? Since technology will eventually invalidate man's tyranny of physical strength, why not anticipate a new age in which the intellectual and moral might inherent in both sexes is the only criterion for leadership, an age when women's particular strength—her moral superiority—is finally recognized, appreciated, and rewarded? In the future, when science, technology, and the influence of politically empowered women have combined to solve the problems of humankind, one will at last find equitable worlds. Given an abundance of time, technology, and feminine input (funding for these projects is rarely discussed), these authors assert, humankind's problems will all be resolved, and the feminist vision will be vindicated.

Futuristic texts such as Amelia Garland Mears's *Mercia, the Astronomer Royal* (1895) enabled readers to look *back* on the successful efforts of militant feminists, who gradually achieved "a wider walk of life, a more extended field of action" (2) and dramatically improved the lot of humankind. *Mercia* details how gradual reformation led to educational, occupational, political, social, and marital equality, resulting in a better world for all humankind. From the perspective of a future century, it is clear that the efforts of nineteenth-century feminists have benefited everyone: even man, "who at the outset bitterly opposed the movement," eventually "reaped the advantage derived therefrom, to his own comfort and content" (5–6).

Victorian advocates of educational, economic, and political reform, who must have felt at times as if their efforts were futile, could be heartened by the thought that they would eventually emerge as the heroines of the feminist revolution, when females would take over existing government models centered in London. The future could validate the present struggle; a future vantage point could link past and future in a history of things to come. Even nowhere must be somewhere, after all, and there was a decided lack of utopian potential in nineteenth-century England. Unable to envision a present-day utopia in London, but unwilling to be driven to a hostile frontier, the British writers in this study were forced by their lack of alternatives into the future.

American writers, on the other hand, enjoyed choices as vast and varied as the West itself. The North American continent had for centuries been a romantic site inextricably linked to optimism and promise—and utopia. The land was seen as nurturing, alluring, female; the English frontier might be perceived as an exclusively masculine prospect, but the American landscape was a feminine bower, a place of refuge and safety. As Annette Kolodny (1975, 136) points out, "The West was a woman, and to it belonged the hope of rebirth and regeneration." Such a motherland afforded a nurturing symbolic environment for women's utopian dreams; the West was no alien space, but an expanded home. Its women were not exiles driven from their homeland—paupers, debtors, debased thieves and prostitutes, unwanted spinsters—but brave frontier wives and mothers. Easterners were familiar with the romantic trope of the female pioneer: "a slender, pale-skinned woman wearing a long-skirted dress and a sunbonnet with pasteboard slats. One of her hands clasps the tiny fingers of a child; her other arm cradles a rifle or perhaps presses a baby against her breast. She is wife, mother, helpmate, and intrepid pioneer personified" (Riley 1988, 14). Her home might be a cabin on the frontier's remotest fringes, but it is an *American* home nonetheless. Neither immense oceans nor androcentric European hierarchical structures isolate or alienate this frontier.

The American frontier was perceived as an unspoiled paradise—at least by those who remained safely at home and wrote utopias[9]—a fertile land that promoted vigorous good health. Reportedly, the soil rivaled that of Cokaygne: wheat and corn sprang forth at the touch of a plow. Animals and people were said to thrive equally well; the climate was considered so robust that many ailing easterners—ironically, the portion of the population least likely to survive—flocked west in search of restoration. Glenda Riley (1981, 6–7) notes that "improved health was apparently a key stereotype of the West" and that Iowa, despite its bitter winters, "was particularly noted for its supposedly salubrious climate." The more westerly the location, the healthier: in 1891, one Kansas pioneer suffering from consumption had so much faith in the benefits of Colorado weather that he crossed the country in the middle of winter with his pregnant wife (Franklin 1986, 335–36). When the disease resurfaced, he considered a second move to California (343) but died before he could make the trip. The West's reputation as a panacea for illness was, of course, illusory; the reality of life on the prairie was most frequently a compendium of illness, danger, and death. The western climate was, if anything, harsher than that of the East. Yet even the cruelest western weather was never perceived as *alien*—there were no nasty foreign typhoons or monsoons. Similarly, the diseases that plagued pioneer families were good, solid, *American* maladies that had conventional (if often useless) remedies—none of those outlandish, exotic malarias or beriberis.

The social climate was similarly familiar and reassuring. It was a comfort to have one's own peers to share the journey west; the negative social stigma attached to British emigration was generally not the case in America. Settlers were most frequently substantial members of the middle class rather than paupers or criminals. As Glenda Riley (1981, 12) affirms, "The very poor rarely migrated. The investment in transportation, animals, tools, seed, provisions, and land was formidable and demanded that pioneers have some means of raising capital such as selling household goods and land, using land warrants or soldier's pay, or negotiating a loan." Most pioneers who ventured west generally did so with a good deal of capital; they were relatively successful people who wished to become more so. James Frazier Reed, for example, a California-bound member of the ill-fated Donner party, left behind a thriving Illinois furniture factory and close friends such as Abraham Lincoln and Stephen A. Douglas (Brown 1958, 95). American trailblazers were good, solid, middle-class visionaries—just the sort one might choose to populate a utopia.

The moral climate seemed equally healthy. Western expansion was seen as a laudable endeavor; the genocide practiced on the native population was perceived not as an act of imperialistic oppression, but as a deliverance: rescuing America from savage natives and distributing the land among its rightful owners. This view was staunchly upheld by middle-class women (at least in part because liminal outsiders' links to centrality were reinforced by the prospect of truly outlandish others). Citing Ronald Quinn, Riley (1981, 177) points out that "white women were socialized by nineteenth-century civilization into seeing Indians as primitive, savage, and dirty. Because society relegated women to the position of 'civilizers,' they had no choice but to visualize Native Americans as 'representatives of an alien and depraved culture, decidedly inferior to their own.' As guardians of public morality, women were given to understand one basic fact before they left their Eastern homes—'The American Indian is a savage.' Once on the frontier, women described the Native Americans they encountered as filthy, foolish, degraded; in all ways a 'symbol of defeat and failure,' the antithesis of the white female, who embodied progress and success." Admittedly, Riley also cites Dawn L. Gherman's assertion that "all white women did *not* see themselves as civilizers and Native Americans as primitive savages . . . that many women actually had a streak of 'wildness' in their makeup which caused them to occasionally long for the natural, the free, and the unrestrained qualities which they perceived in the lives of the Native Americans" (177). Yet while the authors in this study seem to have shared similar longings, the texts do not display any corresponding sympathy for the Native Americans' plight; instead, one finds a recurring elitism of race and class.

The land was not stolen from these savage peoples; it was liberated. Western expansion was not imperialism, after all, but manifest destiny. Indeed, prior to the Civil War, many families had moved West to *escape* a questionable moral climate: Riley (1981, 7) notes that "many people who disagreed with the principle of enslaving another human being were casting about for an area where they could be free of slavery's taint."

Nor did the American frontier share the political alienation associated with British colonial life. The West had the advantage of being simultaneously American and autonomous: it was clearly part of the United States, and thus protected by the imposing might of a powerful nation, yet the territories were not subject to home rule, as were British colonies. The police, judiciary, and civil services tended to be managed locally, and there was a heady commingling of freedom and security: one might escape heavy taxes and unpopular political leaders yet still not be an expatriate. Indeed, the West was not a host on which the eastern states might feed; it was a site of power in its own right. The immense wealth that was so much a part of the western mystique— derived from the incomprehensibly rich gold and silver mines and the huge cattle ranches and farms—had tended to *stay* in the West. Those who had stayed with it were not displaced persons in a displaced place, but creators of new centralities.

As the nineteenth century drew to a close, the American frontier was a magnetic force, an emblem of freedom and empowerment. In a vast country with seemingly endless natural resources and continually expanding frontiers, all things seem possible, and the present holds as many possibilities as the future. There is no need to escape to the next century when utopia might lie just over the next unexplored ridge. Not surprisingly, the majority of 1870–1920 utopian texts by American women are set in contemporary rural or frontier landscapes. Instead of the futuristic, high-tech urban utopias favored by their British cousins, American women's utopias are more comfortable with the present, more reliant on the bounty of nature, and more closely linked to the centuries-long tradition of America as utopia. English authors might refuse to budge from the greater London area; American women's utopian fiction offers the reader a walking tour of rural and frontier America.[10]

Some of women's utopian dreams, after all, were coming true, just over the next hill. Crushing suffrage defeats, such as the Fourteenth and Fifteenth Amendments' failure to enfranchise women, were offset by gains made in other areas and by a scattered, painfully gradual, but steady movement toward female suffrage. During the Civil War, Riley (1981, 134) asserts, "women performed work, carried out responsibilities, and made decisions in the formerly male realm without great impairment to their health, mental capacities or nervous systems. The argument that they were incapable of assuming 'men's work' without serious damage to themselves was becoming anachronistic."[11] In the postwar period, many of these gains were rescinded in the eastern states, but, mainly because of sheer necessity, women continued to enjoy a widened sphere of experience on the frontier. Educational opportunities for women also increased dramatically in the more heavily populated areas of the West: although New England had seen the founding of a number of first-rate preparatory schools for women, including Vassar, Smith, Wellesley, Bryn Mawr, and Radcliffe, only Mount Holyoke enjoyed degree-granting privileges. Yet, as Barbara J. Harris (1978, 99) notes, "as early as 1870, Wisconsin, Michigan, Missouri, Iowa, Kansas, Indiana, Minnesota, and California had coeducational state universities." Admittedly, most women "were enrolled in education and home economics programs and received much less rigorous intellectual training than male students" (99). Yet doors were opened that would be increasingly difficult to shut. The most visible aspect of feminist endeavor, the quest for female suffrage, had also progressed and was inextricably linked to the western frontier: Wyoming enfranchised women on 10 December 1869; Colorado in 1893; Utah in 1896[12]; Idaho in 1898; Washington in 1910; California in 1911; Arizona, Kansas, and Oregon in 1912; Illinois (presidential only) and Alaska in 1913; and Montana and Nevada in 1914. The first eastern state to enfranchise women, New York, would not do so until 1917. American women who looked westward had some proof, however small, that change was possible. This was no utopian fantasy; there were actually places in America where women could work, learn, and vote on a nearly equal footing with men.

The raw materials for an ideal society seemed to be in place; all that was needed was a bit of reorganization. On the frontier, necessity often effected change: one could not be locked into old ways when facing entirely new challenges. Many of the American women in this study drew on this conceptual flexibility and proposed alternative societies that offer radically new models for human interaction. Marie Howland's *Papa's Own Girl* (1874), for example, details the establishment of the Social Palace, a Fourierist institution for social reform, promoting equitable relations between women and men. Other narratives contemplated such innovative social alternatives as cooperative factories, communes for spinsters or working women, inner-city self-help organizations, communal free-love communities, or entire cooperative commonwealths.[13] The real-world flavor of such texts was intensified by their resemblance to actual utopian experiments: sectarian communities such as the Shakers, the Ephrata Cloister, the Moravian Brethren, the Rappites, and the Oneida Perfectionists; reform communities and economic cooperatives such as Brook Farm (based on Fourier's cooperative agricultural model) and various Owenite communities;

and anarchist colonies such as Home and Pacific City. Given such a variety of models, apparently unlimited real estate, and the heady mood of the *en-travers-de-siècle* period, anything—even utopia—must have seemed possible for nineteenth-century American women.

As one might expect, these dramatically differing British and American attitudes toward the appropriate time and site of utopian change resulted in dramatically different types of protagonists. Given her horror of the frontier and political isolation, a twenty-sixth-century British utopienne could not be plucked from her technological wonderland and plunged into the American wilderness; she would be miserable. Similarly, the nineteenth-century down-to-earth pioneer typical of American utopias would be lost and forlorn were she to be thrust into high-tech twenty-sixth-century London.[14]

The typical British protagonist is well suited to her time and place. Intellectually, politically, and frequently physically powerful, she is unwilling to be shunted aside—either to a frontier outland or to the parlor of her London home. She has rejected a maternal, domestic role and thus avoids a position that might impose a subordinate status on her. British women had been banned from mainstream political activity in reality; their heroines would not be similarly sidelined in fantasy. Mature, sophisticated, competent, rational, and very much in the public sphere, the British utopian heroine typically is far too busy for home management and child rearing. Her energies are devoted to the betterment of humankind through political activity. Although both British and American texts tend to agree that woman's moral destiny is to temper man's natural competitive spirit and to lead the world into a bright new age of prosperity and harmony, in British texts the female role is rarely domestic or anonymous. The "angel in the house" is determined to be the angel in the House of Commons.[15]

The highly public and politically savvy Englishwomen of Mears's *Mercia* (1895), for example, avoid the anonymous drudgery of the kitchen and nursery. Either men take over household duties (a task at which they prove surprisingly able), or domestic servants—respected, well-paid professionals—are hired. The rejection of the cult of domesticity is particularly evident in Mears's rather abbreviated version of the maternal role: a single nine-month stint and occasional visits to the nursery. It is maternity without monotony (and, as far as possible, remarkably free of the disruptive presence of children). Mothers-to-be, after deciding whether to have a boy or a girl, follow a grueling regimen, in which the fetus's moral, physical, and professional well-being is seen to: the mother permits herself "no emotion, thought, or action . . . that she would object to seeing reproduced in her child" (13); she keeps "her muscle-power in practice" and devotes herself almost exclusively to the profession she has determined her child shall enter. A mother who wishes musical offspring, for example, will immerse herself in music, indefatigably "practising on the instrument she wished [her child] to excel in; studying the theory of music, attending high-class musical entertainments" (14) and so forth. Once the child is born, the mother is free to channel her energies into nondomestic pursuits that benefit humankind.

American heroines are far more nurturing and private and tend to prevail through their religious and moral strength, rather than political savvy.[16] They view their maternal role as a liberating space, a sacred destiny that simultaneously authorizes and furnishes their self-esteem and authority. As in British utopias, American women are presented as capable, rational, and efficient, clearly well suited for positions of power. American writers, however, tend to link women's "natural" superiority to the very maternal qualities that English heroines distrust. American heroines are more likely to be domestic nurturers, fiercely protective of home and family and disinclined to engage in public activity. Unlike their British cousins, American heroines do not uphold male institutions by participating in them. Instead, they choose alternative lifestyles, frequently communal and cooperative. American utopian heroines lack the fierce individualism of a Mercia; indeed, some texts have no single protagonist, but groups of women united by an indomitable maternal spirit.

Perhaps the most dramatic example of this spirit is Charlotte Perkins Gilman's *Herland* ([1915] 1979), which depicts a community of ardently matriotic sisters who have created a world of "ordered beauty" (11) out of a wrecked, war-devastated society. In the midst of a timbered wilderness not unlike the American frontier, these sisters create an orderly world, "a land in a state of perfect cultivation, where even the forests look as if they were cared for" (11). The nonhierarchical social structure does not oppose traditional political arrangements; it transcends them. Gilman's community is not only the governing body but is the novel's true protagonist as well—individuals are only singled out as spokeswomen for the society. The population is otherwise rather interchangeable, divided loosely into the younger girls who farm the forests and the more mature "aunts"[17] who instruct three male trespassers in the ways of a world grounded in "motherliness." Since the women reproduce parthenogenetically,[18] maternal vitality, rather than patriarchal authority, is worshiped as Creator; mother love, rather than father rule, has "dominated society . . . influenced every art and industry . . . absolutely protected all childhood, and [given] to it the most perfect care and training" (73). The strength of the women of Herland lies in their unifying sisterhood and their ability to generate life: their communal purpose gives them more power than any number of individuals; their generative force enables them to create and maintain a stable population free of poverty, hunger, or war.

The three elements that separate the British and American texts in this study—place, temporal frame, and the nature of their protagonists—reflect differences between British and American women's experience. A small, heavily industrialized island contrasts sharply with a vast continent abundant in natural resources; the frustrations and aspirations of women in urban situations differ greatly from those of pioneer women enjoying a measure of egalitarian life on the open plains; and a century-old legacy of women involved in intellectual and cultural growth directly contradicts a traditional distrust of "bluestockings." Perhaps the best way to demonstrate how these differences are reflected in women's utopian narratives is through a close analysis of two representative utopias, the British Florence Dixie's *Gloriana; or, The Revolution of 1900* and the American Lois Waisbrooker's *A Sex Revolution*.

Gloriana (Dixie 1890) epitomizes the British attraction for urban environments, futuristic settings, and public heroines. From the vantage point of London in 1999, a place of "peace and prosperity, comfort and contentment" (345), the story details how a revolutionary woman's concentrated dedication to female education and political organization brought this utopian world into being. Through highly political acts—first within the system, then through civil disobedience and even rebellion—the heroic Gloriana de Lara actively shapes not only her own history but England's as well. Dixie's *Gloriana* demonstrates how superior women, once freed of the domestic sphere, can not only contribute to their society but also inaugurate fundamental change within it.

Irreproachably feminine, Gloriana nonetheless encompasses the "masculine" virtues of courage and strength and emerges as a figure of imposing wholeness. Donning masculine clothing—she spends a substantial portion of the novel masquerading as the brilliant and noble Hector D'Estrange—Dixie's heroine disproves absolutely the frailties ascribed to her sex by outperforming her male comrades at everything. She gives a sound "drubbing" to a "big, overgrown monster" of a bully, takes high honors at Eton and Oxford, and rides all six winners in a race meet. Dixie argues that any woman not "physically and mentally stunted, both in her intellect and body" (25) is capable of similar achievement, since women's alleged "frailty" is nothing more than the artificial construct of a society that encourages females to be weak and foolish and, by doing so, debases itself. Gloriana is a "militant woman" in the tradition of such heroines as Britannia and Joan of Arc, the idealized allegorical maiden/warrior figure subsequently seized upon as an inspirational symbol by English suffragists.

Dixie argues that the disadvantageous condition of womanhood is largely due to women's disunity and lack of education, and her brilliant, articulate, and politically astute heroine sets about to remedy this situation. To do this, she must devote herself entirely to her cause, forgoing the pleasures of marriage or family: a quintessential British utopian heroine, she demonstrates that her public life is her whole life. Her efforts neatly parallel the work of nineteenth-century reformers and suffragists who attempted to bring women together, using their sheer numbers to generate a strong and vital political unit.[19] Victorian women, divided by a society that forced them to compete with one another for the attentions of men, had to learn to work together. To provide this sort of female bonding, Gloriana establishes an enormous Hall of Liberty in London and subsidiary branches throughout the country, "institutions where women and girls can meet each other" (50) as allies rather than competitors. Here, "for a mere nominal fee" (Dixie is not unaware of women's economic handicaps),[20] a belle can be transformed into a militant woman by learning the skills of the male power elite: instead of coursework in "ladylike" pursuits, these would-be Britomarts study riding, shooting, swimming, and running, along with unspecified classes, "technical and otherwise" (50). No mention is made of abandoned husbands or children; no outraged papas come to reclaim their daughters. The women seem to have no private, domestic histories; they exist only in the public sphere.

Eventually, Dixie's heroine assumes her rightful place as prime minister[21] and leads the country into a new era, in which "the presence and natural companionship of woman will upraise and influence man's character for good" (336). *Gloriana* comforts women who are frustrated with their status as domestic prisoners and who yearn for a public voice. The novel presents egalitarian society as an accomplished fact and even provides an actual schematic for revolution: if women will only recognize their power and come together in united action, they will no longer be at the mercy of an androcentric society but will be in a position to demand rather than request their rights. Women, she argues, have not only a right but a duty to seize and wield political power. In a scathing indictment of the patriarchy, she details its inadequacy as a social structure: "What," Dixie demands, "has the rule of man accomplished? The vain gratification of a few, the misery of millions and hundreds of millions. . . . the fact remains: war is spreading, crime increasing, immorality assuming giant proportions, misery, disease, and wrongdoing growing mightier day by day, while the forces that could and would stay these horrors, still wear the badge of slavery" (323). Dixie's assault focuses on *abuses* of the system, not on the system itself. Her powerful, public women will not abandon the ship of state; to keep it on course, they will supply moral ballast—and clear-sighted navigational skills.

Western prairie schooners, however, seemed to demand an altogether different kind of piloting. American texts such as Lois Waisbrooker's *A Sex Revolution* ([1894] 1985) portray the contemporary frontier as a site of innovation and perceive motherhood as the source of both women's immediate power and of the dramatic change that will immeasurably benefit humanity. Her dream vision, like Dixie's, details how women might ascend to their rightful place in the order of things. Waisbrooker's scenario, however, is set in a contemporary, frontier landscape and employs the very force that Dixie ignores so pointedly: woman's reproductive power.

Although clearly a fantasy, Waisbrooker's dream landscape is neither surreal nor futuristic but is so ordinary that neither the reader nor the dreamer, a young widow whose husband was killed in the Civil War, is aware that the narrator has fallen asleep. Instead, she seems merely to have taken a walk and come upon a "new" (66) bit of quite conventional countryside: a garden, woods, a "vast upland plain" (66) typical of the American Midwest. The inhabitants of this dreamworld, allegorical figures such as Selferedo, the "embodied spirit of the love of power, of selfishness" (73), and Lovella, "the embodiment . . . of protecting love" (73), seem equally familiar. Selferedo is a soldier, "dressed in an officer's uniform and holding a trumpet in his hand" (66), who spouts fairly standard jingoistic rhetoric: his trumpet summons "the warriors of the nation to defend its honor and prevent its disruption" (67); he extols the bravery of those who "died nobly, died defending the flag of their country" (69). He is obsessed with "the importance of preserving this 'glorious nation' intact" (72) and rhapsodizes about "patriotism," "national honor," and "duty to . . . country" (75). He is very much a contemporary of the dreamer, remarkable only for the abundance of his clichés. Lovella, the personification of "womanly beauty, dignity, and power" (67), seems equally at home in her rather prosaic surroundings. She is likened to Wittier's "Yankee Girl" (68), who spun and sang by her cottage—although, for a modern reader, Lovella's views probably would seem more at home in a late 1960s antiwar rally. Leading the women in a chant of "No more war, no more war" (70), she mourns the thousands of fathers, husbands, and sons lost in combat. Although her lament is universal, transcending any age, it certainly responds to the history of the period, when Americans were not only still recovering from the impact of one of the bloodiest wars in history, but also facing the threat of an upcoming conflict with Spain. "Does killing and killing elevate nations, make them glorious?" she demands. "Does not the wail of bleeding hearts drown the shout of victory as well as the cry of defeat?" (71). She calls for a new kind of revolution that will reverse "man's methods," replacing "brute force" with "love guided by wisdom" (71).

As in English texts, Waisbrooker's women use their own superior moral force as a justification to seize power, yet there is at least one crucial difference. British heroines effect change by rejecting their traditional roles as wives and mothers and modifying established political structures such as Parliament; American heroines employ their own reproductive power as an instrument of social change. By threatening a battlefield suicide (they plan to stand passively beside their men until killed by cross fire), the women of Waisbrooker's text are effectively threatening to end the production of new sons for soldiering: dead women will bear no more sons "as an offering to the war demon" nor "daughters whose husbands are likely to be torn to pieces to satisfy that governmental pride which is ready to immolate its citizens on the altar of national ambition" (79). Without women, there can be no more babies; without babies, there can be no more war—or peace either. The doomsday machine that women control is their generative power. By threatening a species suicide, Waisbrooker's heroines exact a grudging authorization from the men to manage the government for fifty years.[22]

Lovella is not stepping into existing male structures; she despises them. Gloriana might solve Britain's problems by achieving a majority in Parliament; Lovella, however, chooses instead to rework the essential machinery of the social order. Rather than utilizing male strategies and hierarchies (for instance, teaching women to form a first-rate army, skilled in weaponry, horsemanship, and organizational systems), Lovella's forces will be armed with the "positive power" of "moral weapons" (82), weapons dependent on neither science nor technology. "The prophecy of a new heaven and a new earth," after all, "is no idle dream, but the conditions which will make things new here must be the work of woman, must be born of woman" (86). Women, Waisbrooker asserts, hold the power of the future in their wombs. They must draw their authority from the maternal role so distrusted by British heroines.

Lovella asserts that the quest for utopia can begin immediately and will be entirely realized within two generations. This "new earth" will quite literally be born of women, since the power of maternal influence is an integral part of Lovella's strategy. "Children will be gestated under the influence of, and with the idea of 'women in the lead,' " and "such children will be a radical improvement on those gestated and born under the influence of the old ideas" (95–96). Waisbrooker's women will also employ eugenics, using readily available disciplines such as physiology and phrenology to ensure that anyone with a "physical or moral defect" (103) will be prevented from siring or bearing children. Eventually, even this check will be unnecessary, since "when we have a knowledge of what perfect motherhood should be, and the conditions to carry it out, we shall have no drunkards and no insane people" (104). These changes can be begun immediately; there is no need to await scientific discoveries.

Neither must one await a religious millennium. Waisbrooker reinterprets Genesis 3:15 ("the seed of woman shall bruise the serpent's head"), seeing it not as the coming of Christ to reaffirm his Father's patriarchal authority but as the triumph of maternal generative force over patriarchal oppression. In a rather painful metaphor, she asserts that women will no longer be "nailed alive to that of which the cross is but a symbol, the masculine organ of generation" (94), but will assume their rightful place as humankind's leaders. Once women achieve "a knowledge of [their] own bodies and brains, together with the conditions under which perfect motherhood can be actualized," and "see to it that such knowledge shall take precedence over all else, . . . then the seed of the [women] shall bruise the serpent's head, and not till then" (106).

This, then, is the American justification for an egalitarian society, one that follows the argument of American feminists such as Elizabeth Cady Stanton, who argued that "we are, as a sex, infinitely superior to men and if we were free and developed, healthy in body and mind, as we should be under natural conditions, our motherhood would be our glory. That function gives women such wisdom and power as no male ever can possess" (Stanton and Blatch 1922, 270). Motherhood is indeed the glory of the American utopian heroine; in sharp contrast to the urbane British bluestocking, American utopian heroines seem patterned after the brave, tough, frontier housewife, the staunch defender of her family and home.

It is home, the traditional "woman's sphere," that finally separates English and American utopias by women. English heroines reject what they perceive as the confinement of the kitchen, the monotony of the nursery, the boredom of the parlor, and the enslavement of the bedroom, preferring the freedom of a public life: only one English text, Jane Clapperton's *Margaret Dunmore* (1888), uses a communal, domestic setting.[23] American protagonists, however, embrace home as a center of female power: the kitchen and nursery are places of nurture and generation; the parlor and bedroom, sites of intellectual and physical communion. Indeed, the American authors in this study almost invariably attempt to extend the comforts of home to entire communities—or worlds. Over two-thirds of American utopias written by women between 1873 and 1920 draw from a national utopian vision of frontier communities (with established models of dynamic, heroic, domestic womanhood) to present familial, cooperative societies that bear the responsibility for the welfare of the individual.

Yet despite these differences, British and American utopias remained united by their late nineteenth-century environment of mingled disappointment and hope. The Enlightenment and two revolutions had made utopia seem conceivable; technological and scientific discoveries made it seem feasible; social critics made it seem desirable. Women had so very little to lose; why *not* challenge the inevitability of male dominance and redefine women's role in society? Women's frustration with their constricted environment was translated into the literature of dissatisfaction, and their impatience with political exclusion resulted in a retelling of history, a reworking of past, present, and future into a revisionary historical panorama.

Dream Weaving (1)

Rationalism, Evangelicalism, and Vaticism

"Utopias," Gary Saul Morson (1981, 87) points out, "characteristically set up a series of homologous oppositions—fact and fiction, possible and impossible, real and fantastic, wakefulness and dream, sane and insane, history and poetry, practical and visionary." Historically, women's movements have been characterized by a similar homologous opposition between private and public: crusading moral feminists asserted that women's duty was to effect spiritual improvement from within the seclusion of the family circle, while egalitarian feminists argued that women should assume their rightful place in the public domain that had been for so long monopolized by men. Until the nineteenth century, women's utopian fiction responded to this apparently irreconcilable division by echoing it; narratives were securely anchored at one of the two philosophical poles. While domestic heroines were invariably strong, intelligent, and capable, and egalitarian heroines were invariably moral (although perhaps rather unconventional), early utopian texts nonetheless depicted women functioning in *either* a domestic or public setting, never in a combination of the two. The men in such narratives might be portrayed as successful public figures who are also devoted to their homes and families, but for women there could be no such homogeneity of public and private life.

One would expect this split to continue in nineteenth-century utopias by women, since movements for social purity and suffrage intensified feminist polarization. After all, as Ellen DuBois (1987, 132) observes, Victorian moral reform "was based in the private sphere and sought to reinterpret women's place within it," while "suffragism focused squarely on the public sphere." In some cases, that is precisely what happened: utopias glorifying the private sphere as woman's true place continued to be written until well after the turn of the twentieth century. Yet many of the rationalist authors in this study initiated a new response to the historical opposition, attempting to reconcile these apparently contradictory philosophies into an innovative model of what I term *vatic* feminism: a prophetic vision of woman as a complex *blend* of the spiritual and intellectual, woman working for the improvement of society in *both* the private and public spheres, woman leading humankind into a new age of *united* morality and reason.[1]

I realize that I am expanding the term *vatic* considerably beyond its rhetorical or tonal sense. The *vates* is here a particularly Victorian prophet whose powers include both synthesis and prediction; such a prophet seeks to unify morality and reason into a balanced secular spirituality. In this sense, Carlyle's attempt "to convert England from the old 'Mythus of the Christian Religion' to the New Gospel of Natural Supernaturalism" (Rosenberg 1985, 4) is vatic, as is Ruskin's belief that "in the spiritual geology of the Bible 'two opposite groups of texts' might enclose and uphold a central intermediate truth" (Quennell 1949, 120) and Matthew Arnold's quest for a "spiritual balance" (276) between rationalist, "right-thinking" Hellenism, and evangelical, "right-acting" Hebraism (268). The vatic utopian authors in this study sought a similar balance between the secular and spiritual: interweaving themes of woman's "natural" equality with belief in her innate moral superiority, these authors present heroines who are at once leaders of and inspirational models for egalitarian societies that offer alternatives to the patriarchal models of female inferiority and gender/class hierarchy.

Vatic utopian narratives reflect women's alarm and frustration with the fragmented condition of the mid-nineteenth-century women's movement and its organizations, dissipated by ideological disagreement and splintered into antagonistic sects. By taking advantage of a genre that presents an existing ideal society already firmly in place (thus sidestepping the rather ticklish question of how such a state is to be achieved), women could present a world in which public and private have been reconciled and have no more meaning for women than for men. This chapter will provide an extremely general overview of the emerging feminist schism to demonstrate how vatic authors used utopia, Gary Saul Morson's "literature of opposition," for purposes of consolidation. By tracing the gradual utopian shift from polarization to integration, one can see how the vatic texts in this study responded to their historical and theoretical climate, weaving divergent public and private agendas into a schematic for unification.

Although the "feminist movement" as such did not even begin to emerge until the 1790s, women's frustration with their dismal status in the patriarchal scheme of things had surfaced centuries earlier. Ironically, one of the few ameliorative models available to them came from the very document that had sanctioned their oppression in the first place: the Bible. Despite the inherent misogyny of a text that blamed humankind's fall on Eve, many characteristics attributed to Christ—meekness, compassion, benevolence, and passivity—seemed more feminine than masculine, and the contemplation of Mary's grace offered solace, as well as a modicum of vindication and sanctification, to all women. As Jane Rendall (1984, 75) notes, women, traditionally "assumed to be more emotional and affectionate than men, were increasingly assumed to be potentially closer to God." In the late fourteenth century, Dame Julian of Norwich (1978, 2:594) drew on this feminine, nurturing aspect of godhead and wrote of "God the Mother," seeing in Christ "all the beautiful works and all the sweet loving offices of beloved motherhood."[2] Heaven, she asserts, is a spiritual womb from which we are born and to which we shall someday return, the place where we were "created by the motherhood of kind love" and where we will be "restored to our natural place by the motherhood of mercy and grace." This link to Christ might not have counterbalanced women's biblical nexus with sin and death entirely, but it did give them a moral leg up on their more worldly husbands and a certain status as moral custodian within the home.[3] An evangelical role enabled women to participate fully, albeit obliquely, in the affairs of humankind, since the moral improvement they engendered in the domestic sphere would eventually spread to the public world—their virtue would lead humankind into a new era of harmony and peace.

This assumed, however, that humankind would *want* to be led into such an era—an optimistic view, given humankind's historic predisposition toward discord and violence. Many women sought out the less passive ameliorative paradigm of Enlightenment era rationalism, which offered "a clearly secular and contractual model of family relationships" and "directly challenged assumptions of divinely ordered patriarchy within the family" (Rendall 1984, 7). Thomas Hobbes's argument ([1651] 1983, 3:123) that "in the state of nature . . . neither [man nor woman] is subject to the command of the other" seemed to be a just rejection of societal paternalism, as was John Locke's contention ([1690] 1969, 159) that "conjugal society is . . . a voluntary compact between man and woman" that "draws with it mutual support and assistance."[4] Such egalitarian ideas would have appealed to many women of the period, even those with a modicum of independence, for although unmarried women and widows might enjoy limited autonomy and married women might be entrusted with the management of large estates or businesses, even these freedoms were tacit, uncodified, and thus still largely dependent on the largesse of men. Moral custodianship—cheerleading for God's team—was all well and good, but it still left women on the sidelines in the mundane game of life. Females had few legal rights and were ultimately subject to the will of a male elite, a lopsided situation that rationalist feminists sought to correct.

By the seventeenth century, rationalist/egalitarian and evangelical/moral models were already in place—and already in opposition. In 1662, Margaret Cavendish attempted to dramatize women's conflicting views of their situation in a series of seven brief "Female Orations." The orations form a suite for disagreeing voices, a dialogue between four advocates of the rationalist argument and three defenders of the domestic sphere. As these women argue among themselves with regard to the relative merits of their opposing views, the dialogic structure underscores the tension between these philosophies (and affords the piece an immediacy and urgency that an essay form might not convey).

The first speaker, a rationalist, laments that women "live like bats or owls, labour like beasts, and die like worms" (Cavendish [1662] 1985, 73). Recognizing the link between exclusion and oppression, she encourages women to engage in noisy, visible, highly public political activity: "make frequent assemblies, associations, and combinations amongst our sex, that we may unite in prudent counsels, to make ourselves as free, happy, and famous as men."

The second speaker, another rationalist, identifies men as both the cause and perpetuators of this unhappy situation. Men, she asserts, are "not only our tyrants but devils" who "keep us in the hell of subjection." She fears that women cannot be free of oppression as long as they remain essentially helpless beings—"our power is so inconsiderable, that men laugh at our weakness" (73).

The third speaker will have none of this egalitarian drivel. She sees the domestic sphere as a paradise for women and the maternal role as their most valuable contribution to society: a staunch defender of the patriarchal scheme of things, she is grateful to be spared the hazards and toil of political responsibility. Men are not oppressors, but the "admirers and lovers . . . the protectors, defenders and maintainers" (73) of women; any inequality is the fault of nature, "who hath made men more ingenious, witty, and wise than women"—indeed, women would be "unprofitable creatures, did they not bear children" (74).

But is nature to blame for women's inequality? And can nothing be done to rectify the situation? The fourth speaker thinks not, arguing that women's lack of physical and mental training is a rather severe handicap. Her reason tells her that women's dismissal as inferior beings is a matter of habit, not logic: "How should we know ourselves, when we never made a trial of ourselves? Or how should men know us, when they never put us to the proof?" (74). She asserts that women must be permitted to be public figures, to "hawk, hunt, race, and do the like exercises that men have," to "converse in camps, courts, and in cities; in schools, colleges, and courts of judicature; in taverns, brothels, and gaming houses." Only then will their "strength and wit" (74) be known to all.

The dialogue continues back and forth: another traditionalist argues that for women to become like men is unnatural; another rationalist insists that if men are indeed the superior sex, then women would be well advised to imitate them in order to improve themselves. The final speaker does little to reconcile the opposing views; she is a firm believer in the domestic sphere, asserting that "our own sex and condition is far the better" (75): woman's submissive nature complements man's aggressive tendencies; woman's sheltered sphere protects her from the perils of warfare, and spares her the heavy toil that would "fade [her] fresh beauty, spoil [her] lovely features, and decay [her] youth" (75).

Cavendish's dialogue demonstrates that the rationalist/evangelical opposition hinges on the schism between public and private roles for women, although certainly not in the sense that one uses the terms today: as Jürgen Habermas (1989, 26) points out, notions of "public" and "private" were largely irrelevant, and certainly not in opposition, until the late eighteenth century, when the rise of the middle class made possible a differentiation between one's private/domestic life and public/political existence. In Cavendish's time there was no real distinction between the two: for the aristocracy, even ostensibly "private" activities such as dressing were frequently rather public matters, a representation of status displayed to numbers of onlookers. In this sense, virtually any highborn woman would have been a more "public" figure than virtually any male peasant, whose most public endeavors would have been politically anonymous. For Cavendish, the public/private dichotomy is more a matter of visibility and invisibility, a contrast between celebrated male spaces, such as the "camps, courts . . . cities . . . schools, colleges . . . courts of judicature . . . taverns, brothels, and gaming houses" of "Female Orations" and relatively secluded female spaces, such as the home or chapel.

In short, all members of the nobility were public figures, but some were decidedly more public than others. The division was drawn along a gender hierarchy: although court women such as Cavendish were very much in the public eye and were often political forces in their own right, their political impact tended toward influence rather than authority; they effected social change obliquely, *privately*, rarely through direct action. A woman might be queen by right of birth, but there were no female prime ministers, cabinet members, or archbishops—and few opportunities for the education and training that might eventually qualify females for such prominent positions. This situation distressed Cavendish, and although "Female Orations" ends ambiguously, with neither side prevailing, she makes her own opinions regarding women's forced anonymity abundantly clear in her "Description of a New World, Called the Blazing World" (1666).

By relating the adventures of a brave young woman who discovers and eventually rules an empire, Cavendish demonstrates her belief that women are fully capable of functioning as highly visible members of society. Her remarkable heroine is profoundly aware of her own intellectual worth and social value: strong, courageous, intelligent, and consummately public, the girl survives trials that kill mere men, overcomes the limitations imposed on her by the patriarchy, and manages to lead an intellectually stimulating, public life on her own terms.

Kidnapped and taken to sea by a spurned suitor, Cavendish's heroine initially appears to be a passive victim, anonymous[5] and helplessly subject to the ungoverned passions of her abductor. Yet she not only endures the tempest that drives her ship to the North Pole but also outlives her captors (who promptly succumb to the arctic climate) and strikes off alone in search of civilization. Cavendish has immediately established her heroine's endurance and courage—essential themes in women's rationalist utopian literature, where strong, meritorious women are invariably rewarded with unusual (but not inappropriate) authority and power. The heroine discovers the Blazing World, a peaceful, technologically advanced society, whose enlightened inhabitants immediately recognize her superior nature and treat her accordingly. In her own world, she was little more than private property, stolen from "her Father's house" (Cavendish 1666, 1) by a thief. In the Blazing World, however, her virtue and mental acuity make her a public treasure, a worthy bride for the emperor, who, in a tribute to her intelligence and beauty, awards her "absolute power to rule and govern all that world as she pleased" (13). To be sure, her complete legislative, judicial, and executive carte blanche does have its limits: she has no power over her husband, and the subjects she rules are not human but a varied group of animal-human amalgams (bear-men, fox-men, bird-men, and so forth). Still, her authority is considerable; she is permitted even to "alter the Form of Government" (120), should she deem it necessary.

Heady stuff indeed, for a seventeenth-century heroine, and, had the tale been told by a man, one might expect the kingdom to degenerate into hopeless frivolity and vanity—something along the lines of Bishop Joseph Hall's *The Discovery of a New World* (1605), which introduced the chaotic woman-run state of Shee-Land and its provinces of Tattlingen, Scoldonna, Blubberick, Cocka-trixia, and Shrewes-bourg. Frivolity and vanity are selfish vices, however—the result of an obsession with one's *private* good. Cavendish's explorer-empress is preeminently *public* spirited and thus admirably equipped to exercise her nearly absolute authority: her first imperial action is not a round of masques and cele-brations, but the founding of a society for the propagation of "profitable and useful Arts" (15). Scorning the usual self-gratifying activities of Restoration heroines—ordering clothes, being seen at plays, and cuckolding husbands—the empress embarks on a strenuous regimen of intellectual self-improvement.[6] She begins by conducting a series of informative interviews with the wisest of her subjects, seeking to obtain as much knowledge as she can about the world around her.

Cavendish's rationalist[7] argument is that if *man*kind would only value women's intellectual nature, free them to develop fully this aspect of them-selves, and encourage them to make full use of their abilities in the public sphere, women would contribute significantly to the progress of *human*kind as a whole. The empress is an intellectual, politically active model for the ration-alist utopian heroine: a highly gifted, mature woman, equal in intelligence to the Blazing World's sagest beast-men, and surpassing them in intellectual curi-osity. Comfortably knowledgeable about such varied topics as law, religion, architecture, astronomy, physics, biology, chemistry, anatomy, alchemy, bot-any, philosophy, medicine, mathematics, and logic, the empress's scholarship is astounding, as she processes information at a dazzling rate. Eventually, she exhausts the combined knowledge of her beast-men teachers and extends her quest for wisdom to the plane of pure intelligence, seeking out as mentors "im-material" spirits uncorrupted by physical existence.

She questions them on a variety of subjects, including one that becomes cen-tral in women's utopias, the myth of Genesis. In the Blazing World at least, God has rescinded woman's banishment: Cavendish's heroine discovers that she has quite literally returned to Eden, that paradise is the Blazing World in which she presently lives, "the very same place where she [keeps] her Court, and where her Palace [stands]" (Cavendish 1666, 71–72). The empress questions the spirits about the events leading to the Fall, and her inquiries are models of delicate rationalist subversion, which subtly shift the focus (and blame) away from Eve and cast Satan as the real villain of the piece. The empress first wonders that "since it is mentioned in the story of the Creation of the World, that Eve was tempted by the Serpent, Whether the Devil was within the Serpent, or Whether the Serpent tempted her without the Devil" (72). Eve's behavior is not discussed, only the relative culpability of Satan and the snake.[8] Woman's reappearance in Eden, and the significant changes that have been made there, underscores Cavendish's point. This time, no armed angels bar her return; this time, her worth has been realized and rewarded; this time, her curiosity is encouraged rather than damned.

This curiosity causes the narrative to take a rather surreal twist. To comply with the empress's desire to examine certain otherworldly documents, the spirits must conscript a "Spiritual Scribe" from Earth[9] to take dictation. The burden falls on none other than the narrative's author, Margaret Cavendish, whose soul is persuaded to leave her body to aid the empress in her quest for learning. Cavendish's superimposition of herself on the text becomes an integral part of the plot: in a dizzying burst of self-referentiality, she trifurcates herself into author (Margaret Cavendish, the historical Duchess of Newcastle), character (the soul of Margaret Cavendish), and narrator (an anonymous persona who refers to Cavendish in the third person). Not content to be the tacit bond between reader and text, she also must be the visible junction between the empress and the spirits. This odd, outrageous (and rather modern) authorial intrusion echoes her soul's assertion that she would prefer to "die in the adventure of noble achievements, than live in obscure and sluggish security" (95).

Highly intelligent and accomplished, often surpassing even the empress in intellectual prowess and appetite, Cavendish's soul hungers for public recognition, reflecting the frustration of a woman who has been sidelined from the world but who refuses to be sidelined in her own utopia. Here, she will brook no restriction, not even physical restrictions on her person. When the empress desires to visit Earth, Cavendish's soul agrees to guide the empress's soul on an extended out-of-body excursion. Free of all restraint, the two finally transcend the liabilities of their gender and function as the essence of pure reason: traveling "as lightly as two thoughts into the Duchess's native World" (103), they journey at the speed of intellect; "in a moment" the empress is able to take in "all the parts" of Earth "and all the actions of all the Creatures therein" (103).

The "parts" are largely unremarkable, but the "actions" of Earth's human inhabitants are characterized by extraordinary amounts of spitefulness, meanness, and corruption. Indeed, Cavendish paints the Earth so bleakly that the reader is hard put to understand the empress's alien enthusiasm for things terrestrial. The planet's inhabitants, for example, seem to represent little more than an impressive catalog of vices: they are "Ambitious, Proud, Self-conceited, Vain, Prodigal, Deceitful, Envious, Malicious, Unjust, Revengeful, Irreligious, Factious, andc." (103). Certainly these failings could be corrected if public-spirited women—such as Margaret Cavendish—were given positions of power. Denied such power because of her gender, she can nonetheless write herself into a utopian world of her own devising, where gender has no meaning or use, where intellect is all: a world "framed and composed of . . . the Rational parts of Matter, which are the parts of my Mind" (159).

"The Blazing World" is a testament to woman's intelligence and capacity to function in the public sphere. It anticipates the rationalist sensibilities of nineteenth-century feminist thinkers who considered the education of women and the reeducation of men the solution to sexist thought and who paved the way for women to take a more active part in public life. The text contrasts sharply with another early utopian narrative, Sarah Scott's paean to domestic virtue, *A Description of Millenium Hall* (1762), which has as its central premise women's moral superiority and duty to influence humankind positively through activity in the private sphere.

Scott's heroines reject all contact with public, worldly life and withdraw into the joys of uncorrupted domestic virtue. Although she considers women's rational nature and desire for self-improvement as valuable assets, her Millenium Hall women function as moral exemplars and spiritual guides who demonstrate that female generosity will eventually overcome male greed, that female purity will triumph over male lust, and that female moderation will temper male excess. Scott identifies the public sphere as a corrupting environment, dominated by irrational, violent males, in which women must constantly defend themselves against attacks on their virtue. Since woman's moral nature is perceived as the single beacon of hope that will lead humankind to a Christian way of life, it is imperative that women be sheltered in the domestic sphere, safely removed from the pollution of the outside world.

This view refutes a great deal of early eighteenth-century literature, which frequently offered satirical portraits of women as silly, vain, materialistic, and often sexually promiscuous creatures. Scott's women have little in common with narcissistic flirts such as Pope's Belinda, whose frivolous life is devoted to clothes, cosmetics, balls, and card parties, and still fewer associations with deceitful bawds such as Jonathan Swift's Corinna, a sluttish wanton who uses artificial hair, eye, eyebrows, teeth, breasts, hips, and complexion to lure prospective customers. Indeed, the women of Millenium Hall seem to anticipate the words of later writers such as George Lyttelton, who in 1776 admonished women to

> Seek to be good, but aim not to be great:
> A woman's noblest station is retreat:
> Her fairest virtues fly from public sight,
> Domestic worth, that shuns too strong a light.
> (3:107, ll. 51–55)

Scott's utopia depicts just such a domestic retreat. Two male travelers, successful by worldly standards (and therefore dangerously removed from a life of virtue), come upon an isolated country estate managed by a group of energetic, artistic, highly virtuous, and celibate women, who have rejected the corrupt male world and its misery. The women have founded an all-female community dedicated to domestic virtue and spend their lives emulating the life and teachings of Christ. The ladies of Millenium Hall find happiness "in fulfilling the design of their maker, in providing for their own greatest felicity, and contributing all that is in their power to the convenience of others" (Scott [1762] 1986, 62). They do this by helping unfortunate people in the area, and, in the pastoral setting of an Adamless Eden, the homeless are sheltered, the sick are tended, poor children are educated, and deformed people are given a refuge.

Although the women of Millenium Hall devote much of their energy to education, Cavendish's empress would feel stifled here: there is no opportunity to explore philosophy, mathematics, logic, law, or the properties of the physical world; instead, these well-bred young women study genteel literature and useful modern languages, draw and paint inspirational subjects, sew and embroider functional articles of clothing, and play and sing uplifting music. Their primary purpose, after all, is not self-improvement. Scott's women need no improvement: they are moral exemplars designed to inspire humankind (and most particularly, one would assume, *man*kind) to leave the folly of its ways. Perhaps this is why most of the text is devoted not to a description of the estate, but to the grim histories of the five patronesses who have come to own and manage the hall. These narratives illustrate woman's duty to draw humankind toward Christ and away from the menace of man's competitive world.

Yet Scott's text is ultimately as subversive as Cavendish's. In the cloistered, nurturing "paradise" (24) that is Millenium Hall, there has been a subtle role reversal: here, it is man, not woman, who is the tempter, the Other. Man, after all, ignores divine dictum when his worldly appetites make him disregard the teachings of Christ, and it is *his* lechery that can lead an otherwise virtuous woman to *her* fall.[10] The men who live beyond Millenium Hall are public, worldly creatures who disobey Christ's command to give all one has to the poor and not pile up the things of the earth; they make no attempt to lead pure and moral lives and spend their time in gambling, drinking, and debauchery. Even worse, their depravities are not confined to the public world and public women but frequently corrupt the domestic sphere as well. Beyond the protective walls of Scott's utopia lies a world so pervaded by vice that the home and family are at tremendous risk: even the most virtuous and vigilant of women are susceptible to worldly contamination from treacherous guardians, dissolute husbands, and perfidious suitors.[11]

Each of the women of Millenium Hall has been personally imperiled by insidious infectors. As a child, the beautiful orphan Louisa Mancel is supported in a private girls' school by the seemingly philanthropic urges of an apparently great-hearted young lord. His true urges, however, are centered somewhat lower than his heart. He is the worst kind of cad, who plans to remove her from the cloistered safety of the school when she reaches sexual maturity, lull her suspicions with a mockery of domestic virtue (a false priest and marriage ceremony), and enjoy her favors. Miss Mancel, whose "notions . . . are too refined for persons who live in the world" (50), passively places her faith in God, "convinced that her innocence would be guarded by that power who knew the integrity and purity of her heart" (48). Her prayers are rewarded: Providence promptly strikes the would-be ravisher dead of apoplexy. Other women at Millenium Hall have learned a similar distrust of a male-controlled private sphere. The history of Lady Mary Jones relates how an innocent young orphan, virtuous by nature, is reared in worldly company, which nearly proves her undoing. Like Miss Mancel, she is nearly ruined by a cad[12] with a false marriage ceremony, but in Lady Mary's case, providential intervention takes the form of a fortuitous carriage accident that forces her into the domestic security of a sickbed.

By founding Millenium Hall, Miss Mancel, Lady Mary, and the other women of the establishment have managed to elude not only the perils of the public sphere but also vice-ridden domestic circles. The women are thus doubly withdrawn, doubly private, in the security of their inviolate paradise. From the safety of this cloistered vantage point, they promote Christian values and work profound changes on those with whom they come into contact. Their self-sufficiency has immunized them against outside corruption; if anything, it is their virtue that has become contagious: the two male visitors who have stumbled upon Millenium Hall are reformed within a matter of days. One takes to reading the New Testament, "convinced by the ladies of the house that their religion must be the true one" (206); the other decides to spread the good news of this female re-vision of Christian life throughout the world. The domestic has emerged triumphant—and its passive proselytizers have not even had to leave the security of the cloister.

Scott's assertion that women must retreat from the corrupting influence of men is in direct opposition to Cavendish's vision of free women who are active in the public sphere and who deal with men as equals. Yet both women would have distrusted the idealized view of the domestic that gradually emerged following the French Revolution. Revolutionary theorists viewed the home as an inviolate sanctuary, where happy, virtuous women could care for their husbands and rear their children. The home was also a refuge for men, who were no longer considered violent and treacherous corruptors of the private sphere but, rather, its gallant and valiant defenders. Women need not rely on their wits for protection, as did Cavendish's empress, nor on the isolation of the convent, as did Scott's heroines. A hearth and its male defender offered ample security.

Ironically, the revolution's egalitarian ideals, which seemed to augur the end of women's oppression, ultimately marginalized women as never before. This was in part due to Jean Jacques Rousseau's tremendous influence on revolutionary architects. Like Locke and Hobbes, he presented a model of society predicated on natural human rights. Unlike that of his predecessors, however, Rousseau's position on gender equality was not in the least ambivalent or ambiguous. He extended these rights only to men, believing women to be naturally inferior creatures whose primary purpose was to serve and please males. In his "Économie Politique" ([1755] 1959, 3:243), he sets up a model for society that extends even to the individual family, arguing that the father should be the *"premier magistrat"* of the home, and that this paternal authority has been established by nature, since the disadvantages peculiar to women are sufficient reason for excluding them from primacy.[13] Woman's duty, he argues in *Émile* ([1762] 1966, 16), is to provide a loving and moral home for her family, to employ her domestic influence for the betterment of humankind: "Once women become good mothers, men will not be long in becoming good husbands and fathers" and, one would assume, better *premiers magistrats.*

This argument implies that the female should by nature be domestic and deferential and that women who seek equality with men are somehow unnatural—a premise that neatly dovetailed with lower- and middle-class resentment of the highly public women of the aristocracy. Joan Landes (1988, 17), in her discussion of the place of aristocratic women before the French Revolution, notes that "elite women achieved a public position that had little if anything to do with their domestic roles." The fall of absolutist government, however, wrenched from these women any connection they had to a public life. The newly emerging public redefined the celebrated *salons* as monuments of frivolity and reinterpreted women's indirect political influence as political corruption.[14] Eventually, this hostility toward the powerful women of the aristocracy extended to any intellectual or political woman, including revolutionary *citoyennes.* It suddenly became very hazardous for a woman to move outside the security of her home and family.

Edmund Burke points out this danger in his "Reflections on the Revolution in France" ([1790] 1973), using the unlikely figure of Marie Antoinette (perhaps one of the most public women of the age) as his exemplar of ideal domestic womanhood. The outrages on her person increase proportionately as she is drawn further and further from the shelter of her home and family and thrust into public view: chased from her bedroom; torn from her husband; dragged, with her "infant children" (84), from her home; and exhibited as a public spectacle. What a contrast to the idealized, almost saintly apparition of Antoinette as the young dauphine, hovering above an earth "which she hardly seem[s] to touch," a "delightful vision . . . glittering like the morning star, full of life, and splendor, and joy," a secure and happy private woman protected from public disgrace by "ten thousand swords" that would leap "to avenge even a look that threatened her with insult" (89). What a contrast, too, to the revolutionary women who abduct the family: the monstrous and highly *public* creatures whose activities are designed to call attention to themselves, creatures whose unnatural unwomanliness is used as a metaphor for what Burke sees as the unnaturalness of the revolution. The "horrid yells, and shrilling screams, and frantic dances" of the bloodthirsty *citoyennes* are a kind of display, a representation of "the unutterable abominations of the furies of hell, in the abused shape of the vilest of women" (85). The revolt of the French masses was not a triumph of Enlightenment thought, but an affront against a newly emerging idealization of domestic womanhood.

This idealization would prevail. As the revolution progressed, Frenchwomen found their participation in public matters systematically curtailed. The Society of Revolutionary Republican Women, for example, formed in 1793 by Pauline Léon and Claire Lacombe, was outlawed by the convention within six months, as was any other form of female political association. Landes (1988, 145–46) chronicles women's increasing exclusion from political activity: "In 1794 all attempts at legal and social reform for women were curtailed. In May 1795 the Convention declared that all women were to be kept out of the galleries. . . . In May 1796 the Council of Five Hundred ruled that 'the interests of society and morality' excluded women from senior teaching positions. The Napoleonic Civil Code of 1804 reinforced the authority of husbands and fathers at the expense of wives and children. It resurrected unequal standards of divorce and deprived women of the right to perform as civil witnesses, to plead in court in their own name, or to own property without the husband's consent." Women, it seemed, must be protected from the insidious contaminating influence of public life—otherwise, they might degenerate into vain and foolish aristocratic bluestockings, debauched and debased actresses and prostitutes, or monstrous and mannish revolutionary viragoes.[15]

This abhorrence of rationalist, public-minded women was to persist for centuries; indeed, to a certain extent, it still exists today. Certainly it had a profound effect in shaping postrevolutionary women's views of themselves and their place in society. Evangelical moral crusaders, who had distrusted the public sphere even before the French Revolution, were horrified by what they perceived as an unnatural, godless, and highly public display—and redoubled their efforts to focus women's energies into genteel, domestic channels. Events in France seemed to reinforce their assertion that women should remain in the private sphere, where their inherently moral nature and maternal instincts would contribute to familial and social well-being. Decent (that is, domestic) women could take advantage of increasing urbanization's tendency to separate workplace and home, using the resulting isolation of the domestic sphere as a shield against external onslaughts on their chastity, piety, humility, and docility.[16]

These women found the concept of gender equality highly disturbing and potentially threatening to their status. Hannah More, for example, argues in *Strictures on Female Education* (1799) that "the imposing term of *rights* has been produced to sanctify the claim of our female pretenders, with a view not only to rekindle in the minds of women a presumptuous vanity dishonourable to their sex, but produced with a view to excite in their hearts an impious discontent with the post that God has assigned them in this world" (2:20).[17] More's assertion reflects her disapproval of the French Revolution, certainly a monument to "impious discontent" with one's position in life. Static societies are at least ostensibly peaceful, and women, as the maintainers of stasis and peace, should work from within the private sphere to promote Sunday schools, distribute uplifting tracts, help the unfortunate learn skills appropriate to their preordained station in life, and perform anonymous acts of charity.[18] Man must use his physical superiority to shoulder the burdens and resist the temptations of a public life; woman should be grateful to be spared the tempests of the outside world and should concentrate her efforts on the spiritual improvement of those within her immediate circle. The domestic sphere, More argues, is the only place in which a woman can achieve happiness, since she "sees the world, as it were, from a little elevation in her own garden, whence she makes an exact survey of home scenes, but takes not in that wider range of distant prospects which he, who stands on a loftier eminence, commands" (2:25).

The only utopia written by a woman at this time was Ellis Knight's *Dinarbas*, a sequel to Samuel Johnson's *Rasselas* (1759). Knight's narrative ([1790] 1993) staunchly upholds mainstream evangelical values: her heroines are domestic angels who realize that women "frequently do hurt by interposing in affairs which seem foreign to their sex" and should instead "turn their thoughts to . . . domestic and natural cares" (123–24). They are serenely happy in the private sphere and "never interfer[e] in public business" (137), unless such business is inherently womanly: they patronize "establishments of charity" (137) and support the arts. Their wifely devotion and spiritual virtue make home such a heaven that even the disillusioned Prince Rasselas eventually reconsiders his gloomy philosophy; he surrenders himself to marital bliss, "which was once beyond [his] hopes, but without which, [he] now could not exist" (136). There were no uncompromisingly rationalist utopias to offset *Dinarbas*, nor would there be, for more than a century.

Instead, as the aftershocks of the French Revolution threatened to relegate all women to the private sphere forever, the rationalist utopian impulse seems to have gone underground, redirected into safer, more acceptable concerns, and focusing primarily on the education of women. Educated women, after all, could function as positive exemplars and, eventually, demonstrate that female equality was not the terrifying specter it seemed to be. This strategy of compromise provides the earliest precursors of the vatic text.

Catherine Macaulay, who rejected the concept of "natural" or "innate" sexual inequality as a male construct, argues in *Letters on Female Education* (1790, cited in Luria 1974) that education will produce more virtuous women, since "all the vices and imperfections which have generally been regarded as inseparable from the female character . . . do not in any manner proceed from sexual causes, but are entirely the effects of situation and education" (202). Macaulay proposes the fairly utopian notion of an identical education for boys and girls, confident that such an arrangement would be in the best interest of humanity. Yet she does not explicitly advocate female suffrage; although she complains that contemporary women "have hardly a civil right to save them from the grossest injustices" (210), there is no suggestion that women should enter the public sphere to redress their own wrongs. Educated women, however, will eventually be able to convince men to effect political and legal changes that benefit society as a whole.

Education is also the foundation of Mary Wollstonecraft's visionary *A Vindication of the Rights of Woman* (1792), which argues that educational inequality perpetuates sexual inequality. Wollstonecraft is a decided advocate of reason, arguing that once both sexes are allowed to achieve their fullest intellectual potential, humankind in general will benefit. She denounces women's economic exploitation, inferior legal status, poor health, educational privation, and personal unhappiness. Yet her work also demonstrates the stirrings of the mediating, synthesizing impulse that made a place for women between the poles of public and private. Wollstonecraft never devalues the domestic sphere; indeed, she presents it as affording the greatest happiness a woman can achieve.

Wollstonecraft's predictions ([1792] 1975) of a future world in which her ideas will have been implemented are utopian in their own right: she envisions legions of healthy, well-educated women, freed of the artificial constraints imposed by society, fulfilling their destinies as public citizens. In Wollstonecraft's "utopian dreams" (36), women's economic exploitation and lack of legal status have been amended: in this "future time," women are no longer limited to menial employment such as millinery or dressmaking (148) or maternal occupations such as nursing or teaching. Instead, they can take full advantage of their improved educational opportunities and, after exposure to a government-run system of free coeducational "day schools" for "all classes," can learn "the elements of anatomy and medicine" along with "the sciences and the arts" and "the political history of mankind" (177). Women afforded such preparation "might certainly study the art of healing, and be physicians as well as nurses." They might also "study politics" and "business of various kinds . . . which might save many from common and legal prostitution [that is, marriage]" (148). In addition, women will be able to take an active part in public matters, "instead of being arbitrarily governed without having any direct share allowed them in the deliberations of government" (147). Wollstonecraft does not go so far as to demand female suffrage, however. No sooner does she touch on this question than she adds that women "need not complain" about their lack of enfranchisement, "for they are as well represented as a numerous class of hard working mechanics" (147), and she then proceeds to attack the lavish lifestyle of the royal family. In 1792, full political equality for women was too radical a concept, even for the radical Wollstonecraft.

A happy woman, it seems, can live without enfranchisement; however, she will not renounce the domestic sphere. Instead, she will be her husband's loving companion and respected "domestic friend" (129); she will be "surrounded by her children, reaping the reward of her care. The intelligent eye meets hers, whilst health and innocence smile on their chubby cheeks" (51). Indeed, Wollstonecraft's severest censure is not directed against men, but against conceited, superficial women who "neglect to discharge the indispensable duty of a mother"; such a woman "sins against herself by neglecting to cultivate an affection that would equally tend to make her useful and happy" (142). Wollstonecraft is no evangelical—she distrusts enthusiasts filled with religious "zeal" (160) and condemns the sentiment and paternalism inherent in the domestic model. Yet she is not willing to renounce the limited status and power women have achieved there.

Despite Wollstonecraft's valuation of the private sphere, her ideas regarding female education were considered far too radical, and possibly far too close to the truth. As Dale Spender (1987, 5) notes, "Many accepted the accuracy of her analysis. This is why those who wanted sexual equality put so much energy into the struggle for educational equality: and why those who did not want sexual equality offered such entrenched resistance to the extension of education to women."

In the early nineteenth century, however, rationalists found a new champion of women's equality: Frances Wright, whose commitment to absolute sexual and racial equality extended even to such radical concepts as free love and interracial mating. Yet even she occasionally felt the need to compromise her otherwise uncompromising stance; her utopia, *A Few Days in Athens* (1822), for example, features a heroine who is not only intellectually brilliant but is also conventionally chaste and virtuous, an asexual woman in the best tradition of the nineteenth-century ideal. Such concessions failed to mollify highly influential evangelicals such as Sarah Josepha Hale,[19] Catherine Beecher, and Sarah Lewis, who believed that woman's mission consisted of regenerating humankind through meek self-sacrifice and evangelical spirituality. Women were civilization's bulwark against barbarity, and their effectiveness was heightened precisely because they had no power to corrupt them. In its place was the mystical force of female influence: legions of pure mothers and wives who would bring about the betterment of humankind. Female equality was a horrifying threat to humanity because it would strip women of the real (that is, domestic) power they had managed to accumulate so far.[20]

Any rationalist leanings found in women's utopian writing of the period were invariably tempered by the awful might of "woman's influence." Jane Appleton's "Sequel to 'The Vision of Bangor in the Twentieth Century'" ([1848] 1971), for example, struggled to depict "womanly" women who function capably outside the domestic sphere. Although Appleton does not support the concept of statutory female political power—no mention of suffrage is made in her text—in her exemplary world of 1978, woman is accepted as strong rather than frail, man's equal rather than his helpmeet. She is no longer "petted and pacified with adulation, while her true dignity is forgotten" (251); neither is she merely "the 'companion to cheer *his* pathway,' the 'angel to soothe *his* sorrows,' the 'wife to adorn *his* fireside,' etc. etc." (252). Respected for her moral strength and intellectual prowess, she is no longer demeaned as a living objet d'art. She is admired "not for the fair hair, or the azure eye, nor yet for the graceful manner, or elegant accomplishment alone" (252), but for the inner force that Margaret Cavendish had recognized as early as 1666: "the *soul* that burns within her, and now only has freedom to show itself" (252). Educated, impervious to flattery, financially independent, and freed from the drudgery (if not the responsibility) of domestic chores by technological advances, she is man's virtual equal in all things.

In midcentury, the blending of rationalist and evangelical precepts could be seen in the work of apocalyptic feminists such as Eliza Farnham and Margaret Fuller. Farnham's *Woman and Her Era,* for example, argues that legal, political, religious, and educational reforms for women will not destroy the domestic sphere but will instead result in the spiritual purification of humanity. The woman's movement, Farnham (1864, 1:311) prophesies, is the harbinger of the "COMING ERA—the ERA of spiritual rule and movement; in which, *through* [women], the race is destined to rise to a more exalted position than ever before it has held," to a world "of purer action and diviner motion, which lies above the . . . selfish purpose wherein man has held and exercised his long sovereignty." Farnham never considers the possibility of gender equality; as an apocalyptic feminist, she knows that woman is far superior to man. The reasoning abilities in which males take such pride are in fact a sadly inadequate means for understanding; true knowledge requires intuition. Science must give way to spirituality; women must be allowed to take their rightful place as humankind's leaders.

In *Woman in the Nineteenth Century* (1855), Margaret Fuller exhorts women (à la *Millenium Hall*) to use their inherently moral natures to save man from his own masculine competitive nature and aggressiveness. "Women of my country! You see the men, how they are willing to sell shamelessly the happiness of countless generations of fellow-creatures, the honor of their country, and their immortal souls, for a money market and political power. Do you not feel within you that which can reprove them, which can check, which can convince them?" (166). Yet although the evangelical tasks of reproving, checking, and convincing might well be carried out from the security of the domestic sphere, Fuller longs to "have every arbitrary barrier thrown down" and "every path laid open to Woman as freely as to Man" until "inward and outward freedom for Woman, as much as for Man, shall be acknowledged as a *right,* not yielded as a concession" (37). Her rationale is that only free women will have the courage and strength to "tell these men that you will not accept the glittering baubles, spacious dwellings, and plentiful service, they mean to offer you. . . . Tell them that the heart of Woman demands nobleness and honor in Man, and that, if they have not purity, have not mercy, they are no longer fathers, lovers, husbands, sons of yours" (166–67). Fuller first clarifies the tension between the rationalist and the evangelical—which she represents as the "two aspects of Woman's nature," an inspirational "Muse" and an intellectual "Minerva" (115)—and then argues that they are a dual incarnation, a synthesis that demonstrates woman's fitness for the dual spheres of private influence and public participation. Fuller closed the circle: the blend of private and public that began as a conciliatory response to the postrevolutionary suppression of female equality finally emerged as a defense of female supremacy.

It would be taken yet one step further, however. The 1830s and 1840s saw tremendous social upheaval on both sides of the Atlantic: in England, the passage of the First Reform Bill in 1832 was a response to years of pressure for increased political rights; in America, the growing abolitionist movement stressed the need to extend civil liberties to the black population. For years, words such as liberty, fraternity, and equality had been tainted by the atrocities of the French Revolution, but now it seemed that the quest for human rights was afoot once again—and this time, many women were determined not to be left behind. As agitation for women's rights increased and women realized the need to form a unified political front, the synthesis of private and public spheres would become crucially important.

The growing climate of disunity in the woman's movement had been undermined by apparently irreconcilable differences between rationalists and evangelicals. Their divergence was deeply ingrained, often extending considerably beyond philosophy to their essential way of life. As Alice Rossi (1971, 248) points out, rationalist American "Enlightenment feminists" were most frequently "highly urban, sophisticated solitary thinkers and writers" (248) who supported themselves by their writing. Evangelical "Moral Crusader" feminists, on the other hand, were "almost all native-born, middle-class Americans from rural areas or small towns . . . decidedly not cosmopolitan, urban, worldly in their thinking or life styles" and not generally self-supporting.

This, of course, was less the case in England, where some of the most dedicated exponents of woman's domestic sphere led highly public lives: Hannah More, for example, was witty, urbane, and sophisticated, a fashionable, outspoken bluestocking whose literary output of plays, novels, and essays was prodigious and whose reputation was considerable on both sides of the Atlantic. Nevertheless, evangelical Anglicans such as More were more likely to predominate in rural districts, while rationalist Unitarians and Quakers typically inhabited urban areas. Lenore Davidhoff and Catherine Hall (1987) point out that in Birmingham, for example, "a number of influential Quaker and Unitarian families . . . were central to the town's economic and political life" (43), while rural areas such as Essex and Suffolk were dominated by aristocratic gentry, resulting in "a higher profile of the established church" (51).

Attitudes toward formal religion divided the two groups further: rationalists were frequently "extremely suspicious of religious institutions, quick to see scheming on the part of the clergy for their own personal and institutional advantage, and skeptical about any 'truth' concerning man or woman in the Bible"; evangelicals, however, generally worked with the church and clergy, and even while they might be "critical of clerical interpretations of the Bible," they nonetheless accepted it as the source of "great moral teachings" (Rossi

1971, 248–49). Finally, and perhaps of most significance, the groups were in fundamental disagreement about goals. Rationalist feminists wished to bring women into the public sphere through education, employment opportunity, and, most importantly, the vote. Although many evangelical objectives might seem public in nature—they sought, for example, the closing of brothels, the abolishment of all intoxicating beverages, and the elimination of slavery— these issues were ultimately domestic, derived from their impact upon the home and family. Husbands who frequented brothels brought home venereal disease that could infect wives and unborn children; husbands who drank heavily wasted money needed for the family (and were often wife and/or child beaters); slavery was associated with the separation of families and the sexual debasement of black women.

By 1870, the ideological battle lines were clearly drawn, and the opposing forces seemed irreconcilable. Indisputably, women should be public figures who initiate change through rational argument; indisputably, women should be domestic heroines who inspire change through moral influence. Obviously, enfranchisement was the answer to women's oppression; obviously, enfranchisement was a burden that would ultimately cost them the small amount of status they had managed to accumulate. Clearly, individual autonomy was women's prime concern; clearly, women were primarily moral custodians destined to inspire and purify civilization. How could these opposing convictions be incorporated into a single vision of unified feminism? What was needed were visionary strategies for reconciling the apparently irreconcilable. Many sought the answer in utopia, which could circumvent real prejudices through the use of conceptual landscapes. One might envision a successful socialist community that has eliminated all oppositions or a Martian society that has blended its oppositions into an harmonious whole; one could transcend opposition through allegorical dreams or could imagine a world of the future that has finally achieved unity. Utopian fiction wove the rationalist weft and evangelical warp into a vatic tapestry, paving the way for the reconciliation of nineteenth-century feminist views and helping women forge themselves into a single force for change.

Dream Weaving (2)

Vaticism and Women's Utopian Fiction, 1870–1920

Nearly all of the utopian literature written by late nineteenth- and early twentieth-century women reflects the ongoing schism between opposing forces in the women's movement. Some texts are openly evangelical: Augusta Drane's *The New Utopia* (1877) features a hero who glorifies docile, domestic women as models of feminine perfection and ridicules female intellectuals as confused and misguided bluestockings; Lucia Mead's *Memoirs of a Millionaire* (1889) details the efforts of a devout and idealistic young woman to establish a "Christian Missionary Fund" to help the downtrodden people of the earth, promote Christianity, and diminish slavery and alcohol usage. Other narratives, such as Florence Dixie's *Gloriana* (1890) and Amelia Mears's *Mercia* (1895), are frankly rationalist, featuring capable, politically adept heroines who compete on an equal footing with men (and generally triumph). A number of the authors in this study, however, perhaps sensing the danger inherent in a polarized feminist movement, strove to blend evangelical and rationalist perspectives into a harmonious vatic whole.

Admittedly, they were not always successful: many of these texts are tentative, awkward, and ultimately rather lopsided, drifting to one ideological pole or the other despite their attempts at balance: in Marie Howland's *Papa's Own Girl* (1874), for example, even the strongest women must ultimately defer to the weight of their biological imperative, while Jane Hume Clapperton's *Margaret Dunmore; or, A Socialist Home* (1888) extends the delights of an idealized domesticity to the public sphere. As the century progressed, however, and the division in the feminist ranks showed little sign of reconciliation, vatic utopian narratives developed increased confidence, urgency, and equilibrium. Alice Ilgenfritz Jones and Ella Merchant's *Unveiling a Parallel: A Romance* (1893) and Olive Schreiner's "Three Dreams in the Desert" (1890) are at once cautionary and inspirational fables that delineate the hazards of polarization and the delights of unity; Winifred Harper Cooley's "A Dream of the Twenty-First Century" (1902) and Charlotte Perkins Gilman's *Moving the Mountain* (1911) offer specific strategies to forge discord into unity.

The first true example of a vatic utopian text is Howland's *Papa's Own Girl* (1874). Her account of the evolution of the Social Palace, an institution for social reform, attempts to blend a rationalist agenda with an evangelical valuation of the domestic sphere. *Papa's Own Girl* would give any self-respecting moral crusader fits: it proposes absolute equality for women in education and employment opportunity, advocates women's full economic independence, and promotes unrestricted adult enfranchisement. Yet Howland's characters are at heart remarkably conventional and consistently seek out a traditional, patriarchal social framework; once these educated, professionally, financially, and legally secure women meet Mr. Right (or, in one case, Count Right), they happily return to the joys of anonymous domestic bliss. Although Howland's utopian community strives for a perfect vatic balance between public and private, the scale is ultimately tipped by the weight of domesticity (and biology).

This domestic bias did little to mollify more conservative readers, who were outraged by what seemed to be a remarkably unflattering portrayal of marriage (the cause of the book's banishment from the Boston Public Library). The noble, virtuous heroine, Clara Forest, is trapped in a loveless marriage with a cruel husband who publicly humiliates her, while Clara's gentle, benevolent father is bound forever to a cold woman who controls him through guilt and sexual manipulation. The novel is peppered with similarly wretched couples. The only happy marriages are contracted by the heroines who have evidently flown in the face of conventional morality: Clara Forest leaves her husband, and then, when the court grants him a divorce but forbids her to remarry, she defies the law and weds a European count; her friend Susie Dykes has a child out of wedlock, rejects the father, and marries a penniless young man. The heroines' apparent unconventionality extends to every facet of their lives. These are highly visible, shrewd businesswomen, who move freely in the public sphere. Clara and Susie, "ruined" women according to conventional standards, do not conventionally drown themselves in the nearest river; instead, they establish a highly profitable florist/nursery business. Nor do they immerse themselves in shame and sorrow; instead, they reject the "conventional morality" (Howland [1874] 1975, 145) that censures them.

Yet the underlying structure of *Papa's Own Girl* is one of strict moral orthodoxy. The heroines are not brazen harlots, mannish termagants, or threatening Amazons, but womanly women who champion domestic values. Susie Dykes is a naive, trusting young girl with a "good nature" (31), a "little woman even among the rather diminutive," with "pretty soft grey eyes, a slender, well-shaped waist, and a wealth of light yellow hair" arranged in a "pretty and simple way" (73). She is indeed an unwed mother, but Howland has orchestrated the events leading to her fall so that her pregnancy is ultimately a testament to her goodness and moral worth. Clara's morally bankrupt brother lures Susie to his rooms by begging her to come and pray with him and then brutally rapes her. Later, his father pressures him to marry Susie, but his habitual drunkenness and abusiveness arouse her protective maternal instincts: concerned far more with the welfare of her unborn child than the censure of society, she rejects her unwilling beau absolutely and finally and embarks on a career in gardening, an activity traditionally associated with genteel feminine creativity. Paradoxically, Susie's unmarried state and public endeavors are triumphs of the domestic: she preserves the sanctity of the family by refusing to admit a drunkard and moral degenerate into its hallowed circle—martyring her reputation for the sake of her maternal responsibility—and shields her daughter from the shame of poverty by engaging in an activity firmly rooted (as it were) in the domestic sphere.

Clara Forest is no more a Jezebel than Susie. Blinded by feminine devotion, Clara is lured into marriage by a cad who subjects her to endless humiliation and cruelty. She endures stoically, even when her husband systematically violates each of his marital vows. His public adultery, however, is finally too much for her, and, heartbroken, she returns to her parents. She has not abandoned her marriage; she has been driven from it. Indeed, it is her highly developed moral sense and exalted views of matrimony that prevent her from living a socially acceptable lie.[1] "I have no husband," she asserts, and to live with a man who "longs only for the presence of another woman, shocks my sense of morality" (289).

Still, she longs for the bliss of domesticity; although she spends the next several months industriously reclaiming fallen women, closing saloons, and assisting Susie in the nursery business, she does not feel fulfilled until she meets and eventually weds the wealthy Fourierist utopian, Count Paul von Frauenstein.[2] Once Clara encounters a man worthy of her love, Howland's apparently unconventional heroine is revealed as a "true woman" in the best evangelical tradition. The virtues that facilitated her venture into an active public life— honesty, intelligence, strength of character—now become a passive force for good: she inspires the count to devote his pecuniary, intellectual, and moral might to benefit humankind. Yet as she shifts from her public, active role to a private, passive one, Clara gradually fades from the novel, eclipsed by her powerful, dynamic husband. Men—Clara's father, brother, and husbands—are the organizers and arrangers in this novel; women merely react to male cruelty and kindness.

Paul von Frauenstein, for example, is a legitimizing force. Susie and Clara might ignore the petty censure of society, but they cannot overcome it; Frauenstein does so with his name and his wealth. He adopts Susie's illegitimate child, canceling out the combined moral outrage of an entire community. He invests money in Susie's flower business, a gesture that does not even begin to tap his immense financial resources. Yet Susie believes that this casual act of charity somehow "atones for all I have suffered—for every tear I have ever shed. I have been happy many times, but I have never felt the stimulus of pride" (382). Her pride, however, is completely dependent on him: on *his* ability to write a large check, on *his* confidence in her ability to succeed. His power is absolute: when Clara looks at him, "her eyes . . . fell before the magnetic power of his" (382).[3] Her devotion to him borders on worship, for "to doubt Paul would be to lose faith in the operation of natural laws" (459); he is a quintessential patriarch, whose powerful condition is a part of the natural order of things.

When he marries Clara, their wedding service reinforces the power of patriarchy. The bride is delivered from one man to another: her father, a judge, presides over the ceremony, after which his daughter joyfully sobs in his arms "for some time," until he "hand[s her] over to Paul" (490). Now, wearing the count's name like a talisman, Clara finds the doors once shut against her magically opened; she is welcomed back eagerly into society. Frauenstein's authority extends throughout the area, touches everyone, and is finally made manifest when he spends four million dollars (a not inconsiderable sum in 1874) to create the Social Palace, a Fourierist cooperative that provides food, housing, and employment. He watches over it with paternal conscientiousness and benevolence.

Clara's sole role in the development of the palace is passive: the count assures her that he has spent years attempting to devise "some plan that might leave the world better for my single effort, but I needed an inspiration that would not come to me" (503). Clara's "divine presence" (that is, her spiritual, true-womanly nature) is the catalyst for the long-awaited "miracle" (503). There is a miracle for Clara as well. During her first marriage, she was unable to produce children and was constantly upbraided for her inadequacy by her husband. Once Frauenstein establishes her in her rightful position as inspirational domestic heroine, however, Clara is at last able to fulfill her destiny as a woman: in what seems to be a providential endorsement of her union with the count, she produces a son to carry on his father's work. This, after all, is her highest purpose in life, and when the child is born, Clara effectively disappears from the text: in the courtyard outside the birthing room, the members of the Social Palace congregate to wave handkerchiefs and shout, "God bless the child!" "Long live Frauenstein!" and "Long live the heir" (547). No mention is made of the passive and silent figure withdrawn into the anonymity of the private sphere.

Ultimately, *Papa's Own Girl* seems to advocate that withdrawal. What began as a story about Susie Dykes and her flower business and Clara and her marital woes has evolved into the tale of the count and his Social Palace (even Susie's hard-earned capitalist enterprise is swallowed up by his own Fourierist communal scheme). The androcentric social view is still firmly in place, and Howland's rationalist utopia is finally an evangelical treatise, as its unconventional women doggedly pursue the conventions of the domestic sphere.

Jane Hume Clapperton's *Margaret Dunmore; or, A Socialist Home* (1888) introduces a similar communitarian scheme but places a female at the head of the social unit. Margaret Dunmore, a wealthy young Englishwoman who establishes a socialist commune, retains her authority by embracing only the *idea* of the domestic sphere, while eluding its physical entanglements. Highly intelligent and strongly committed to egalitarianism, she is fully in charge of her extremely visible communal project: she initiates it, funds it, and manages it herself. There is no Frauenstein to commandeer it; there is not even a patriarchal deity to oversee the community, since the members reject formal Christianity (and, tacitly, the patriarchal Christian injunction against women) in favor of humanist agnosticism. Nor will male members of the commune predominate, since absolute equality is the rule: "an executive committee, consisting of two male and two female members" is "elected by ballot at the end of each six months" (88).

Like Howland, Clapperton uses socialism to reconcile public and private roles for women. Clapperton's particular brand of vaticism, however, avoids the patriarchal bias of *Papa's Own Girl* by situating her heroine's rationalist establishment firmly in the domestic sphere, the traditional site of whatever authority nineteenth-century women had managed to accumulate. The Socialist Home is indeed a socialist commune, but it is primarily a *home;* its members are indeed egalitarian socialists, but they are primarily a family. Margaret does not so much found the community as give birth to it, and her politics are invariably described in maternal terms: "the Socialism of the new era, which she carries as a babe in her bosom," is a "modern domestic system, favorable to the bringing into the world humanity of a new type" (22). Her certainty that "defects of English character" can be traced to "defects in the English home" (72) parallels the beliefs of the cult of "true womanhood": that women contribute to a better society through the performance of their maternal role.

Margaret is a vatic blend of the rational and evangelical ideal. Although she does not conform physically to the "type" of the true woman—she has "too much breadth between the eyes [an indication of her intellectual capacity] to be lovely in form"—she does possess the semirequisite "depth and purity of expression" and "above all the tender sensitiveness of the rich, full lips" (48). She is both a competent businesswoman and an inspirational figure: not only does she manage commercial matters expertly (purchasing real estate, handling bookkeeping, running a school), but her inspirational "moral enthusiasm" (157) prompts one of her comrades, a brilliant chemist, to forgo the self-indulgent pleasures of the laboratory and dedicate himself to the study of scientific amelioration and "social economics" (157).

Clapperton's valuing of the domestic is a highly effective vatic strategy, which not only mitigates socialism's more radical associations but also keeps the novel firmly focused on its female characters. Vera Ward, for example, could be easily lost in domestic obscurity. Her surname reflects her dependent nature; she describes herself as "stupid" (4), and her friends agree that, while she is good-hearted, she is not particularly bright. Rose Karratray, another member of the community, is far more intellectual and inventive, but these rational excellencies are balanced by her docile, sympathetic, motherly nature: "her sweet nature [makes] her do what others would like best"; she is "emotionally of a high type of womanhood; the best fruit of an advanced civilization" (15), with a "docile disposition" (16) and "genius for loving" (17). Were they characters in *Papa's Own Girl,* they would quietly evaporate, absorbed by dynamic male characters.

Yet Clapperton does not permit Vera or Rose to disappear as Susie Dykes and Clara Forest did. The women of *Margaret Dunmore* never relinquish control of themselves or their enterprise—or their novel. Both Vera and Rose are loyal and loving wives, but they are empowered, rather than overwhelmed, by these roles. Childbirth brings Vera's "powers of responsive affection" (118) into full force as her self-centered, child-hating husband gradually comes to recognize not only her goodness but also the importance of the domestic sphere. "Awed, reverent, before the mystery of womanhood" (126), he ultimately decides to forgo his selfish ways and tries to "develop the paternal instinct" (127). Rose's husband initially feels suffocated by marriage, but under her tutelage, his "domestic instincts . . . budded and flowered" (195). *Papa's Own Girl* is vatic but is weighted toward the patriarchal scheme of things: women seek success in the public sphere, aided (and eventually assimilated) by men. *Margaret Dunmore's* women draw men into the rewards offered by the home; the text is vatic because it dissolves the boundary between public and private, between autonomy and domestic selflessness.

Other texts, however, exploit the ideological distance between evangelicalism and rationalism to make their vatic point. Alice Ilgenfritz Jones and Ella Merchant's *Unveiling a Parallel: A Romance* (1893), for example, attacks purely evangelical or rational models as lopsided and dangerously unsound. This satirical utopia presents three societies: the conventional nineteenth-century world, which restricts women to an inspirational role within the domestic sphere, and two "Marsian" communities—Paleveria, a society founded on purely rationalist principles, and Caskia, a vatic community that promotes enlightened evangelicalism. Although the Marsian communities are used primarily to point out women's unequal status on earth, they also serve to identify the disadvantages of a polarized society and the advantages of a community in which women's spirituality is combined with active participation in the public sphere.[4]

The unhappy Earth women of the novel have been reduced to nonparticipants in society; they are totally at the mercy of their men. As the male earthling visitor boasts, "We humor them, patronize them, tyrannize over them. And they defer to, and exalt us, and usually acknowledge our superiority" (35). He is convinced that this state of things occurs because terrestrial women are essentially passive creatures who "lack the inclination to assume grave public duties" (43). Natural female aptitudes and inclinations, he asserts, tend toward the evangelical ideals of religious devotion and moral excellence; although women are not "political equals" (49), they are nonetheless morally "very superior" (52). Men recognize and value this superiority of virtue, the narrator assures his Marsian host, and defer to women in all things domestic: indeed, women benefit from their exclusion, for they are treated "more as princesses than as inferiors,—they are angels" (52). Male solicitude not only ensures that females are relieved of all political responsibility but also frees them to devote themselves entirely to their homes and families. With a paternalism reminiscent of Rousseau, the earthling explains that women are safe and happy in their domestic bower of bliss. They reign absolutely, "honored with chivalrous devotion, cared for with the tenderest consideration. We men are their slaves, in reality, though they call us their lords; we work for them, endure hardships for them, give them all that we can of wealth, luxury, ease. And we defend them from danger and save them every annoyance in our power. They are the queens of our hearts and homes" (85).

Severnius, the skeptical Marsian, finds this a bit difficult to swallow. He is, after all, a Paleverian, and his people traditionally "let no statement pass without examination . . . they scrutinize facts closely and seek for causes" (45). The earthling's idealized view of woman's state does not satisfy Severnius's logical sense (nor would it be likely to coincide with the experience of most nineteenth-century women, for that matter). The Paleverian's inquiries force the earthling to admit grudgingly that most women are not treated quite so regally, that many resent their dependent status, and that some are engaged in a struggle for personal autonomy and political representation. Although Severnius is in deep sympathy with the women's cause, the earthling considers the entire suffrage movement an incomprehensible attempt to disrupt "the idea of masculine pre-eminence and womanly dependence" (159). Despite the Marsian's systematic deconstruction of earthly androcentricism, the earthling clings stubbornly to his belief in the "paternal right to cherish, and restrain, and protect, the weaker sex, as they should be cherished, and restrained, and protected" (160)—whether they will or not. His justification for man's oppressive benevolence is couched in terms that demonstrate woman's gendered evangelical role: he asserts that it is man's "office" (a public word, linked to business and politics) "to buffet with the world, to wrest the means of livelihood, of comfort, luxury, from the grudging hand of fortune" (168). On the other hand, it is woman's "highest grace" (a term associated with internal, private virtue) "that she accepts these things at his hands," for "she honors him in accepting, as he honors her in bestowing" (168).

Given his rather provincial worldview, it is no wonder that the earthling is a bit overwhelmed by liberated Paleverian women, who enjoy perfect equality with men. He is amazed at the ease and informality of male/female relationships: no one is humored, patronized, or tyrannized; no one is expected to lead a purely private or public existence. Men and women treat one another with mutual respect, and equality extends to social, political, and legal matters. Primogeniture is dismissed as an irrational concept, since all children are equally their parents' offspring; all children, whether male or female, inherit the fortunes of their parents in equal shares. If preference is given a particularly gifted heir, it is done without respect to gender: a daughter who is best equipped to take over the family business will do so as a matter of course. Severnius's sister Elodia, for example, manages all the family affairs. She is a "public-spirited" (41) woman who exemplifies the Paleverian ideal: intelligent, capable, articulate, energetic, and able to function as man's equal in all things, thanks to the "one common nature" (185) shared by women and men alike.

Yet this "one common nature" is unbalanced, skewed in favor of rationalist materialism. Paleverians are primarily concerned about worldly affairs and are fairly apathetic about matters of the spirit. In a sense, their society is very like that of the visitor's Earth—if one can imagine such an Earth totally lacking the moral influence he claims its women exert. Vices such as drinking and smoking are accepted (although there is supposedly a Paleverian "anti-intoxicant element" [114], its influence is at best negligible). Hunger and privation are facts of life for many Paleverians; although some citizens amass great wealth and live in incredible luxury, their less fortunate fellows grapple with dire poverty. Prostitution is as common in Paleveria as on Earth.

Indeed, there is only one crucial difference between terrestrial and Paleverian debauchery. Paleveria is a man's world—for both genders. Since woman's nature is "of a piece" (133) with man's, it is subject to the same weaknesses. Lacking the alleged spiritual vigor of their terrestrial counterparts, Paleverian women share men's vices along with men's rights. Females not only drink intoxicating beverages but also frequently overindulge and suffer massive hangovers. Although the women do not smoke tobacco, they have discovered an equally loathsome substitute in the practice of "vaporization": they fill a small cup with alcohol and pulverized valerian root, light the mixture, and inhale it. While supposedly soothing to the nerves, the habit is nonetheless hazardous to one's health; like tobacco, it is associated with disease and even death.

In addition to these private vices, Paleverian women engage in public excess. Elodia, for example, has a tendency to display. She indulges her luxurious tastes freely: her home is a glittering showplace, and she belongs to a sororal organization devoted to gala parties and parades. Like terrestrial fraternal leagues, this erstwhile charitable organization has degenerated into "a very costly and elaborate sentiment" (67). Members costume themselves in gaudy uniforms and parade the streets "for the avowed purpose of being seen and making a sensation" (77). The organizational headquarters are housed in a lavishly appointed hall, where women frequently meet to dine sumptuously and engage in behavior that horrifies the earthling: "Jokes abounded and jolly little songs were sung,—O, nothing you would take exception to, you know, if they had been men; but women! . . . the preservers of our ideals, the interpreters of our faith, the keepers of our consciences! I felt as though my traditional ideals were shattered, until I remembered that these were not my countrywomen, thank heaven!" (80–81).

Even more unsettling, however, are the licensed houses of prostitution where women seek pleasure in the company of male harlots. The earthling maintains a typical nineteenth-century view of sexual desire: women's innate spirituality frees them from carnal cravings, but men have enormous sexual needs.[5] A terrestrial female can do little more than be secretly grateful that her lord and master seeks to satisfy his baser urges elsewhere; she will wait patiently until he eventually tires of the pleasures of the brothel and tavern. A Paleverian female visits brothels and taverns of her own: to his horror, the visitor discovers that Elodia maintains a highly active sexual life. Equally unnerving is her apparent lack of the maternal impulse; when Elodia remarks offhandedly that she has an unacknowledged illegitimate six-year-old daughter, the earthling is appalled by Elodia's unnatural nature, "no finer, no holier than man's" (182). Despite her beauty and intellect, she is "devoid of the one supreme thing,—the sense of virtue"—and is thus a "temple without holiness" (188). Jones and Merchant have made their vatic point: the dismal plight of terrestrial women demonstrates the consequences of spirituality without equality; the decadent condition of Paleverian women demonstrates the repercussions of equality without spirituality.

Only in Caskia, a far more spiritual yet equally egalitarian Marsian community, are evangelical and rationalist blended, as people integrate their private and public interests into a civic concern for general welfare. The rationalist "idea of equality" exists in Caskia, but because the Caskian "plane of life is so much higher" (185), female liberation leads not to license but to spiritual elevation. Private, domestic virtue is a public way of life: since generosity and mutual respect reign, there is no need for laws, and no one is left to live in poverty. Caskians of both sexes "train themselves toward the highest culture and most perfect development of which mankind is capable" (93). After centuries spent struggling to eradicate hereditary evils, they have finally triumphed, eliminating their "baser natural propensies" (93) by blending warring faculties into a united whole. Their belief in a triple nature, composed of spiritual, intellectual, and physical unity, parallels the vatic union of the spiritual and rational. Caskians, after all, have achieved their ideal society through a systematic erasure of a series of dichotomies (that is, wealth and poverty, power and weakness), most of which are linked to the male/female dichotomy and tend to form hierarchical imbalance. Painstaking attention to the development of all facets of human nature has resulted in equilibrium, a vatic blend of private spirituality and public egalitarianism epitomized by the Caskian doctrine that "every soul shall be absolutely free" (112).

This evangelical rationalism may spring in part from the Caskian creation myth, which eliminates the complications of ribs, apples, and serpents in favor of simple equality: two creatures, "male and female, sprang simultaneously from an enchanted lake in the mountain region of Caskia, in the northern part of this continent. They were only animals, but they were beautiful and innocent. God breathed a soul into them and they were Man and Woman, equals in all things" (57–58). There is no Fall to alienate the Caskian Adam and Eve from their Creator; there is no guilt to alienate them from one another. Of most importance, there is no blame—and thus no need to set up a punitive hierarchy that limits woman to the domestic sphere.

A female Caskian is a true daughter of the vatic Eve, a woman "of such fine proportions, of such nice *balance*, that her noble virtues and high intelligence did not make her forget even the smallest amenities" (152, emphasis added). Such a woman is a being in harmony, who is able to fuse her mind, body, and spirit into a triple self. This personal harmony extends to every facet of Caskian existence. Nature must coexist with humankind, and humankind must be in balance with itself. Caskians know neither physical nor spiritual privation, for they realized, "generations ago, that Mars was rich enough to maintain all his children in comfort and even luxury."[6] They "sought out and cultivated nature's resources," meanwhile seeking out and cultivating within themselves "corresponding resources . . . namely, generosity and brotherly love" (218). The intellectual, physical, and spiritual natures of man have become so closely joined that there are no dividing lines within the soul; neither can there be dividing lines that cut off individuals from their surroundings. Homogeneity is central: "there is no point where the Mind may say, 'Here my responsibility ends,' or where the Body may affirm, 'I have only myself to please' " (218). Public and private simply cease to exist, as reason and emotion, spirituality and physicality, selfhood and otherness blur into a single vatic whole.

One need not travel to Mars to discover vatic unity, however. Olive Schreiner's "Three Dreams in the Desert" (1890) uses allegory to blend the discordant forces of rationalism and evangelicalism. Each of her three dream visions represents a different feminist ideological model: the rationalist dream allegorizes woman's historical oppression and demonstrates that an androcentric society restricts the advancement of the race as a whole; the evangelical dream depicts woman as a spiritual force who will lead humankind into a better world; and the vatic dream provides a prophetic glimpse of the future land of liberty, equality, and sisterhood.

In the rationalist story, man and woman are two great beasts of burden yoked together, woman stretched on the sand, man standing uncomprehending and immobile beside her. Centuries ago, she roamed as man's free, unbound partner, but "the Age-of-dominion-of-muscular-force found her" and bound the "burden of subjection" to her back, tied "with the band of Inevitable Necessity" (70). She lies mute and helpless, half-crushed beneath the terrible weight of her oppression, and man stands powerless beside her. Her bondage has fettered him as well, yet he remains unaware of the profound impact of her situation on his own. Suddenly, however, the Age-of-dominion-of-muscular-force is slain by the knife of Mechanical Invention. The woman, unaware that this has happened, at first continues to lie motionless for a time; then "the body quivered, and a light came into her eyes, like when a sunbeam breaks into a dark room" (72). She struggles to rise, as man watches impassively: "he cannot help her: *she must help herself*" (73). Indeed, he is at first confused by her exertions; frightened, he pulls away from her and, in doing so, tightens the bond that unites them and drags her down once again. Finally, however, as she staggers to her knees, he understands what she is attempting to accomplish and stands close to her, looking into her eyes "with sympathy" (74).

The evangelical dream examines the sacrifices women must make to forward humankind's progress. A woman comes to the steep bank of a river, which she must cross to reach the Land of Freedom. To cross it, she must go down the banks of Labour and through the water of Suffering. There is no bridge, and the water is very deep; there is no track to show the best ford. She can take almost nothing with her: she must remove "the mantle of Ancient-received-opinions" and the "shoes of dependence" (78); all that is left to her is the thin white garment of Truth. As she moves down the dark path to the river, she realizes that she will not cross; she will be swept away by the strong current and "heard of no more" (82). The track she makes to the water's edge, however, will show the way for those who follow, and over the bridge that will someday be built will pass *the entire human race* (83). She is the pathfinder for humanity.

These two visions are followed by a third, vatic dream describing a future egalitarian utopia that will come about through the fusion of rationalism and evangelicalism. It is brief enough to cite in full:

> I dreamed I saw a land. And on the hills walked brave women and brave men, hand in hand. And they looked into each other's eyes, and they were not afraid.
> And I saw the women also hold each other's hands.
> And I said to him beside me, "What place is this?"
> And he said, "This is heaven."
> And I said, "Where is it?"
> And he answered, "On earth."
> And I said, "When shall these things be?"
> And he answered, "IN THE FUTURE."
> (84)

Schreiner's text is vatic because each dream is an integral part of a unifying, prophetic whole. Reason enlightens oppressed woman and gives her the courage and strength to struggle until she is strong enough to rise; her mission as humankind's deliverer shows her the path she must forge to the faraway Land of Freedom. A future world of "brave women and brave men" lies before her, but only after she realizes her potential through reason and fulfills it through confidence in her moral authority can the schism between rationalist and evangelical be reconciled and a heaven on earth achieved.

Yet Schreiner's chronology is indeterminate, and her future heaven on earth might be centuries away. Many authors wished to see a more specific timetable for relief, vindication, and reconciliation. Winifred Harper Cooley's "A Dream of the Twenty-First Century" (1902) looks forward quite precisely to 1 January 2001, when women's morality and spirituality have been instrumental in reforming the "corrupt, subsidized government" (511) of the nineteenth century. The reform has not come from within the domestic sphere, however; it is thanks to the changes brought about by women's suffrage that America's healthy, vigorous population enjoys advanced (although unspecified) technology, five-hour workdays, uncrowded cities, and increased longevity. Since the government owns and controls all basic resources and utilities, the slums, sweatshops, and monopolies have been abolished.

Cooley's narrative works as a sustained effort to alleviate women's political estrangement from one another. Nineteenth-century moral purists would not be put off by the appearance of her "new woman," a "radiant creature, in flowing, graceful robes," a "fair Feminine Type" (511). They would recognize their own evangelical efforts in the unselfish work of her foremothers, women who realized that their maternal responsibilities extended past "their own loved children" to "all little ones, in the alleys as well as on the boulevards" (513). After all, nineteenth-century women had already realized "that the rising generation should not begin life hampered by unclean bodies and tainted morals" (513). A moral crusader would certainly be gratified to learn that the halcyon future will justify her efforts in the grim present: the "abolition of slums," for example, will indeed be brought about "chiefly by women" (513)—women very like herself. Twentieth-century men have finally recognized women's inherent right-mindedness and joined them in improving "the minds and hearts of their youth"; thus, "the character of children has increased marvelously" (514). The family unit is not only still intact but has finally realized that its highest duty is to nurture its sons and daughters: the "tender love and congeniality existing between parents" is not merely beneficial to man and wife; of more importance, it provides a "finer type of childhood" (514) for the next generation.

Cooley, however, credits these advances to two changes that would horrify any conservative evangelical: unqualified equal suffrage and a rational "Religion of Humanity" (515). Moral zeal, she argues, is not enough to effect positive change; for centuries, women attempted to work (with varying degrees of failure) within "the insidious, left-handed influence that always was recommended to them by men" (513). Indirect influence was, after all, a rather haphazard methodology for the reform of humanity. Women needed something a bit more substantial: "official power" (513). Once they were given political freedom, women were free to use the primary " 'influence' *necessary* to effect transformations—the ballot" (513). Female enfranchisement was enhanced by society's emancipation from biblical "dogmatism, superstition, ritualism, emotionalism and conservatism" (514), which had for so long sanctioned women's repression. Rational humanism, based on "simplicity and sense" (515), is the new religion, and the new Word of its disciples is education. Since their energies are no longer devoted to placating an implacable Old Testament God, people can now devote themselves to ethical and philanthropic endeavor.

In addition, since the new faith incorporates "the best that has been worked out by every people that has struggled and suffered and aspired beneath the sun" (515), it is now truly universal, and humankind is finally at peace. In 2001, feminine influence has metamorphosed into female power; spiritual and logical have fused into a single ameliorative force.

For nineteenth-century women, however, the year 2001 was depressingly far away. Some writers were unwilling to wait a century for progress and unity and attempted to create a plausible vatic utopia from the admittedly skimpy materials on hand. Perhaps the most immediate (and tantalizing) glimpse of unified, empowered womanhood is presented in Charlotte Perkins Gilman's *Moving the Mountain* ([1911] 1968) set only thirty years in the future. Nineteen forty-one seems to have witnessed the triumph of rationalism and the public sphere: both sexes share identical educational opportunities, political involvement, and representation. A sophisticated child-care system liberates women from the drudgery of child rearing, and technology has been harnessed to deliver women from the toil of household responsibilities. Women are free to pursue careers as doctors, architects, engineers—no employment is denied them on the basis of gender. The patriarchal name is no longer a legitimizing force, since women retain their maiden names and pass the matronymic on to their daughters.

Rationalism has also triumphed in matters of faith: there is a skepticism about any organized religion and a particularly abiding distrust of the androcentric "old tribal deity of the Hebrews" (244). There is no longer a belief in sin, for immoral or criminal activities are considered to be the result of congenital deformities or mental illness (these are being scientifically eliminated, with what modern readers might consider a chillingly detached efficiency).[7] Creation is seen as an earthly process of eugenics and environmental control: "we make better people now" is a constant refrain. Without sin, there is, of course, no need for hell, but Gilman's utopians do not posit any sort of afterlife; their paradise is achieved on earth. A healthy, useful life is all they desire, since "every living thing dies; that's part of living" (254). Theirs is ultimately a faith based on reason: "In place of Revelation and Belief," the heroine asserts, "we now have Facts and Knowledge" (199). Indeed, reason is the foundation of Gilman's entire society, and, as in Jones and Merchant's Paleveria, once men and women recognize each other as intellectual equals, it is only reasonable to recognize their social, political, and legal equality.

Yet this is no Paleverian moral wasteland. *Moving the Mountain* is a vatic text because Gilman uses her rational utopia to promote a blend of evangelical reforms, such as the abolition of prostitution, the moral and physical protection of children, and the promotion of temperance. The sanctity of motherhood and the family has finally been recognized, and women have been given the power to make humankind better: although her citizens are all intellectually, socially, and politically equal, women still maintain a moral and spiritual edge.

Prostitution, a central concern of evangelical women involved in the nineteenth-century Social Purity movement, has been absolutely eradicated in this world of the future. Recognizing the practice as a "social crime of the worst order" (111), one that corrupts the body, the mind, and the soul, women have done what men had been unable or unwilling to do for centuries past: they have simply "stamped it out" (111). Once society was free of prostitution's debilitating force, "physical purity" became the norm rather than an ideal, as "young women learned the proportion of men with syphilis and gonorrhoea and decided it was wrong to marry them" (108). This vatic meld of education and purification protected those who had been previously most vulnerable to injury—the wives, mothers, and unborn children who were helpless victims of the ravages of venereal disease. These innocents are now defended by law, for "it is held a crime to poison another human being with syphilis, just as much as to use prussic acid" (113).

Politically empowered and spiritually powerful, these women of the future have the right to choose who they will or will not marry, and thus they can fight disease not only with their minds and hearts but with their wombs as well. Gilman sees woman's reproductive capacity as the ultimate source of her power: the true value of equality and morality is that they enable her to develop the maternal force to its fullest capacity. With such a valuation of motherhood, it is no wonder her new women are still "sweet and modest" (37), no wonder mothers still look "proud and happy and matronly and motherly" (65), no wonder monogamous marriages are alive and well and function, like those of the Caskians, "on a much purer and more lasting plane than [those of] a generation ago" (102). Women who champion suffrage, Gilman argues, do not necessarily wish to escape the domestic sphere; many wish only (à la Margaret Dunmore) to extend its advantages to the public sphere for civic benefit.

Once this vatic premise is accepted, it does not seem paradoxical that, in this socialist, rationalist, high-tech society, whose inhabitants have rejected the Bible and the androcentric social model in favor of rationalist freethinking, the moral crusade has finally emerged absolutely triumphant. There is no poverty, disease, or crime—women simply will not permit their babies to be imperiled by such unhealthy forces. Rather, there is an emphasis on education, ecology, and cooperation: children are raised in gardens; the air and water have been cleansed; work is done for communal good. There is no "sex problem" (48), no war, no overwork, no business cheats, no insanity (51), no overpopulation, no immigration problems. Evil is systematically being bred out of humanity, although "moral sanitariums" (271) care for the odd atavistic criminal. Alcoholism, that "race evil of the worst sort" (121), has been abolished, and even tobacco use has diminished dramatically, for "women disapprove of tobacco-y lovers, husbands, fathers; they know that excessive use of it is injurious, and won't marry a heavy smoker" (120). This has all come about because the moral influence of women has been set free to do its work. In all the ages past, man effected historical change only "as a destructive agent" (189); women's centuries of "constructive industry" (189) went unrecognized and despised. Now the coming age has arrived, and woman's true worth is at last acknowledged. The terrible imbalance that discomfited the world for so long has at last been overcome. Equilibrium and harmony have come about through the fusion of public and private, rational and spiritual.

Nineteenth-century women's utopian fiction reveals what women felt they lacked in their lives—yet the authors in this study, influenced by ideological divisions in the feminist movement, perceived considerably different deficiencies. Vatic utopian texts attempted to offer a meeting ground to women with widely differing political and social agendas, and suggested that reason and morality were not competing philosophies but were complementary elements that could be woven into a unified whole. Vatic texts underscore feminism's fundamentally utopian nature: both rationalism and evangelicalism, after all, envision a world in which the lives of the female half of humankind are directly ameliorated, while arguing that the lives of the remaining male half of the population will be improved as well. Admittedly, these texts did not *resolve* the splits and apparent contradictions within feminist thinking; often, they merely overrode or simply ignored them. Yet vatic texts used the force of desire and fantasy to provide a hypothetical meeting ground where both branches of nineteenth-century feminism could be seen as valuable alternatives for humankind—alternatives that, when integrated, offered new ways of imagining human relations. Vaticism responded to the polarization of women and attempted to weave their disparate dreams into a unified pattern of reconciliation.

SEVEN

Nightmares and Reawakenings
Post-1920 Women's Utopian Fiction

For the most part, women's utopias written between 1870 and 1920 are of a piece, reflecting their authors' homogeneity of race, class, gender, and, to a large extent, attitude. The majority of texts are characterized by a fundamental optimism, a confident reliance on technological and evolutionary progress, and a gradually increasing certainty that equal rights for women are necessary and inevitable. After 1920, however, women's utopian texts began to take on a considerably darker tone: dreams became nightmares, technology an enemy, progress an illusion, and feminism a forgotten issue. The chaos, brutality, and barbarism of the First World War seemed to prove incontrovertibly that humankind was not ready for (and perhaps not worthy of) utopia, and women's long-sought enfranchisement did not bring about long-anticipated change. In the decades following World War I, the production of optimistic feminist utopias diminished almost to the vanishing point. Dystopias were ascendant, no longer a subgenre of a subgenre.

It was not until the 1960s that a renewed interest in feminism led to a renewed production of confident, egalitarian utopian texts by women—texts which, in many cases, bear startling resemblances to their Victorian prototypes, although rejecting the middle-class worldview that characterized nineteenth-century texts. This chapter will first provide a brief overview of women's utopian writing between 1920 and 1960, then examine certain nineteenth-century utopian themes that resurfaced in the twentieth, and finally delineate several remarkable similarities, as well as fundamental differences, between the narratives.

Paul Fussell (1977, 24) paints a vivid picture of England at the onset of the First World War: "Out of the world of summer, 1914, marched a unique generation. It believed in Progress and Art and in no way doubted the benignity even of technology. The word *machine* was not yet invariably coupled with the word *gun*." This sublime innocence and self-assurance extended to war itself:

in a world where "glorious" and "death" were not necessarily oxymoronic, armed combat was a romantic notion and was still greeted with the enthusiasm generally afforded a particularly thrilling athletic contest.[1] The Great War must have seemed a fitting culmination to the utopian dreams of the previous century—it was, after all, the war to end all wars, the triumph of right-thinking humanity over all that was base and regressive.

Yet the optimism of 1914 was short-lived. Confronted with the ghastly European landscape of mustard gas and dismembered bodies, humankind once again began to doubt its own perfectibility. Civilization had progressed with Escher-like disorientation, taking an appalling leap forward into primitive barbarism: less than a hundred miles from London,[2] men were using the very latest in modern weaponry to slaughter one another in unprecedented numbers. Technology, which had promised to make life so much easier, proved equally competent at expediting death; social Darwinism, which promised an inevitable ascent of the species, was forced to reacknowledge humankind's beastly origins; Freudian theory, which seemed to offer freedom from postlapsarian guilt, shackled the psyche to even more fearful and base desires; and socialist dreams, which promised a new world of peace and harmony, brought only new blood and sorrow and privation.

The end of the war saw a brief surge of international romanticism, which grew out of the evanescent hope that such conflicts could be rendered obsolete by the League of Nations. Yet even this bit of respite was overwhelmed, first by economic depression and then by the gradual realization that the world was moving inexorably toward yet another global conflict. World War I was not the war to end all wars, but World War II must have seemed to be the war to end all utopias, a compendium of human brutality that would have been inconceivable to the nineteenth-century authors in this study. Their limited analogues could have encompassed neither a holocaust nor a Hiroshima, neither the horrible spectacle of millions dead nor the appalling impersonality with which they were slain.[3]

Innocence and optimism were not the only casualties of the First World War, however. Despite, or perhaps because of, women's political triumphs,[4] feminism seemed to have been dealt a killing blow as well. Yet it would have been hard for women to foresee a decline in feminist activity in the years immediately following the First World War. British women seemed particularly well off; for a time, it appeared that Englishwomen's rights were simply to be had for the asking. The Sex Disqualification Act of 1919, for example, stated that women could not be excluded from any civil or judicial office or from any civil profession or vocation simply because of their gender or marital status. This seemed to open a tremendous amount of professional, academic, and political doors for women, and subsequent legislation reformed divorce laws and awarded protection to unwed mothers. In 1920, American women were enfranchised, and the two major women's associations, the National American Woman Suffrage Association (which would become the League of Women

Voters) and the Woman's Party, were fairly well united in their goals. Indeed, both groups joined together for a time as the Woman's Joint Congressional Committee and, during the initial years of the decade, carried out successful campaigns in support of the Sheppart-Towner Maternity and Infancy Protection Bill, prohibition, and child labor laws.

Yet, even amid this heady atmosphere of political unity and legislative success, a philosophical disagreement as to woman's essential nature reemerged. Were women truly equal to men? Or, given their physical and spiritual delicacy, did they require special treatment and protection? British feminists were divided into two camps: a small group of egalitarians such as Rebecca West, who wanted nothing more (or less) than the end of sexual discrimination, and "new feminists" such as Dora Russell, who argued that women "had a range of special needs which as equal members of society they had every right to demand should be met" (Spender 1984, 40). This "new feminism," however, was really little more than the old evangelicalism, for it glorified maternity and woman's moral preeminence and, in doing so, situated her once again in the private, domestic sphere. The only difference was that women might now be granted pecuniary compensation for their biological and spiritual labors: just as Edward Bellamy ([1888] 1966, 158) proposed that twenty-first-century women be paid for "bearing and nursing the nation's children," new feminists such as Eleanor Rathbone suggested that mothers given sufficient governmental financial support could avoid the economic imbalance that had historically kept them powerless and thus could be better able to fulfill their maternal role.

There was a similar schism in America, as women's groups began to reencounter the historical rationalist/evangelical split, but this time without the unifying vatic impulse. Lacking this model for compromise, women's groups drifted increasingly toward the more conservative, and hence apparently safer, evangelical model. Early campaigns for an equal rights amendment met many of the same arguments that the ERA would face in the 1960s: such an amendment would not give women true equality; it would only force them to become ersatz men and would strip away the legal protection they had sought for so long. This was a terrifying prospect for women who had only recently shed their dependent status, and, as Olive Banks (1981, 157) points out, support for equal rights eventually dwindled to "a small group of activists that failed to recruit new members and became smaller and more exclusive as time went by."

Economic upheaval characterized much of the 1920–60 period and significantly contributed to the reprivatization of women. In 1915, Clementina Black had suggested that society might be evolving toward "a family supported financially by the earnings of both parents, the children being cared for meanwhile and the work of the house being performed by trained experts" (14). After the First World War, however, such ideas seemed hopelessly unrealistic. Returning soldiers needed employment, and the global depression of the 1930s made work all but impossible to find. Working women—especially married working women, who could presumably rely on the wages of their husbands—

were expected to give up their jobs and return to the home and hearth. Failure to do so was selfish, unpatriotic, and unwomanly: as Carol Dyhouse (1981, 7) points out, British "women reluctant to relinquish jobs were castigated by the national press, accused of greed and avarice, ingratitude to war-heroes, of stealing the bread out of other (dependent, womanly) women's mouths." The situation was the same in America, where working women were seen as posing a double threat to the social order: not only was she neglecting her own duties as wife and mother, but she was also costing some man work that would feed and clothe his own wife and children. This view was reflected in the way in which welfare began to be split along gender lines: programs associated with work (unemployment relief or make-work employment) provided funds with which males were expected to support their families; programs associated with charity (pensions and protective legislation) were directed toward married women who had lost their male protectors (that is, abandoned wives and widows). Unemployed, unmarried women had few avenues other than marriage available to them.

Yet charity and protective legislation alone were insufficient to keep women at home and away from the job market. Additional incentives were needed. It would be difficult to lure women who had had a taste of public life back into the monotonous, endless drudgery of the Victorian home. A new model of domestic bliss had to be created and marketed: the home as an attractive, modern place in which the "new woman," a strictly twentieth-century homemaker, could find the fulfillment her mother had foolishly sought in the wide world. Housework need not be old-fashioned drudgery. It could be *scientific* drudgery, making full use of innovations such as prepared foods, inexpensive ready-to-wear clothing, and labor-saving devices such as the carpet sweeper and washing machine.[5]

Of course, there were a few drawbacks. Modern women lost some of the consolations their mothers enjoyed—pride in one's cooking or sewing, for example. And housework, despite the high-tech innovations, was still housework. And servitude was still, well, servitude. Men, who earned money, continued to decide how it was to be spent; women remained dependent on the protection of their male relatives and husbands. Young single women might find employment for a brief, badly paid fling at independence,[6] but they were still expected to settle down and marry—or face the humiliations of spinsterhood. The new age was little more than a ghastly mockery of the old, drained of the fierce hope that had fired so many nineteenth-century women. All that they had fought for had come—and had come to nothing. Just as technology had not ushered in a new age of plenty for all, suffrage had not brought about the promised land women had sought.

In a despairing world that seemed determined to force women back into the private sector, it is not surprising that women's utopias underwent a great deal of remodeling. In England, women's optimistic nineteenth-century utopias, hopelessly naive by postwar standards,[7] were replaced by anti-utopian satires mocking flawed humanity's futile struggle after the ideal and by dystopias offering grim views of a future world in the grasp of barbarism, socialism, or fascism. The heroic Glorianas and Mercias who might have saved their country from such a fate virtually disappeared, replaced by debased females stripped of all autonomy, "breeding machines" (Albinski 1988, 79) who live imprisoned not only by men, but by their own female biology. Pessimism dominates these years,[8] its focus gradually moving from fascism to Nazism and on to the threat of nuclear war.

A good example of the rather abrupt forsaking of optimistic feminist utopias is the work of Cicely Hamilton, a teacher, novelist, actress, pamphleteer, essayist, journalist, and political activist. In 1909, Hamilton cowrote a confident prosuffrage utopia, *How the Vote Was Won*,[9] detailing the political triumph of dignified and noble public women; thirteen years later, her despairing dystopia, *Theodore Savage: A Story of the Past or Future* ([1922] 1928; originally titled *Lest Ye Die*), refuted that confident vision. In Hamilton's bleak postwar landscape, dignity is an impossibility, nobility a dangerous liability, and woman a domestic slave.

The heroic Victorian Englishwomen of *How the Vote Was Won* (Hamilton and Marshall [1909] 1910) join together in a rationalist crusade and revolt against the inane fiction used to deny them enfranchisement: that women are essentially domestic and rather helpless creatures, incapable of supporting themselves, and thus totally dependent on men. Hamilton's heroines, hardworking and forced to support themselves by necessity and pride, expose the fiction by engaging in a nationwide "work to rule." They quit their jobs and apply to their nearest male relative for financial support. As the play opens, a number of newly unemployed female relatives descend on the living room of Horace Cole, a smug, impatient, middle-class, and decidedly antisuffrage "English master of his own house" (10), whose comfortable world is about to be turned upside down. First, his housekeeper and maid abandon their posts to join their male relations; Horace can only fume as his overwrought spouse, a flighty caricature of the "belle-ideal," valiantly but unsuccessfully attempts to make his tea. Then a bewildering array of females, representing a broad spectrum of women's experience, arrive on his doorstep.

Hamilton's widely differing group of individuals undercuts the stereotype of working women as a uniform group of selfish, antidomestic androgynes. Horace's fiercely independent (and highly attractive) niece Molly may indeed write scandalous books for a living, but his weary sister Agatha seems to have stepped out of a Brontë novel: she has been forced by her genteel poverty to seek employment as a governess. His shrewd second cousin Madame Christine has parlayed her skill with a needle into a highly successful dressmaking shop, his maiden aunt Lizzie Wilkins (accompanied by her noisy parrot and malevolent spaniel) keeps a boardinghouse, and his first cousin Maudie Spark is an "aggressively cheerful" (21) music hall singer. Faced with the sudden prospect of caring for all of these women, Horace realizes that he is not only unwilling but also unable to bear the responsibility. At last, he fully comprehends what enormous benefit men derive from women's work. He metamorphoses almost immediately into a most dedicated advocate of women's rights.

The tone of Hamilton's economic *Lysistrata* is confident, optimistic, and rather jolly overall—the product of a writer who not only expects the vote (and soon) but also foresees an improved society as one result of female enfranchisement. Her confidence is embodied in characters such as Winifred, Horace's militant sister-in-law, a distinguished and capable young woman absolutely in control of herself and admirably in command of a delicate political situation. Everything she predicts happens exactly as she has anticipated, even her seemingly unlikely assertion that "by tomorrow, perhaps before, Horace will be marching to Westminster shouting out 'Votes for Women' " (5).

Hamilton's optimism might seem a bit naive to modern readers, based as it is on an underlying middle-class certainty that people are fundamentally good and will ultimately do the right thing. Her women are paragons of virtue and industry, and, although the male characters appear in a considerably less than flattering light, there is nonetheless an underlying honor that dictates their actions. Horace, for example, insufferable chauvinist and pompous egoist though he might be, draws the line at setting his relatives out to starve. One might argue that his concern is only for what the neighbors might say. Yet, even if this is so, at least the norms of society are firmly grounded in decency: neighbors would censure such an act. It might also be argued that there is some division in the female ranks; Horace's wife, Ethel, for example, "a pretty, fluffy little woman who could never be bad-tempered, but might be fretful" (4), clings stubbornly to the security of the patriarchy throughout. Yet, like her husband, she is eventually overwhelmed by the united force of the women's movement, which sweeps all before it. In Hamilton's optimistic view, the weight of such unity[10] can bring an entire government to its knees: within hours of the strike, even the most powerful men have been thrown into a panic; the prime minister, for example, cannot keep important appointments because he is otherwise employed, "making his bed with the assistance of a bootboy and a Foreign Office Messenger" (25).[11]

Hamilton's confidence extends even to her relaxed, gentle tone. There is nothing particularly strident in this play; the only long, didactic speech is Horace Cole's hilarious closing monologue, a transparently self-interested attempt at feminist rhetoric, punctuated by the sly running commentary of his female audience. Since the author sees female enfranchisement as inevitable, she is less concerned with its mechanics and more interested in the impact it will have on people—especially on men hopelessly out of step with what she considers the realities of existence. Horace is a foolish Old King Cole, a relic of an outdated way of life, and inevitably plays straight man to witty women. Patronizingly, he chides Madame Christine for giving the movement her money and smugly plays the patriarchal ace: "It's a pity you don't have a husband," he remarks, "he'd very soon stop your doing such foolish things." Madame trumps him easily: "I had a husband once. He liked me to do foolish things—for instance, to support him" (21). Horace is a straw man, beaten back on every front by the women's moral and intellectual superiority; as the play ends, his monumental self-importance has withered, and only his selfishness remains intact. He eventually becomes the most enthusiastic—and vocal—proponent of suffrage in the play, because it is in his own self-interest to do so. The final curtain closes on Horace, beribboned and bedecked with emblems of the woman's movement, waving a banner calling for suffrage, crying, "Votes for Women," as he marches off to picket Westminster—a ludicrous figure who nonetheless draws dignity from the distinguished and honorable women who surround him.

How the Vote Was Won is the work of a woman secure and positive enough to joke about momentous issues. Yet, thirteen years later, Hamilton's optimism was virtually undetectable: her grim dystopia, *Theodore Savage: A Story of the Past or Future* ([1922] 1928), presents an inverted world in which dignity and honor have been sacrificed to self-interest. Humankind has reverted to a savage existence, predicated on the law of might. Women are no longer a positive force for change; instead, they are cowering slaves who compete for male protection.

After a prolonged and particularly brutal war reduces England to a state of savagery, civilization crumbles first into anarchy, with each individual fighting desperately for his own survival, and then into primitive barbarism. The narrative is the memoir of Theodore Savage, who mourns a lost age of decency (the fact that Savage is looking *backward* from his barbaric present precludes any romantic notion of a happy ending). He reminisces about happier days before the war—the period of time, one would imagine, in which *How the Vote Was Won* was set—when people were blissfully oblivious to the impending disaster awaiting them and faced their nightmarish future with "blind confidence" (43). Hamilton no longer perceives generosity and idealism as essential components of the human psyche but instead dismisses them as superficial, ephemeral qualities—self-sacrifice is nothing more than a "fleeting impulse," and idealism invariably degenerates into "bestial cunning" (45). Instead of brave individuals giving up their personal comforts for the good of the many (as Madame Christine gives her property to the suffrage movement), humankind is now a selfish and greedy species bent on eliminating all competitors and willing to use devastating explosives, poisonous gasses, or even lethal "plague-germ" (57) to accomplish this. As a friend of Savage explains, human beings are all "potential combatants" (60); the word "neighbor," he asserts, historically has been synonymous with "enemy" (60). Civilization, Hamilton argues, is little more than a thin veneer, which can be stripped away at any time: as the war progresses, Savage is appalled by how quickly social order collapses; "laws, systems, habits of body and mind" all crumble away, "leaving nothing but animal fear and the animal need to be fed" (87). The only remnant of cooperative behavior is a primitive tribalism that seems more analogous to a wolf pack than to civilization.

Admittedly, the germ of disillusion can be seen in Hamilton's 1909 text. The selfish men of *How the Vote Was Won* are, after all, embryonic versions of the greedy monsters who inhabit her postwar world; they are roused to action only when their own comforts are at risk. The barbaric men of *Theodore Savage* are deadly serious Horace Coles, free to indulge themselves completely, free to impose their wills on weaker beings, and quite willing to do both. Hamilton's earlier confidence in the controlling moral force of social opinion relied on the maintenance of a society: selfish men can be shamed into generous acts only when there exists a moral norm by which they can be judged. Strong women, united into a powerful sisterhood, can help ensure such a norm. The women of *How the Vote Was Won* are triumphant because they ignore class distinctions and band together for society's common good. They are willing to face ridicule and abuse, willing to risk whatever they have—in Agatha's case, employment, which she desperately needs to survive; in Madame Christine's, her entire fortune—because they consider their cause to be just. They believe that their duty is to effect change not only for themselves but also for future generations: as Agatha asserts, "When women become citizens I believe that daughters will be given the same chances as sons, and such a life as mine will be impossible" (16).

Hamilton worried that the daughters of the future would not be given such chances. In 1927, she would warn against assuming that gains made by women were irreversible. "Hard-won liberties," after all, have been given up before, "and history, in the shape of a neo-Victorianism, may well repeat itself ere many years have passed" (cited in Spender 1984, 79). The women of *Theodore Savage*, crippled and debased by a diseased society founded on gender oppression, exemplify Hamilton's fears. Savage's prewar love interest is the refined, cultivated, and decidedly neo-Victorian Phillida Rathbone, a delicate young woman "whose daintiness demanded like surroundings" (20). Phillida would seem hopelessly out of place at a nineteenth-century feminist rally, for she never actually *does* anything, and her assets are almost exclusively decorative—"a straight-cut profile; gray, humorous eyes, with dark lashes up-curling; and a sweet trick of movement, most rhythmical movement" (16). Her sole accomplishment is piano playing, which adds greatly to her charm but in no way contributes to her utility: she plays only to please her father and would-be husband. Were her servants to walk out, she would be as helpless as Ethel Cole—indeed, once the war breaks out, they do, and Phillida is quite literally lost, disappearing from the novel without a trace. She is hardly the stuff of rationalist heroines.

Yet she is no evangelical, either. There is no high-mindedness about Phillida, no concern for spiritual improvement. She is a creature of the patriarchy who absolutely supports not only its hierarchical structure but also the ceaseless struggle to emerge as high on the hierarchical ladder as possible. Her dovelike delicacy does not prevent her from being a political hawk: "this porcelain maiden, delicately moulded—was alive to the war-spirit, throbbing with it" (49). For her, the term "pacifist" is nothing more than a synonym for "coward and backslider" (51), and she is openly contemptuous of those who do not rush to the battlefront.[12] Yet the androcentric system that she champions will not be her champion in return. Phillida is swallowed up by the very hierarchy she helped engender, lost in a nightmare of poison gas, plague, and famine.

Savage mourns her loss, especially when another woman enters his life—Ada Cartwright, surely one of the least appealing heroines of fiction and the antithesis of the dignified, honorable heroines of *How the Vote Was Won*. Ada is a product of her age, a catalog of human shortcomings who manages to survive the war through a combination of absolute self-interest, animal cunning, and blind luck. Savage discovers her hiding in a ruined city, while he is fleeing a band of marauders. Ada, also attempting escape, seizes upon him for protection, wailing and howling so loudly that he fears she will reveal his hiding place. To quiet her, he permits her to stay with him (proof of his superior nature, since any other male in the book would have simply killed her on the spot). From that point on, she functions as a degraded, degenerate version of Phillida: completely dependent on him, she is rather like a child or pet who, "having learned to look to him for food, for guidance and protection . . . could be cast off only by direct cruelty and the breaking of a daily habit" (133). She is never his equal and is even an incompetent servant. Although Savage is occasionally amused by "her little feminine antics" (153) and "giggling allurements" (155), he is more frequently irritated "by her infantile helplessness" (162) and sullen antipathy to work. Eventually, he begins to beat her and discovers that abandoning "the code of civilization in dealings between woman and man" (172–73) makes his life a great deal easier. Reasoning with Ada is pointless, and she takes advantage of his kindness, but beating her works "wonders" (173). Despite his strenuous application of the rod, however, she remains a spoiled and stupid child, "essentially a parasite, a minor product of civilization, machine-bred and crowd-developed" (263).

The only similarities between Ada and the women of *How the Vote Was Won* are biological. One would be hard put to imagine Ada accomplishing anything of consequence on her own—she is not even a particularly competent follower, and it is inconceivable that she could lead others. She is not "tall and distinguished looking," like Winifred, nor does she share her "capable manner and . . . emphatic diction" (Hamilton and Marshall [1909] 1910, 4); instead, she enjoys a "comeliness of the vacant, bouncing type" (Hamilton [1927] 1928, 142) and speaks with a Cockney accent so thick that Savage has difficulty even understanding her name (for a while, he believes it to be "Ida"). She has neither the pride nor pluck of Agatha; instead, she wails and howls at the slightest provocation, constantly bemoaning her plight. She lacks Molly's independence, Madame Christine's shrewdness, Maudie's good nature, and Lizzie's "native intelligence" (Hamilton and Marshall [1909] 1910, 24); she is a groveling, clumsy, whining fool. Yet she seems to be distressingly typical of Hamilton's postcata-clysmic new woman. The debased females of the future world have no need for heroic qualities; such attributes would be liabilities in slaves who must attend to an endless round of cooking, washing, child rearing, and working in the fields with the men, punctuated only by curses or blows from their husbands. Nor have they any use for generosity, since their energies must be directed to-ward their own survival. The last vestiges of unselfishness take the form of a primitive sisterhood that is directly linked to the survival of the tribe. When a pregnant Ada is brought into their midst, the tribal women feed her, warm her, and make a place for her to sleep; she responds to their mindless "clack of tongues" and is comforted by "loud voices raised in chatter" (234). Yet even this tiny bit of comforting solidarity is frequently upset by the specter of self-interest. Wives are absolutely dependent on their husbands for food, shelter, and physical protection and must fight to retain their men in order to survive. When Ada, bored with the dull, grueling monotony of her life, seeks distrac-tion by flirting with another woman's husband, the threatened wife attacks her and tears out her hair.[13]

This violent female possessiveness forms a sardonic counterpoint to the male view of women as virtually interchangeable. When Ada dies, worn out by childbearing and domestic drudgery, Savage remarries almost immediately—not out of love, but "simply as a matter of business" (265). He needs a replace-ment slave, a piece of property who will in turn care for the remainder of his property: a woman to "help in *his* field-work, cook *his* food, look after *his* children, and satisfy *his* animal desire" (265, emphasis added). No one chal-lenges these arrangements because there is a good deal of historical precedent. Oppression had been woman's traditional lot for centuries, and, in Hamilton's grim dystopia, there does not seem much hope for change. Men are in control, and men will seek to retain that control. Even Savage, by far the most sympa-thetic character in the novel, is hopelessly mired in misogyny: when he at-tempts to explain to his son the reasons for the barbarity of their age, he relies on the most misogynic of etiological myths, the tale of Pandora. Fascinated, the boy asks, "Is it a true story?" "Yes," his father replies (246), validating women's oppression for yet another generation.

This pessimistic, despairing spirit continued in British women's utopias throughout the 1920–60 period, producing a series of gloomy narratives testi-fying to the crippling consequences of male dominance. In the United States, however, women's post–World War I texts tended to be far more hopeful, per-haps reflecting the conflict's milder impact on America, which, after all, had suffered far fewer casualties than Britain and had emerged in much better finan-cial shape as well.[14] Yet utopia was no longer sought over the next ridge—nor anywhere in the contemporary world, for that matter. Nan Bowman Albinski (1988, 106) has observed a tempered American optimism, and a shift away from the "depiction of an imminent, domestic, communitarian setting to a fu-ture America often affected by a world-wide cataclysm (war or natural calam-

ity) that begins in Europe, and acts as the clearing-house for an age of peace."
Woman's place in this new age is markedly conventional: mainstream America,
after all, had traditionally perceived feminists not as admirable figures but as
unnatural, mannish viragos. The postwar campaign to return women to the
domestic sphere was marked by the replacement of heroic utopian heroines
with more ladylike (that is, passive and submissive) protagonists. Carol Farley
Kessler (1984) remarks on a troubling "narrowing of focus after the wide-
ranging visionary alternatives before 1920" (14); indeed, she finds only "three
twinkling candles glimmer[ing] between the slats of a bushel basket stretching
across four decades" (15).[15]

Albinski considers Ayn Rand's *Anthem* (1938) to be the most representative
work of this period (with the exception of its atheistic bias). Set in a bleak
socialist world of the future, the novella depicts a society in which all human
relationships are controlled by the state and individuality is a criminal act. The
very word "I" has disappeared from use: "There are no men but only the great
WE" (19). The narrative details how the street cleaner Equality 7-2521 gradually acquires a forbidden realization of self and flees his society. Eventually, he
establishes a utopia based on selfishness, which he shares with the book's heroine, Liberty 5-3000.

At first, Liberty 5-3000 seems reminiscent of the proud, determined feminist heroines of the nineteenth century. Certainly, when Equality first sees her,
she does not seem particularly passive or domestic: "Their [read *her;* all individual pronouns have been outlawed] eyes were dark and hard and glowing,
with no fear in them, no kindness and no guilt. Their hair was golden as the
sun; their hair flew in the wind, shining and wild, as if it defied men to restrain
it" (39). The couple's initial clandestine meetings commence on what seems to
be fairly equal terms: although he has taken it upon himself to name her—he
calls her "the Golden One" (41)—she has named him as well—"the Uncon-
quered" (56).

Yet as the two grow to know one another, Equality moves into an increasingly dominant role and takes a rather proprietary interest in his prospective
mate. He is tremendously relieved to learn that Liberty is still a virgin, un-
stained by use and hence more valuable. She, on the other hand, seems indif-
ferent to his sexual experience: he has several times visited the Palace of Mating, where, once the Council of Eugenics has selected suitable partners, men
over twenty and women over eighteen are sent to breed—yet this in no way
detracts from his attractiveness. Liberty's purity is, however, a considerable
part of her value, and since Equality plans to keep her for himself, he vows that
he will "not let the Golden One be sent to the Palace of Mating" (44). The
Golden One's views on the matter are not sought out.

This imbalance becomes even more pronounced once Equality escapes the
city. Liberty's subsequent escape is not a similar blow for personal autonomy:
she has fled the city only to follow *him;* had he remained, one assumes, she
would have also stayed. After trailing him for days, she finally comes upon

him, yet, instead of taking pride in her considerable tracking skills, she acts as if *he* has found *her*. Absolutely submissive, she pleads, "Do as you please with us, but do not send us away from you" (83), and, as if these words were not sufficient proof of her deference, she kneels and bows her head before him. He permits her to stay, partly to gratify his own sexual appetites: that night, he learns that "to hold the body of women in our arms is neither ugly nor shameful but the one ecstasy granted to the race of man" (84). His sexual partner's ecstasy (or lack of it) is not mentioned.

They proceed to explore the Uncharted Forest and eventually come upon an ancient abandoned house, a relic of the Unmentionable Times.[16] At this point, any lingering illusions of an egalitarian relationship for the couple vanish altogether: Equality becomes the quintessential patriarch, and Liberty completes her descent into passivity. Perhaps the best evidence of this occurs when Equality renames himself—and her. "Let us choose our names" (98), he suggests, and then promptly chooses names for both of them. He wishes to be called Prometheus. "It shall be your name" (99), she agrees. He wishes her to be called Gaea. Once again, she assents and, in doing so, tacitly agrees to bear his children as well; the name has been given her because she is "to be the mother of a new kind of gods" (99). Equality/Prometheus has taken naming (Adam's prerogative) into his own sphere, while Liberty/Gaea has accepted childbearing (Eve's punishment) as her own.

If this pair represents the wave of the future, the "new kind of gods" are going to be uncomfortably reminiscent of the old kind of mortals. The new Prometheus seems clever enough, despite his tendency to bully: he is an inventor, a reader, a seeker after truth. His wife, however, is not particularly bright and is absolutely devoted to her husband in all things—a latter-day "belleideal," an updated version of Bellamy's Edith Leete. Too submissive to be a rationalist and too passive to be an evangelical, the new Gaea is overwhelmed by a closet full of brightly colored garments—gasps at the sight of them—and is totally in thrall to her husband. She does not challenge or question but obligingly submits, assuring him, "Your will be done" (92).[17] Her only awareness of self is infantile, a passive narcissism: when she discovers a mirror, she is so transfixed by her own image that she gives way to unreasoned disobedience; not even the words of her husband can take her eyes from the reflection of her body in "the big glass which is not glass" (92). Later, as her husband studies, she falls asleep on the floor,[18] "amidst jewels, and bottles of crystal, and flowers of silk" (92), gewgaws of the patriarchy, traditionally awarded to its most dutiful daughters. In Rand's Promethean utopia of the ego, the female "I" is an odd subset of its male counterpart, heard only once and then in direct reference to another: Liberty tells Equality, "I love you" (98). Ultimately, Rand's utopia makes no place for woman and offers a chilling evaluation of female nature.

It seems to make little difference whether women are kept as slaves in *Theodore Savage* or as beloved household goddesses in *Anthem*. In the majority of English and American utopian texts written by women between 1920 and 1960, an androcentric society has situated women in the private sphere. As Albinski (1988, 111) points out, American utopias are thus "similar to the parallel dystopias of British women": both are hierarchical, set in "traditional, stratified societies, territorially aggressive, and often with an Aryan racial bias"; both reflect the pervading pessimism of their age.

The 1960s, however, was a time of renewal—renewed interest in feminist concerns, renewed frustration with existing social structures, and, in America, a renewed production of feminist utopian texts. English utopias still lacked both the optimism and the heroic females so typical of Victorian antecedents, but utopias by American women gradually moved toward a guarded optimism and toward views of strong women that had not been seen for decades. Like so many nineteenth-century texts, these narratives blame the ills of the world not on humanity but on society's hierarchical structure.

Those familiar with women's nineteenth-century utopias might experience a sense of déjà vu when they come upon these optimistic, profeminist twentieth-century utopian narratives. So many of their concerns—women's clothing, exercise, education, work—seem to mirror those of the previous century. Yet there is also a sense of déjà vu in the situation of mid-twentieth-century women, still defined by their biological roles and still limited by their social, political, and educational restrictions.

Consider the spectacle of a stylish American female of the early 1960s, teetering on stiletto-heeled shoes, still a size or two too small (and so pointed that rumors circulated regarding the amputation of toes to accommodate the more exaggerated styles). The outdated corset had been replaced by the modern but equally confining girdle, and the lumpy, derriere-exaggerating bustle by a pointy, bosom-exaggerating brassiere. The enormous, ridiculous hats of the Victorians had given way to smaller but equally useless headgear, which now topped up to a foot of lacquered, stiff hair.[19] And the purpose of all this modern discomfort remained distressingly traditional: to attract a man and thus carry out one's biological imperative. Unmarried women scoured college campuses and business offices in search of prospective husbands: "coeds" frankly admitted that they were pursuing an MRS. degree, and secretaries would have preferred marrying their employer to taking over his job (in the unlikely event that they were given such an option). Women had seen so much progress, and so little change. Their society was still androcentric, competitive, and hierarchical.

Consider also the American political climate of the 1960s and its striking similarity to that of a hundred years earlier. In both cases, wars had been fought under unusual and immediate circumstances: the United States was not under attack by a foreign power, yet young American men were fighting and dying in alarming numbers. Nor were these gallant lads falling gloriously and abstractly on some faraway battleground; instead, they were slaughtered horribly and conspicuously before one's eyes. Civil War battles were typically fought in cornfields and pastures; the bodies of the dying crowded farmers' parlors, and corpses lined the roadways. The screams and agonies of Vietnamese sorties were similarly immediate, beamed into American homes via the nightly news. Both wars became a series of horrifying images, frozen in the mind: cadavers piled waist-deep on a peaceful Pennsylvania country lane; a terrified naked child in flames, fleeing down a wagon path near Saigon. Such images, although separated by a century, were witnessed firsthand by the non-combatant public and generated similar pacifist responses[20]: well-organized antiwar movements, of which many middle-class women were members.

In addition, both the 1860s and 1960s were characterized by a heady climate of civil libertarianism. The nineteenth-century abolitionist movement was at its height as the Civil War began, and many distinguished women who worked and spoke for the rights of blacks saw their efforts rewarded by the ratification of the Fourteenth and Fifteenth Amendments. Middle-class women also participated in the civil rights activism of the 1960s and, like their foremothers of the previous century, learned political and strategic maneuvers.

This crash course in activism, however, also provided women with an increased awareness of their political inferiority. Women working in peace and civil rights movements discovered that their participation was limited to traditionally gendered roles: secretarial work, coffee fetching, errand running, and so forth. The supposedly revolutionary army in which they served maintained a distressingly traditional authoritarian hierarchy. Men were still the generals; women were foot soldiers—and not even frontline troops, but litter bearers, mess attendants, and camp followers. Despite tumultuous social upheaval, women's subordinate place in the world remained stable; male authority seemed as inescapable as gravity.

Except, of course, in utopian literature. Unselfish human relationships based on motherhood and sisterhood still presented exemplars to the cutthroat world of the patriarchy, and societies based on gentle partnership models still offered arguable alternatives to hierarchy. The optimistic feminist utopias of the 1960s tend to echo nineteenth-century forms and concerns; although separated by a century, women were united by similar climates of activism and frustration.

One response to this frustration was the separatist utopia, which simply eliminated men altogether. Nineteenth-century separatist texts such as Mary Bradley Lane's *Mizora* (1880–81) and twentieth-century narratives such as Suzy McKee Charnas's *Motherlines* (1978) make use of a single simple equation: no men equals no war, no poverty, no disease—just throngs of competent, self-sufficient women coexisting contentedly in highly matriotic and communally organized communities. Both texts use women's generative power as the foundation of their utopias—and focus on remarkably similar aspects of maternal force. In both texts, female societies are the direct result of a fierce desire to protect life: since man's dystopian, androcentric, hierarchical society seems bent on the total annihilation of humanity, women must salvage civilization by using technology to make possible a single-sex, separatist society. In such a community, traditional, hierarchical social mechanisms are overthrown.

The androcentric societies these utopias reject have little to recommend them: they are dystopian worlds ravaged by pestilence, famine, and war. Lane's ancient society ([1880–81] 1889, 198) of men "continually striving for power" was a place of "plots, intrigues, murders and wars"; while in Charnas's Hold-fast society, where even superficial examples of male loyalty were rare and de-spised as weakness, murder was a fairly acceptable political stratagem.

As these nightmare societies staggered toward race extinction, men seemed oblivious to the impending disaster: either they did not realize their danger, or their craving for power was so great that they ignored it. Women, however, realized that the patriarchal world was doomed and that an alternative society must be created. Although they lacked physical, economic, and political power, women nonetheless managed to penetrate a male bastion of power—science—and use it to ensure the survival of the race. Mizoran females infiltrated colleges and laboratories and managed to discover the secret of life. Parthenogenesis became a reality, enabling women gradually to take charge of themselves and their world; mothers produced only daughters, and the male gender eventually died out. Charnas's Holdfast women (1978, 72), used as experimental labora-tory animals, managed to learn a similar secret: how to produce "seed with a double set of traits," that is, both sets of chromosomes, which were passed on to the resulting female offspring. The women then fled and established their own separatist, virtually parthenogenic Riding Woman society.[21]

In both cases, women manage to take control of the authority afforded by "science," that arcane study from which they had been traditionally excluded. In the nineteenth century, the exclusion was legal (and, maddeningly, women were also denied the legal training that would help them redress the situation); in the twentieth, the exclusion was psychological and social, for girls were not expected to be "good" at science and mathematics. Of course, with no under-standing of scientific principles, women were forced to rely on "experts": the men of science who created and perpetrated myths of female inferiority, fe-male frailty, female inadequacy. How could an uneducated woman challenge Professor Joseph Le Conte's assertion that the concept of "women's rights . . . is certainly in direct conflict with the law of evolution," or Sir James Crichton Browne's declaration (in the medical journal *Lancet*) that female education causes women's brains to consume themselves and results in "nervous distur-bances, insomnia, anaemia . . . general delicacy" and "*anorexia scholastica*" (cited in Kinnard 1986, 302)? Such terms were daunting enough to the unini-tiated, especially when accompanied by the "scientific facts" that female brains are smaller, less complicated, and receive poorer quality blood—blood that is directed to sensory rather than cognitive functions (304). Doctor William Goodell's medical degree lent credence to his cool certainty that "prolonged brain-work" is "injurious" to women's "physical and sexual development," while Dr. S. Weir Mitchell's renown made his certainty that female study is "sexually incapacitative" even more certain (233). Nineteenth-century science was used as a bludgeon against women well into the twentieth century: in 1964,

Harvard's Erik Erikson still claimed that female identity is "defined in her kind of attractiveness and in the selectivity of her search for the man (or men) by whom she wishes to be sought"; in 1965, the University of Chicago's Bruno Bettelheim insisted that women "want first and foremost to be womanly companions of men and to be mothers" (cited in Weisstein 1971, 144–45). Feminists challenged such assertions by redefining scientific terms: Barbara Ehrenreich and Deirdre English (1979, 315) note that "where sociologists saw 'roles' and 'institutions,' psychiatrists saw 'feminist adjustment' and the medical authorities saw 'biological destiny,' feminists saw *oppression*."

Perhaps this oppression could be overcome by infiltrating the institutions that promoted it. The women of *Mizora* and *Motherlines* gain access to science and use it to set themselves free. Nineteenth- and twentieth-century feminists defied social expectations, went to school, and learned that many "scientific truths" were quite simply false—especially those based on clinical theories that lacked hard evidence. Naomi Weisstein (1971, 147) explains: "The problem with insight, sensitivity, and intuition [the tools of psychology], is that they can confirm for all time the biases that one started out with. People used to be absolutely convinced of their ability to tell which of their number were engaging in witchcraft. All it required was some sensitivity to the workings of the devil." The Victorian myths of the inferior female brain, the deleterious effects of education, and the unwomanliness of suffrage lacked any form of empirical evidence—as did similarly ridiculous twentieth-century scientific myths such as the "immutable maternal instinct," the "sanctity of vaginal orgasms," the "child's need for excessive mothering," and the "theory of female masochism" (Ehrenreich and English 1979, 315). Nineteenth- and twentieth-century women realized that they must appropriate science—its terminology, its logic, its precepts—and use it to forward their own political agendas. The free women of *Mizora* and *Motherlines* did just that.

In doing so, they have dramatically improved their quality of life. If there were any doubt that men were the source of humanity's ills, the all-female societies that survive would seem to dispel it. In Mizora, war, disease, and poverty have died out with the competitive society of man, replaced by the peace, health, and abundance of an all-encompassing sisterhood whose main concern is the welfare of the community. In a world of mothers and daughters and sisters, there can be no servants or menials; there is no power parasitism to leech the efforts of others. A hierarchy of wealth is out of the question: some individuals may indeed accumulate more personal property than others, but no one is poor, and, in the long run, personal fortune is inconsequential: one might say of a Mizoran citizen, "*She* is a fine scholar, or mechanic, or artist, or musician," but never, "*She* is rich" (Lane [1880–81] 1889, 47). Similarly, Riding Women accord the highest respect to citizens such as Palmelar, who is "poor in horses because she [gives] away her wealth to needier women" (Charnas 1978, 28). A great Mizoran teacher will most probably live in palatial surroundings, yet she is so honored because of her ability to pass knowledge on to succeeding generations. Similarly, since food and horses are the key to survival in the Riding Women's Long Valley, the most skillful hunters and horse trainers earn a special respect from their sisters. These societies, founded as they are on generation, have as their primary concern the future of their race. An individual's value is determined primarily by her contribution to her vast family of sisters, mothers, daughters, aunts, and cousins. Individual gain is a trivial matter, individual power an obscenity.

Both societies are founded on interdependence rather than power. This arrangement is understandable. Historically, women have fared poorly in hierarchies; almost invariably, men view themselves as higher links on the great chain of being. United sisterhood, however, is a tremendously powerful force, and one that patriarchy considers threatening: as early as 1662, Margaret Cavendish complained that men do not "suffer us freely to associate amongst our own sex" (73). Nineteenth-century society was set up in such a way that women were forced to compete rather than cooperate, but women still recognized the value of female friendship. Janet Horowitz Murray (1982, 82) argues that women "relied on one another for support and advice," and that "sisters and friends often shared intense emotional commitments," which "could become more reciprocal and mutually supportive than economically unequal relationships with parents, brothers, and husbands." In the twentieth century, the yearning for female friendship and the urge for communal interdependence would metamorphose into the concept of sisterhood.[22]

The rejection of power hierarchy in favor of community is especially evident in religious matters, which is not surprising when one considers that the hierarchy established in Genesis was used for centuries to explain, endorse, and perpetuate women's subordinate status. The women of *Mizora* and *Motherlines* reject any notion of a Supreme Being or hereafter: they find their deity in nature's generation and their immortality in their own reproductive force. Mizorans assert that "Nature is God, and God is Nature" (Lane [1880–81] 1889, 255) and that death is merely a returning of the body "to the elements from which it came" (258). The concept of an immortal soul is nothing more than a belief born of an "agony of longing for happiness" (260). "When our lives are ended, the Great Mother gathers us in. *We* are the harvest of the centuries" (310). The Riding Women celebrate "the pattern of movement and growth and [their] place in it, which is to affirm the pattern and renew it and preserve it" (Charnas 1978, 212). Like the Mizorans, they scorn the petty consolations of paradise—as an elderly Riding Woman explains, "After I live my life and die, I'm still part of the Motherline, with women of my flesh before me and behind me. Death is nothing to get excited about" (89). Life, on the other hand, is something to get very excited about indeed, particularly the production of new life.

Generation is all: it has supplanted the old hierarchies of patriarchal religion, replacing them with the reproductive force pulsing within every living creature. Godhead no longer comes from above, but from within. In Mizora, "the

MOTHER is the only important part of all life" (219); among the Riding Women, the Motherlines are an integral part of their being. Women in both societies reject the atrocities and inequities that a power-mad hierarchy seems to engender. Selfish cravings for individual gain and glory give way to an altruistic maternal impulse that offers an alternate form of social organization based on harmony rather than rule.

Yet generation is not a strictly female prerogative. There is life in the earth and in all its creatures. Man, too, carries life within him and, with it, the potential to recognize its worth. Many utopias by women present societies that imitate nature's nonhierarchical arrangements and that coexist in harmony with the world around them. Plants, animals, and people live in consonance rather than conflict, in communities based on a nurturing ecofeminism. Although Charlotte Perkins Gilman's *Herland* (1915) and Marge Piercy's *Woman on the Edge of Time* (1976) are separated by just over sixty years, the texts are united by their presentations of people who seek to live in partnership with the earth, its creatures, and one another.

Both texts demonstrate a reverence for the natural force that creates and sustains all life. Humankind and nature are no longer at war with one another but now peacefully exist in a state of compatibility and perfect cultivation. Gilman's Herlanders are skillful agriculturalists who have managed to nourish their community without plundering the land. There is no monotony of furrowed, overplanted earth, no dreariness of bleak cities; instead, the forests surround "parklike meadows and open places" (10). Enrichment of the earth is an essential part of their holistic approach to agriculture; composting, for example, is seen as "refeeding the soil with all that came out of it. All the scraps and leavings of their food, plant waste from lumber work or the textile industry, all the solid matter from the sewage, properly treated and combined—everything which came from the earth [goes] back into it" (80). Herlanders are involved in a constant effort to increase production efficiency while minimizing the strain on the earth that feeds them. Marge Piercy's citizens of Mattapoisett[23] have also abandoned the idea of cities, after establishing that such social arrangements simply "didn't work" (68). Villages now seem to grow out of the landscape, and small buildings are "randomly scattered" in Herlander fashion, "among trees and shrubbery and gardens" (69). The society is agricultural, largely vegetarian, and obsessed with ways to achieve optimally efficient cultivation. As in Herland, all wastes are composted, for Mattapoisett's citizens "can afford to waste . . . nothing" (125). Energy, a rare and precious commodity, is carefully drawn from fire, air, water, and earth: solar power, windmills, water-driven turbines, and decomposing wastes. It is hoarded and spent only on projects that substantially enrich the community's quality of life.

Both societies realize the need to avoid ecological imbalance and to pay strict attention to population control: environmental concerns extend to the quantity and quality of human beings as well as animals. In Herland, selective eugenic breeding helps to ensure "the standard of peace, comfort, health, beauty, and progress [Herlanders] demand" (68). In Mattapoisett, highly advanced technology enables the inhabitants to maintain a strict control over population size and genetic makeup: one baby is created to succeed each person who dies, and the death of a particularly gifted and humane person is marked by the production of a genetically identical replacement.

Harmony has been established because no one wishes to assume control over nature or power over one another: just as humankind and nature exist in partnership, human and human live in mutual respect. Social arrangements are strictly egalitarian. Herlanders have "no kings and no priests, and no aristocracies"; the society is governed "not by competition, but by united action" (60). Similarly, Mattapoisett citizens have "no final authority" (153); community problems are discussed at length in town council meetings, which frequently last for days, until a mutually acceptable solution is worked out. There are no laws as such, merely an awareness that power and greed are inherently evil and that it is wrong to take from others "their food, their liberty, their health, their land, their customs, their pride" (139). Since the androcentric hierarchical model is no more acceptable for couples than for groups, male/female relationships are predicated on mutual concern and respect. In both texts, the basis for this respect is a reworking and revaluation of traditional gender roles, a process that parallels Olive Banks's (1981, 244) assertion that "feminist goals cannot be achieved without changes in the relationship between men and women that entail the transformation of traditional sex roles and the traditional family."

Both texts recognize woman's power of generation—the power that forms the basis of separatist narratives such as *Mizora* and *Motherlines*. In a truly equitable society, however, this generative power must be yielded along with man's dominant status and must be blended into a new model of consolidated human energy. The parthenogenic Herlanders are eager to relinquish their absolute power of regeneration: when three American men stumble upon their land, the possibility of dual parentage is acclaimed as "the Great New Hope"; when a Herlander becomes pregnant in the traditional manner, her sisters await with "deep awe and warm expectancy . . . this new miracle of union" (140). In Mattapoisett, the exclusively female mechanics of maternity have been turned over to science: embryos are grown not in bodies, but in brooders; babies are mothered by men and women alike (males are given hormones so that they can nurse their children). Connie, a time-traveling visitor from the long-past twentieth century, laments that women have "given it all up" and "let men steal from them the last remnants of ancient power, those sealed in blood and milk" (134). Yet she is assured that such is not the case, that the surrender of the power to give birth is "part of women's long revolution," an essential part of "breaking up all the old hierarchies. Finally there was that one thing we had to give up too, the only power we ever had, in return for no more power for anyone. . . . So we *all* became mothers" (105, emphasis added).[24] Now males and females are united by a "social faith" predicated on generation: "the children are everyone's heirs, everyone's business, everyone's future" (183).

Yet, while parallels between nineteenth- and twentieth-century utopias by women frequently seem to eradicate the intervening century, there are significant dissimilarities between these narratives, reflecting significant divergences between nineteenth- and twentieth-century feminist ideology. In both eras, women's movements were pioneered by white middle-class women and supported by liberal males, but the 1960s saw the emergence of a radical feminism that rejected the limited goals of liberal feminists as hopelessly bourgeois and conventional and condemned the supposedly radical goals of the New Left as oppressively patriarchal. Radical feminists disdained the protection afforded them by the liminal shadow world of racial and class centrality and opted instead for an entirely new model of female experience.

In 1970, Shulamith Firestone (36–37) argued that the National Organization for Women (NOW), long associated with white middle-class women, tended to concentrate on bourgeois concerns: "the more superficial symptoms of sexism—legal difficulties, employment discrimination, and the like." Firestone likened the organization to turn-of-the-century suffrage movements, because of "its stress on equality with men . . . rather than liberation from sex roles altogether, or radical questioning of family values." Since radical feminists argued that middle-class values reinforced the oppression of women, NOW's bourgeois perspective was seen as dangerously atavistic. Neither could one rely on the New Left to vanguard the woman's movement; Robin Morgan condemned "the counterfeit male-dominated Left" as an operation overseen by men who profess to champion " 'Women's Lib,' as they so chummily call it," but "then proceed to degrade and destroy women by almost everything they say and do" (cited in Eisenstein 1983, 126).[25]

This distrust of middle-class norms and male protection emerges dramatically in women's utopian writing. Twentieth-century heroines are no longer exceedingly proper, heterosexual, religious, Anglo-Saxon matrons, thoroughly attentive to the value of the domestic sphere; instead, they tend to be earthy, bisexual or lesbian, atheist, multiracial, radical feminists who denounce traditional social arrangements as the source of women's oppression. There are no more mantels laden with bric-a-brac to dust, no more Houses Beautiful requiring so much unpaid and unnoticed effort; individuals clean up after themselves, and larger housekeeping projects are communal responsibilities. Conventional child-rearing arrangements have been succeeded by communal child care, and living arrangements are dramatically simplified through a return to the basics, which frequently takes the form of primitive tribalism. Men need not trouble themselves to protect women, for utopian females manage nicely on their own: skilled hunters and fierce warriors, they are men's equals in all things and superiors in many; and alternative sexual arrangements—bisexuality or homosexuality—help break the patriarchal pattern of domestic dominance. The middle-class, fundamentally hierarchical worldview that permeated nineteenth-century utopias is rejected as classist, racist, and sexist; in its place is an egalitarian synergy.

Both *Mizora* and *Motherlines* feature separatist, single-sex communities, yet these societies maintain decidedly incompatible philosophies. Mizora is the epitome of middle-class values: a respectable nineteenth-century woman would probably be quite comfortable in a Mizoran home, luxuriously furnished and copiously ornamented, featuring the latest in technological innovation. She could live in harmony with her female offspring, secure in the knowledge that purity and decorum were not only encouraged but also quite literally bred into the members of the community—along with acceptable physical characteristics such as blond hair and white skin. In the absence of power-mad males, Mizoran women live in an atmosphere of order, purity, and goodness. Everyone is noble and fine; life is peaceful, serene, and morally uplifting.

Genteel Mizorans would be horrified at the lusty, noisy, semibarbaric lifestyle of the Riding Women. Charnas's earthy heroines eschew the placid isolation of private houses, preferring to share primitive communal tents. Their daughters do not live decorously at home, but in the "childpack," a "skinny, grimy mob" (Charnas 1978, 38) of prepubescents that roams at will, fed by the community but otherwise living apart from adults. There is nothing particularly decorous about life in the Long Valley, and the fierce Riding Women would be perceived as obscenely coarse by Mizorans: a racial hodgepodge of colors and features, they are rough, uncultivated, and savage. While fiercely loyal, they are not particularly chaste, engaging in both lesbian relationships and ritual sexual union with stallions. Mizoran gentlewomen are "never arrogant, never supercilious, never aggressive," but always "tolerant, humane, sublime" (Lane [1880–81] 1889, 133); Riding Women are frequently insolent, often conceited, fight and hunt for pleasure, and tend to be narrow-minded, fierce, and unrefined. These warrior Amazons need no middle-class morality or males to shelter and shield them; they are perfectly capable of defending themselves.

Gilman's Herlanders are also quite self-sufficient, and, if one of their number were suddenly transplanted to the Mattapoisett community of *Woman on the Edge of Time*, she might be assumed to fare quite well—until she encountered their views on religion and sexuality. Herlanders are consummately devout, and their pious spirituality infuses every facet of their culture: although Gilman ([1915] 1979) rejects the patriarchal Father in favor of a nurturing Mother, her ideal community is permeated with "the power of mother-love . . . raised to its highest power" (57). Worship of this maternal force is the essence of Herland, integral to "every art and industry" (73); it is the fundamental basis of the society's existence. Mattapoisett is far more humanistic and materialistic. There can be no centrality of religion, for their culture recognizes no religious beliefs. Instead, the community has "ideas" about human partnership "with water, air, birds, fish, trees" (Piercy 1976, 125). The citizens have no Great Mother to work miracles for them but only their hard work, common sense, and the miracle of an earth rich enough to feed them.

A Herlander's Victorian sensibilities would also be outraged by Mattapoisett's rather relaxed sexual arrangements. Although Gilman's utopians revere generation in general, they have decided reservations about the specifics of procreation. Sexuality is not a passionate, impetuous matter: the male narrator and his Herlander bride enjoy intercourse only after a religious wedding ceremony and an extended period of platonic cohabitation. In Mattapoisett, on the other hand, people reject the construct of marriage as limiting and inhibiting and couple with whichever consenting being they wish; a varied diet of frequent sexual activity is considered essential to human health and happiness. Herland and Mattapoisett, like Mizora and the Long Valley, are finally disjoined: women's understandings of eutopia, dystopia, centrality, and otherness are transformed as nineteenth-century middle-class values give way to a radical feminist distrust of all things bourgeois.

Yet despite this divergence, fundamental similarities of purpose and form remain: new political exertion and new expectations, it would seem, engender new women's utopias, and old frustrations frequently draw on old strategies. The narratives of the present leap across the intervening hundred years and help illuminate the texts of the past; their striking parallels eclipse the niceties of convention and style and point starkly to what women hunger for. Lane's and Charnas's texts show that feminine "weakness" is really a powerful force for good, a gentle strength directed away from control, toward nurture, peace, and harmony. Gilman and Piercy close the circle, taking the revalued feminine, no longer other but central, and sharing it with both genders, to their mutual joy. At long last, Plato's long-despised "management of pancakes and preserves" can be seen for what it really is: the nurture and preservation of humanity.

APPENDIX

Women's Utopian Fiction, 1621–1920
A Chronological Annotated Bibliography

Although nineteenth-century utopias by women provide abundant alternatives to the limited patriarchal vision, they have been all but lost to modern readers. The following bibliography is an attempt to make these narratives more accessible, to help scholars avoid the blind alleys so frequently encountered in any study of obscure texts.[1] It is admittedly broad in scope, yet certainly not exhaustive—fortunately, new texts are constantly being rediscovered.

The works are listed chronologically, each according to its earliest date of publication; subsequent editions are cited in the cases of serials reprinted as books and modern editions that may be more accessible than the original texts. Whenever possible, the author's full name is cited: names not appearing on the title page of the work and variant spellings are bracketed.

1621 Wro[a]th, Mary [Sidney], Lady. *The Countess of Mountgomeries Urania.* London: Joseph Marriott and John Grismand. Reprint, London: John Morphew and J. Woodward, 1709.

    Wroth's romance, a response to her uncle Sir Philip Sidney's *Arcadia* (1590), is set on the pastoral island of Pantalaria. Here, in spite of cruel fathers, faithless lovers, and brutal husbands, women enjoy a relatively unfettered existence (at least by seventeenth-century standards): some seek adventure on their own and engage in such masculine pursuits as writing poetry, hunting, fishing, and even fighting.

1651 Cary [Rande], M[ary]. *The Little Horns Doom and Downfall; or, A Scripture-Prophesie of King James, and King Charles, and of This Present Parliament, Unfolded. Wherein it appeares, that the late tragedies that have bin acted upon the scene of these three nations: and particularly, the late kings doom and death, was so long ago, as by Daniel predeclared. And what the issue of all will be, is also discovered; which followes in the second part.* London: The author.

    The title says it all; of particular interest to utopian scholars, however, is Cary's detailed description of life during the millennium. The second title page (with the imprint London: W. H.) reads: "A new and more exact mappe or, description of New Jerusalem's glory when Jesus Christ and his saints with him shall reign on earth a thousand years, and possess all kingdoms. Wherein is discovered the glorious estate into which the church shall be then put both in respect of externall and internall glory, and the time when. And also, what hath been done these eight yeares last past, and what is now a doing, and what shall be done within a few years now following in order to this great work. Wherein also that great question, whether it be lawfull for saints to make use of the materiall sword in the ruining of the enemies of Christ, and whether it be the mind of Christ to have it so, is at large debated and resolved in the affirmative from clear scripture, and all others answered." London: W. H.

1655   [Cavendish, Margaret Lucas, Duchess of Newcastle] Lady Margaret Newcastle. "The Inventory of Judgements Commonwealth, the Author Cares Not in What World It Is Established." In *The World's Olio*, 205–12. London: J. Martin and J. Allestrye.

The duchess offers a brief schematic for an ideal commonwealth in which a "Carefull and Loving" monarch contracts with his people to rule justly, eschewing favoritism and greed, giving wit precedence over beauty, and honoring poets. Specific reforms include the duties and responsibilities of the full spectrum of society. Traditional gender roles are preserved but are characterized by courtesy and decorum: men should avoid prostitutes, treat their wives with respect, and provide for their children; women should avoid gossip and intrigue; both husbands and wives should avoid public displays of affection, amours with servants, and dancing.

1659   Montpensier, Anne Mary Louisa d'Orleans, Duchesse de. *La Relation de L'Isle Imaginaire, et l'histoire de la Princesse de Paphlagonie*. Bordeaux: [Jean Regnauld Segrais].

Like the later satires of Manley (1709) and Haywood (1725), Montpensier's description of an Arcadian island offers thinly disguised satiric observations of her society, especially the French court of Louis XIV under the regency of Cardinal Mazarin. The author herself appears as the queen of the Amazons.

1666   [Cavendish, Margaret Lucas] Duchess of Newcastle. "The Description of a New World, Called the Blazing World." Pt. 4 of her *Observations upon Experimental Philosophy*. London: A. Maxwell.

In this allegorical tale, a young woman discovers the Lost Eden, a world attached to Earth at the North Pole. She marries its emperor, who rules a land guaranteed peace by its few laws, unified religion, and single language. The explorer-queen is permitted an unusual amount of authority and freedom: she exercises her considerable scientific curiosity through interviews with her subjects (a varied group of animal-human combinations) and extended out-of-body excursions.

1687   Behn, Mrs. Aphra [Amis]. *The Emperor of the Moon: A Farce*. London: R. Holt, for J. Knight and F. Saunders.

Utopia is a peripheral element in this brief comedy: in an attempt to distract his beloved's possessive father, a rogue assumes the guise of a cabalist from Eutopia and expounds on the supposed nature of the Moon-World to the gullible philosopher. Lunar inhabitants are all-knowing and immortal:

stars and "little Daemons of the Air" give them information about the past, present, and future; beauteous sylphs and nymphs grant them eternal life. A second rogue, masquerading as the lunar ambassador, tells the old man of a moon society full of intemperance, vanity, whoring, adultery, and political corruption—a society, marvels the philosopher, identical to fashionable London's.

1688   Behn, Mrs. A[phra Amis]. *The History of Oroonoko; or, The Royal Slave, a True History.* London: Will Canning. Reprint, in *Shorter Novels: Seventeenth Century,* ed. Philip Henderson, 145–224. London: J. M. Dent, 1967.

The introductory section of Behn's narrative offers a brief description of a West Indian society whose inhabitants seem "an absolute *Idea* of the first state of Innocence, before man knew how to sin." The naturally modest natives live happily without religion, laws, or clothes and enjoy the full bounty of nature in their prelapsarian Eden. There is some sexism and ageism, however: women are little more than slaves, and the older wives must serve the younger ones.

1709   [Manley, Mary de la Rivière]. *Secret Memoirs and Morals of Several Persons of Quality of Both Sexes, from the New Atalantis, an Isle in the Mediterranean.* London: John Morphew and J. Woodward.

"The New Atalantis" is England; the "memoirs" are thinly disguised contemporary scandals. Astraea (the goddess of justice, innocence, and purity) has long since abandoned the world but visits Earth to see if humankind is still "defective." Alighting on Atalantis, she encounters her bedraggled and neglected mother, Virtue, who describes society's deplorable state. While not a true utopia, this text reflects a satirical use of the genre later perfected by Swift. It is of particular interest because it replaces the conventional dialogue between men with a dialogue between women.

1725   [Haywood, Eliza Fowler]. *Memoirs of a Certain Island Adjacent to Utopia, by a Celebrated Author of That Country.* London: Booksellers of London and Westminster. Reprint (facsimile ed.), New York: Garland, 1972.

As in Manley's *Secret Memoirs and Morals* (1709), the "certain island" is England, and the "memoirs" are a series of satirical anecdotes. A young man who has "ranged o'er almost all the habitable Part of the globe in search of Pleasure and Improvement" arrives in England and encounters a mournful Cupid, who laments the island's preoccupation with "blind Gratification of unlicens'd wishes." The god leads the young man to an enchanted well, where the foibles of the famous and infamous are revealed. Finally, the Genius of the Island, aided by Astraea and Reason, destroys the well; Beauty and Virtue regain their authority—at least in a "small Part" of the isle.

1762   [Scott, Sarah Robinson]. *A Description of Millenium Hall, and the Country Adjacent: together with the character of the inhabitants, and such historical anecdotes and reflections, as may excite in the reader proper sentiments of humanity, and lead the mind to the love of virtue, by a gentleman on his travels.* London: J.

Newbery. Reprint (facsimile ed.), New York: Garland, 1974. Reprint, New York: Virago, 1986.

An epistolary fiction, describing Millenium Hall, a pastoral country estate in Cornwall inhabited by a group of energetic, artistic, and highly virtuous celibate women, whose grim histories graphically illustrate women's dismal condition in eighteenth-century society. They have dedicated themselves to helping unfortunate people in the area: the homeless are sheltered; the sick are tended; poor children are educated; deformed people are shielded. This text may have been influenced by Mary Astell's *A Serious Proposal to the Ladies, for the Advancement of Their True and Greatest Interest* (London: K. Wilkin, 1694), an essay that suggests the establishment of an institution in which women would be able to live, study, and work independently of men.

1790   [Knight, Ellis Cornelia]. *Dinarbas: A Tale, Being a Continuation of Rasselas, Prince of Abyssinia.* London: C. Dilly. Reprint, ed. Ann Messenger; East Lansing, Mich.: Colleagues Press, 1993.

In this sequel to Dr. Johnson's *Rasselas,* the prince returns to war-torn Abyssinia and eventually assumes the throne, discovering along the way that life offers more pleasure than pain and that God is a support during periods of trial. Despite the negative assessment of marriage offered in Johnson's original narrative, the prince and his sister each find satisfaction in wedded bliss: Rasselas marries the beautiful, intelligent, virtuous Zilia; Nekayah weds the noble, heroic Dinarbas. Although the novel encourages education for women, they are limited to traditional roles: Queen Zilia, for example, knows she must "never interfere in public business"; instead, she establishes charities and patronizes the arts.

1822   [Wright] D'Arusment, Frances, Mme. *A Few Days in Athens, Being the Translation of a Greek Manuscript Discovered in Herculaneum.* London: Longman, Hurst, Rees, Orme and Brown.

In Athens of the third century B.C.E, the young Stoic Theon overcomes his prejudice against the supposedly debauched Epicureans. He discovers that their pastoral gardens, offering a nonmystical blend of rationality, materialism, and intellectual pleasure, may be even more conducive to virtue than Zeno's spartan, urban porticos. Of particular interest is the sympathetic portrait of Leontium, a beautiful, intelligent, and highly articulate young woman who studies and lives (virtuously) with Epicurus and is mislabeled a prostitute by unenlightened outsiders. Frances Wright's liberal views on religion and sex were similarly misunderstood and censured.

1824   Sedgwick, Catherine Maria. *Redwood: A Tale.* 3 vols. New York: E. Bliss & E. White. Reprint, New York: Garrett, 1969.

This three-volume novel describes the differing social climates in America's northern, mid-Atlantic, and southern regions. Chapters 15–16 explore a Shaker community in Massachusetts and detail the efforts of its members to persuade a young woman to join. Unable to accept the society's harsh restriction on sexuality, however, she ultimately flees and returns to the world and the passionate young man who loves her.

1826   [Shelley, Mary Wollstonecraft]. *The Last Man*. London: Henry Colburn. Reprint, Lincoln: University of Nebraska Press, 1965.

Set in the twenty-first century, this dystopian, apocalyptic vision tells of a future in which nature inexplicably turns on mankind, loosing a plague that ravages Earth for seven years. The novel is the narrative of Lionel Verney, the sole survivor, who details the events of the last three decades of man's existence on Earth. Shelley's portrait of women is rather ambiguous: most are meek, passive, and intolerably dull; the strong-willed, independent exceptions (a domineering, power-hungry countess and a militant, passionate princess) seem somehow linked to the blind malevolence of the plague.

1827   [Loudon, Jane Webb]. *The Mummy! A Tale of the Twenty-Second Century*. London: Henry Colburn.

The mummy is none other than King Cheops, who, resuscitated in 2130 by means of a galvanic battery, hijacks a balloon and flies to London. Twenty-second-century England, after recovering from the strife brought about by democracy and universal education, is now Roman Catholic; its figurehead is a celibate, reclusive English queen (chosen by male electors). The society is technologically advanced: moving houses glide along the road, saving their owners the trouble of packing for a trip; balloons and "aerial horses, inflated with inflammable gas," fill the air. Gender roles, however, remain traditional; woman's place is in the home (wherever it may be), surrounded by her modern conveniences, inflating her air mattresses and using feather fan vents to recycle the air.

1836   [Griffith, Mary]. "Three Hundred Years Hence." In *Camperdown; or, News from Our Neighborhood: Being Sketches by the Author of "Our Neighborhood,"* 91–92. Philadelphia: Carey, Lea and Blanchard. Reprint, in *Three Hundred Years Hence*, ed. Nelson F. Adkins, Philadelphia: Prime Press, 1950. Reprint, in *American Utopias*, ed. Arthur O. Lewis, Jr.; New York: Arno Press and the New York Times, 1971.

A dream vision anticipating Edward Bellamy's *Looking Backward* (1888) in form: thirty-two-year-old Edgar Hastings fancies himself buried alive by an avalanche in 1835 and awakened three hundred years later. He encounters a United States dramatically improved by technology and morality. Trains, ships, and farm machinery are powered "by some internal machinery"; a passage to India is accomplished in only twenty days. War, capital punishment, monopolies, child abuse, and slavery have been abolished—thanks to the "influence of women." Women enjoy economic equality and improved educational opportunities, although no mention is made of enfranchisement.

1837   Fox, Mary, Lady. *Account of an Expedition to the Interior of New Holland*. London: Richard Bentley. Reprint, in *The Southlanders: An Account of an Expedition to the Interior of New Holland*, London: John W. Parker and Son, 1860.

To avoid the chaos of the Reformation, a group of European seamen migrate to Australia, where they intermarry with the inhabitants and establish an English-speaking Christian society. Racial equality, education, and moral laws are stressed; traditional gender roles are preserved.

1838   Browning, Elizabeth Barrett. "An Island." In *The Seraphim, and Other Poems.* London: Saunders and Otley. Reprint, in *Complete Works of Elizabeth Barrett Browning,* 6 vols., ed. Charlotte Porter and Helen A. Clarke, 2:37–44; New York: Thomas Y. Crowell, 1900.

> Barrett Browning dreams of a pastoral earthly paradise where women co-exist happily with nature, free of the tyranny of men. The land is a place of forests and caves, fertile, peaceful, and life affirming, soothed by "Nature's way and tone" and "steadfast sympathies." Eventually, however, the poet is wakened from her reverie by the reality of church bells, which knell her obligations to the patriarchal God: "Thy will be done."

1841   [Chamberlain, Betsey] Tabitha [pseud.]. "A New Society." *Lowell Offering* 1:191–92. Reprint, in *The Lowell Offering: Writings by New England Mill Women (1840–1845),* ed. Benita Eisler, 208–10; Philadelphia: J. B. Lippincott, 1977.

> A female millworker envisions an egalitarian Society for the Promotion of Industry, Virtue and Knowledge, which champions equal education and wages for both sexes, equitable labor practices (such as the eight-hour work day), and a balance of intellectual and physical employment.

1845   Martineau, Harriet. *Dawn Island: A Tale.* Manchester, England: J. Gadsby.

> Martineau's fable promoting the benefits of free trade is set on a tropical island paradise, made hellish by the barbaric customs of its natives. Filthy dwellings house lazy men who have reduced women to the status of slaves; barbaric rites include human sacrifice, cannibalism, and infanticide. The society is in a constant state of war with surrounding islands. When a European ship arrives, however, the sailors engage in trade with the natives, exchanging emblematic items such as tinderboxes, spectacles, and spoons for food. The natives learn that trust and honesty are essential—not only in matters of trade but in human relationships as well. Ultimately, the savages realize the wastefulness of their savagery and turn to commerce and Christianity as a way of life.

1848   [Appleton, Jane Sophia]. "Sequel to 'The Vision of Bangor in the Twentieth Century.' " In *Voices from the Kenduskeag,* 61–73; Bangor, Me.: David Bugbee. Reprint, in *American Utopias,* ed. Arthur O. Lewis, Jr., 243–65; New York: Arno Press and the New York Times, 1971.

> This response to Edward Kent's 1848 "vision" presents America in 1978—a society free of war, religious bigotry, and poverty. Women, freed of the second-class status imposed by the Genesis myth, are seen as each "in *herself* the 'image of God.' Not 'God's last, best gift to *man,*' but *with* man." Sexual difference is acknowledged and cherished, but the rank of each sex is equal. Educated, impervious to flattery, financially independent, and freed from household drudgery by technological advances, women no longer see suffrage as an issue; at one time, they were "obliged to take part in government," because man's greed had turned society "topsy-turvy." Once women had

restored "order and beauty," however, they took no further part in political activity.

1853   Hale, Sarah J[osepha Buell]. *Liberia; or, Mr. Peyton's Experiments*. New York: Harper and Brothers. Reprint, New Jersey: Gregg, 1968.

Charles Peyton, a humane plantation owner in Virginia, attempts to improve the lives of his slaves. His experiments grow progressively larger in scope: after freeing his slaves, he first establishes Rocky Run Farm, a small farm collective and model community. When this operation proves unsuccessful, Peyton helps the blacks establish a prosperous African colony in Liberia. Traditional gender roles predominate.

1866   Davis, Rebecca Harding. "The Harmonists." *Atlantic Monthly* 17:529–38.

In this dystopian view of an actual utopian movement, Zachary Humphries recalls his youthful trip to a Rappite colony in Economy, Pennsylvania. The stern idealism of this celibate religious communal group has degenerated into hopeless repression and materialism: lonely withered women are virtual slaves, whose only creative outlet is cooking for gross male masters obsessed with obtaining capital. This text is the first of several such attacks on communitarian societies (see Alcott [1873], McGlasson [1891], Orpen [1897]).

1869   Corbett, Elizabeth T. "My Visit to Utopia." *Harper's New Monthly Magazine* 38:200–204.

A woman visits her friend in Utopia, where men and women marry and live together with kindness, courtesy, and mutual respect. Women are men's comrades rather than servants: "honoring" and "obeying" are omitted from the marriage service; men share household chores and child-rearing duties. Female suffrage is the natural outgrowth of such respect.

[Ives, Cora Semmes]. *The Princess of the Moon: A Confederate Fairy Story, by a Lady of Warrenton, Va*. Baltimore, Md.: Sun Book and Job Office. Reprint, Louisville, Ky.: Lost Cause Press, 1970.

This children's book is set in Virginia, after the American Civil War. Young Randolph is a Confederate hero who longs to escape the ravages of postwar Yankee invaders. A lunar fairy gives him a magical horse called Hope, which carries him to the moon, a utopian kingdom ruled by a hereditary monarch. Randolph falls in love with and weds the king's daughter. However, not even the moon is safe from Yankee carpetbaggers, who appear with Randolph's still-loyal slave in tow. The Fairy of the Moon, pleased at finally having these "demons of cruelty" in her power, plans to destroy them, but generous Randolph intercedes and gains their pardons. The book concludes with the hope that the South shall rise again.

1870   Alcott, Louisa May. "The Sunny Side." Chap. 13 from *An Old-Fashioned Girl*. Boston: Roberts.

Four young women, whose "religion" is based on caring for and helping one another, turn their shared rooms into a cooperative home.

Cridge, Annie Denton. *Man's Rights; or, How Would You Like It? Comprising Dreams.* Boston: William Denton. Also printed with four additional "dreams" in *Woodhull and Claflin's Weekly* 1 (1870).

In a series of nine rather Swiftian dream visions, a woman describes a Martian society in which traditional gender roles and stereotypes are reversed: pale, feeble "gentlemen-housekeepers," either overworked and nervous or vain and lazy, must stay at home, while stately, dignified women rule. Attempts to begin a man's rights movement are initially dismissed as silly, since women's grace, beauty, ability to produce children, and mental superiority make them the "naturally" superior sex. The detailed, sympathetic view of the men's plight satirically reflects on the dismal situation of terrestrial gender relationships and offers a tantalizing glimpse of empowered womanhood.

Woodhull [Martin], Victoria C[laflin]. *A Page of American History: Constitution of the United States of the World.* Cheltenham, England: Norman Sawyer. Reprint (slightly revised), retitled *A New Constitution for the United States of the World, Proposed for the Consideration of the Constructors of Our Future Government,* New York: Woodhull, Claflin, 1872. Reprint, in *The Victoria Woodhull Reader,* ed. Madeleine B. Stern; Weston, Mass.: M S Press, 1974.

While not a true utopia, Woodhull's constitution offers a schematic for an egalitarian society. The document emphasizes the "full and unrestrained" rights of all individuals (as long as the exercise of those rights do not infringe on the rights of others) and advocates financial, educational, and judicial reform.

1871   Harbert, Lizzie Boynton. *Out of Her Sphere.* Des Moines, Iowa: Mills.

Strong-minded Marjory Warner is a prototype for the successful career woman/homemaker. Although she champions the "power of womanhood" and the benefits of the domestic sphere, she rejects its limiting gender stereotypes. As a respected preacher and beloved wife, she demonstrates that "womanly" women *should* work and vote to extend female spirituality and morality to the public sphere.

1873   Alcott, Louisa M[ay]. *Work: A Story of Experience.* Boston: Roberts. Reprint, New York: Schocken, 1977.

In the final chapter, reformer and retired nurse Christie Sterling envisions a future in which women will become "a loving league of sisters, old and young, black and white, rich and poor, each ready to do her part to hasten the coming of the happy end," when humanity will enjoy universal "independence, education, happiness, and religion."

Alcott, Louisa May. "Transcendental Wild Oats: A Chapter from an Unwritten Romance." *Independent* 25 (18 December): 1569–71. Reprint, ed. William Henry Harrison; Harvard, Mass.: Harvard Common, 1975.

Alcott pokes fun at the pretensions of her father's (Bronson Alcott) socialistic Fruitlands community. Abel Lamb desires "to plant a Paradise, where Beauty, Justice, and Love might live happily together, without the possibility of a serpent entering in." The narrative satirizes the Alcotts' marriage as well: women perform most of the labor, since the men are too concerned with spiritual issues to deal with "trivial" matters such as food, clothing, and housing. Fruitlands (which Mrs. Lamb eventually rechristens "Apple Slump") is a dismal failure: "the exiles [leave] their Eden and [face] the world again."

[Thomas, Bertha]. "A Vision of Communism: A Grotesque." *Cornhill Magazine* 28 (September): 300–310.

This dystopian dream vision equates communism with the pursuit of mediocrity. Human equality is impossible, since nature will produce the "intellectual millionaire" or grant a "large musical fortune" or "enormous stock of beauty" to a fortunate individual. True communists, therefore, must treat life as "a handicap race" and ensure absolute equality by denying such natural inequalities: the mentally acute, for example, should receive far less education than their duller fellows; the musically gifted should play only out-of-tune instruments; the physically attractive should wear only unflattering clothing.

1874   Fawcett, Millicent Garrett. *Tales in Political Economy.* London: Macmillan.

A small island gradually undertakes trade with its neighbors and, eventually, becomes a utopian paradise, thanks to the twin blessings of free trade and the free market.

Howland, Marie [Stevens Case]. *Papa's Own Girl.* New York: John P. Jewett; Boston: Lee and Shepard. Reprint, retitled *The Familistère: A Novel,* Boston: Christopher, 1918. Reprint (original title), Philadelphia: Porcupine, 1975.

Clara Forest, the daughter of a Massachusetts physician who encourages female education and liberation from the "custom" of female oppression, escapes her stifling marriage and philandering husband through divorce. Dr. Forest helps Clara and Susie Dykes (the unmarried mother of his son's child) to begin a florist business, which, aided by the wealthy feminist Count von Frauenstein, evolves into the Social Palace, an institution for social reform, promoting equitable relations between women and men. The Social Palace stresses education and cultural enrichment, the dignity of work and economic independence, and full adult enfranchisement. This text is an early positive response to actual American communitarian societies (see also Douglas [1879], Campbell [1886], Cruger [1888], Mason [1889, 1898], Mead [1889], Woods [1889], Bartlett [1891], Winslow [1893], Graul [ca. 1897], and Clarke [1898]).

Phelps [Ward], Elizabeth Stuart. "A Dream within a Dream." *Independent* 26:1.

In this brief dream vision, a woman envisions herself as a pastor, performing an egalitarian marriage ceremony that eliminates references to obedience and property in favor of assurances of true love. In such a union, women could find an earthly paradise.

1877   [Cobbe, Frances Power] Merlin Nostradamus [pseud.]. *The Age of Science: A Newspaper of the 20th Century.* London: Wars, Lock and Tyler.

England in 1977 is vaguely reminiscent of Jonathan Swift's island of Laputa. Religion has given way to "the sacred doctrine of Evolution," and

God has been replaced by Science. Art has suffered considerably: the poet laureate describes the pangs of arthritis in "The Gout, and other Poems"; the Royal Academy exhibits the work of manufacturers. Women are forbidden to read or write, but a Simian Educational Institute instructs apes of both sexes.

[Drane, Augusta Theodosia] Mother Frances Raphael. *The New Utopia*. Serialized in *Irish Monthly* (fifth yearly volume), 160–69, 181–91, 241–54, 299–313, 359–68, 419–32, 479–86. Reprint, London: Catholic Truth Society, 1898.

John Grant, a devout Catholic, inherits an estate and sets about to improve the lifestyle of miners in a nearby town. His concern is limited to the men and boys of the community; "model women" (that is, docile and meek) are "a commodity" in scarce supply; the world is overrun with "girls of the period"—confused and misguided bluestockings, cursed "with that joyless intellectualism which mars all beauty on the face of woman."

1879   Douglas, Amanda M[innie]. *Hope Mills; or, Between Friend and Sweetheart*. Boston: Lee and Shepard. Reprint, New York: Charles T. Dillingham, 1880.

John Grant, a devout Catholic, inherits an estate and sets about to improve the lifestyle of miners in a nearby town. His concern is limited to the men and boys of the community; "model women" (that is, docile and meek) are "a commodity" in scarce supply; the world is overrun with "girls of the period"—confused and misguided bluestockings, cursed "with that joyless intellectualism which mars all beauty on the face of woman."

Jack Darcy, the college-educated son of a millhand, is inspired by Adam Smith, Ruskin, Mill, and English and French utopias to establish an industrial cooperative. Eventually, he marries the aristocratic heroine. Traditional gender roles prevail.

Phelps [Ward], Elizabeth Stuart. *An Old Maid's Paradise*. Boston: Houghton, Osgood; London: James Clarke.

Corona, a spinster of thirty-six, tires of living with her brother's family and seeks a home of her own. She builds Paradise, a small house in the seacoast town of Fairharbor. Other single women, attracted to this "free, delightful, manless" Eden, visit and remain; they sail and savor the beauty of nature, heartily relishing the freedom of their single status. Eventually, however, Paradise is lost: first, a visitor named Mr. Sinuous persuades one of the women to marry him; then, after the fall, the "Flaming Sword" of winter drives the remaining women back to the world of men.

1880–81 [Lane, Mary E. Bradley]. "Narrative of Vera Zarovitch: Being a true and faithful account of her journey to the interior of the earth, with a careful description of the country and its inhabitants, their customs, manners and government." Serialized in Saturday installments of the *Cincinnati Commercial*, 6 November 1880–5 February 1881. Reprint, retitled *Mizora: A Prophecy: A Mss. Found among the Private Papers of the Princess Vera Zarovitch, being a true and faithful account of her journey to the interior of the earth, with a careful description of the country and its inhabitants, their customs, manners and government*, New York: G. W. Dillingham, 1889. Reprint, Boston: Gregg Press, G. K. Hall, 1975.

Vera Zarovitch, a Russian princess, escapes from a Siberian prison. After a series of brief adventures, she arrives in Mizora, a feminist utopia situated near the North Pole. Mizora is an all-female Eden created by the "Great Mother," Nature; it is consecrated to Science, "the goddess who has led *us* out of . . . wretchedness." Technology is advanced, and education is the society's major concern. Men, considered the source of all evil, have been extinct for three thousand years, allowed to "die out" (along with disease, war, and poverty) when women learned the secret of life. Masculine characteristics in women have been gradually eliminated, through eugenics and environmental control, and the result is a race of healthy, blond, Aryan women, living in single families and presumably celibate. Government is a democratic meritocracy, an enlightened hierarchy of intellect and moral tone.

1881   [Twing, Carolinn E[dna] S[kinner]. *Experiences of Samuel Bowles, Late Editor of the Springfield (Mass.) Republican in Spirit Life; or, Life As He Now Sees It from a Spiritual Standpoint.* Springfield, Mass.: Star.

     According to the late Mr. Bowles, heaven is remarkably mundane: Spiritual Congresses, composed of elected officials, oversee the welfare of the various heavenly nations; heavenly churches, places of amusement, and schools abound (education is compulsory for child-spirits); homes, furnished much like those on Earth, are surrounded by the spirits of flowers and trees and are designed to match individual taste (although each dwelling's level of beauty is in keeping with the spiritual enlightenment of the owner). Celestial chic is also determined by one's spiritual capital: those lowest on the scale wear "the plainest garb"; more enlightened spirits are "gorgeously clothed."

1882   Linton, E[lizabeth] Lynn. *The True History of Joshua Davidson, Communist.* New York: R. Worthington. 2d ed., retitled *The Life of Joshua Davidson; or, The Modern Imitation of Christ: A Theoretical Novel,* New York: R. Worthington.

     Led by young Joshua Davidson, a group of young men attempt to follow the teachings and example of Christ, engaging in a form of primitive communism and striving to help those "men and women of what the world calls the worst kind." The plot and characters roughly parallel the New Testament: Davidson's apostolic gospel is shouted down as communism, and he is martyred when a mob tramples and kicks him to death.

     [Wood, J., Mrs.]. *Pantaletta: A Romance of Sheheland.* New York: American News.

     In this dystopian, misogynistic, sex-role reversal satire, General Icarus Byron Gullible searches for the North Pole and accidentally discovers Sheheland and the Republic of Petticotia—a society that, because of the granting of equal rights to women, is now composed of effete, enslaved males (Heshes) and dominant females (Shehes) who smoke, drink, and secretly hunger for the attentions of an old-fashioned, "manly" man. Gullible is first arrested as a spy, but, thanks to his machismo and the longings of the man-hungry females, he eventually reinstates the "natural" order of things.

1883   Phelps [Ward], Elizabeth Stuart. *Beyond the Gates.* Boston: Houghton Mifflin.

     This heaven-as-utopia dream vision presents a woman's account of her visit to Paradise during a severe illness—an account that eerily prefigures the out-of-body experiences reported by modern survivors of legally dead status. In her reverie, the narrator first encounters deceased friends and relatives and then is drawn through space to a wooded garden where birds sing hymns. She sees and is blessed by God but is forced to return to Earth. When she awakes, her physician assures her that she will live, and her brother wonders why she looks "so disappointed."

1884   Webster, [Julia] Augusta Davies. *Daffodil and the Croaxaxicans: a Romance of History.* London: Macmillan.

In this fantasy, reminiscent of Carroll's *Alice in Wonderland* (1865), a young girl discovers the underground kingdom of the Croaxaxicans, a race of over-sized frogs ruled by a sleepy king and a vain queen obsessed with fashion, political machination, and social rank. Although the frogs and "frogesses" spend most of their time singing, dancing, and engaging in theatrical "hop-pades," there is a certain oppressive quality to this rather totalitarian society: anticipating Orwell's *1984*, the frogs are subject to capital punishment for even minor crimes and, after their executions, become nonentities who are quietly written out of history.

1885   Campbell, Helen Stuart. "Mrs. Herndon's Income." *Christian Union.* Reprint, Boston: Roberts, 1886.

After the disappearance of her husband, Margaret Herndon finds herself in possession of a substantial fortune. She uses it to help transform the Ulti-mates, a group of intellectual and artistic dilettantes, into a philanthropic unit, which rejects large-scale charities such as missionary establishments and orphan asylums in favor of "individual action for each individual" in need.

Shelhamer, Miss M[ary] T[heresa]. *Life and Labor in the Spirit World, Being a Description of the Localities, Employments, Surroundings, and Conditions in the Spheres.* Boston: Colby and Rich.

The spirit of young Katie Kinsey, speaking through Miss Shelhamer, de-scribes in considerable detail the utopian kingdom of Heaven. It is a bustling, cooperative society, a "Summer-Land" free of sexism, racism, strife, and, of course, death, a place of education, peace, and spiritual development. The inhabitants of the afterworld are devoted to "the amelioration of suffering on earth, as well as . . . the elevation of lowly, undeveloped beings in the spirit world."

1886   Campbell, Helen [Stuart]. *Miss Melinda's Opportunity.* Boston: Roberts.

Miss Melinda is an elderly spinster who has lived under the domineering influence of her older sister, Matilda. When Matilda dies, the lonely Melinda takes an interest in the plight of several young shopgirls and helps them to rent a house and establish a highly successful cooperative, the Working-Women's Guild.

Phelps [Ward], Elizabeth Stuart. *Burglars in Paradise.* Boston: Houghton Mifflin.

In this sequel to *An Old Maid's Paradise* (1879), the spinster Corona returns to her feminine Eden and attempts to defend it against a series of male intruders: burglars who pilfer a hatchet and knife, horse traders who hawk a bewildering variety of disreputable equines, a "cracksman" who steals a bond, and a parade of policemen and detectives who seek to retrieve it. Finally, however, the fortifications of her paradise are breached by a former suitor, now a widower who wishes to be Corona's friend and companion. Adam was given such a companion; one wonders if Corona's male Eve will precipitate a second Fall.

W[aterhouse], E[lizabeth]. *The Brotherhood of Rest*. Reading, England: E. Langley, Lovejoy's Library.

In this borderline utopia, a physician prescribes "Change, Rest and Happiness" for an overworked lawyer and sends him to an isolated monastic community. Here, wearing simple clothes and eating simple foods, his occupations are limited to light literature, music, walks in the woods, pleasant conversation, and gardening. Restored by the peace and tranquillity of his surroundings, he eventually returns to work refreshed and renewed.

1887   Blake, Lillie Devereux. "A Divided Republic: An Allegory of the Future." *Phrenological Journal and Science of Health* 84, no. 2:76–78; no. 3:139–42. Reprint, in *A Daring Experiment and Other Stories*, 346–60; New York: Lovell, Coryell, 1892.

New England women, disgusted by the "ancient customs which oppress" them, abandon the East Coast and form a feminine republic in the state of Washington. The abandoned men gradually become "unshaven, and slouchy"; homes become dilapidated; churches serve as gambling saloons. The women's republic, making full use of female architects, plumbers, and the like, is a place of absolute order—no dirt, poverty, or jails. Finally, the men seek a truce, offering female suffrage, equal pay, and equal work. The women return home.

Dieudonné, Florence [Lucinda] Carpenter. *Rondah; or, Thirty-Three Years in a Star*. Philadelphia: T. B. Peterson.

Clearly patterned after the novels of H. Rider Haggard, this adventure/romance/borderline utopia tells of Parzelia, a small planet inhabited by winged vegetable-people who grow from pods. Their existence is fairly idyllic (they have no envy, hate, anger, treachery—indeed, no sin of any sort) until four terrestrials invade the place. The leader, Regan, assumes control of the island and proceeds to introduce money, religion, writing, and culture. In an attempt to control his subjects more fully, he engages in brutal "experiments," such as cutting off their wings. It is only with the arrival of a fifth earthling, the highly spiritual and moral title heroine, that harmony is restored.

Dodd, Anna Bowman [Blake]. *The Republic of the Future; or, Socialism a Reality*. New York: Cassell. Reprint, New York: Irvington, 1968.

This epistolary antisocialist dystopia records the observations of Wolfgang, a Swede who visits America in the winter of 2050. New York has become a socialistic city. Schools are state controlled; traditional religious and family values have been destroyed. Romance is seen as a casualty of equality, since "husband and wife are in reality two men having equal rights, with the same range of occupation, the same duties as citizens to perform, the same haunts and the same dreary leisure." The society's advances—war and poverty have been abolished, and technological improvements have led to a two-hour workday—seem to be outweighed by its regimentation and lack of excitement.

Phelps [Ward], Elizabeth Stuart. *The Gates Between.* Boston: Houghton.

Esmarald Thorne, an impatient, rather insensitive man of science, dies in an accident. After death, he first wanders the earth, miserable and alone, and then ascends to a heavenly plane. There, entrusted with the care of his recently deceased infant son, he learns humanity and devotion and is eventually reunited with his beloved wife.

W[aterhouse], E[lizabeth]. *The Island of Anarchy: A Fragment of History in the 20th Century.* Reading, England: Miss Langley, Lovejoy's Library.

Dangerous anarchists and revolutionaries are transported to an island. Although the majority engage in vice and quarreling, a few find salvation through their conversion to Christianity.

1888   Clapperton, J[ane] H[ume]. *Margaret Dunmore; or, A Socialist Home.* London: Swan, Sonnenschein, Lowrey.

A wealthy young woman establishes a socialist commune, providing a home for many people who would otherwise suffer. Conflicts that arise from old-fashioned ideas about property and privacy are overcome; the community is a success. Traditional gender roles predominate.

Cruger, Mary. *How She Did It; or, Comfort on $150 a Year.* New York: D. Appleton.

This do-it-yourself utopia relates the tale of Faith Arden, who, despite the warnings of her friends, determines to survive on less than $300 a year. Hard work, economical housekeeping, imaginative invention, and unflagging good cheer (along with painfully detailed bookkeeping) enable her to build a snug home and turn a "lonely, dreary spot" into "a very Eden of beauty and bloom"—and come in considerably under budget.

[Oliphant, Margaret Wilson]. *The Land of Darkness, Along with Some Further Chapters in the Experiences of the Little Pilgrim.* London: Macmillan.

The author's wandering protagonist encounters the dystopian horrors of hell and eutopian blessings of heaven.

1889   Corbett [Elizabeth Burgoyne], George, Mrs. *New Amazonia: A Foretaste of the Future.* London: Tower.

In a socialistic land of peace and vegetarianism, capable and intelligent women have assumed the responsibility of government. The resulting society, while a bit severe (improvement is brought about through strict moral laws, eugenics, and censorship of any dissenting ideas), is presented as vastly superior to that of nineteenth-century London.

Ford, Mary H. "A Feminine Iconoclast." *Nationalist,* November, 252–57.

In a critique of Edward Bellamy's *Looking Backward,* two young women aboard a streetcar discuss the annoying paternalism implied by Bellamy's Nationalist sexual separatism. Bellamy's banner, they agree, is a double standard that permits men to rule the world and expects women to be satisfied with only a modicum of self-determination.

Mason, Eveleen Laura [Knaggs]. *Hiero-Salem: The Vision of Peace.* Boston: J. G. Cupples.

Mason's epigraph is Coleridge's "The truth is, a great *mind* must be androgynous." Althea Eloi and Daniel Heem join their lives (and last names) and form the Eloiheem Commonwealth, a spiritual community that attempts to abolish inequities of sex, class, and race. Althea is the "father-mother," the breadwinner; Daniel is the "mother-father" who cares for the home and children.

Mead, Lucia True [Ames]. *Memoirs of a Millionaire.* Boston: Houghton Mifflin.

Young, devout, and idealistic Mildred Brewster inherits thirty million dollars from a former suitor and establishes a Christian Missionary Fund to help the downtrodden people of the earth, promote Christianity, and diminish slavery and alcohol usage. She sends out male and female missionaries; both sexes preach and administer the sacraments and receive equal pay. In America, Brewster's millions help to establish reading rooms and circulating libraries and provide model homes for workers. She eventually marries, journeys to Europe for her honeymoon, and (like radical feminist Margaret Fuller) is drowned at sea. Her story, narrated by her companion-chaperon, is told through a collage of letters, diary extracts, and newspaper clippings.

[Woods, Katherine Pearson]. *Metzerott, Shoemaker.* New York: Thomas Y. Crowell.

In the poor quarter of the city of Micklegard, the shoemaker Karl Metzerott, "Socialist bred and Socialist born," learns to reconcile communism and Christianity. He helps his neighbors form Prices, a Christian socialist urban commune. Despite the antagonism of the wealthy classes (ranging from snobbery to murderous violence) and a series of disastrous misfortunes, the group continues and eventually succeeds, thanks in part to the sacrifice of Metzerott's Christlike son, Louis. The plot revolves around the actions of the male characters: women are relegated to secondary roles as spoiled but goodhearted children, hardworking housewives, or simple, elderly spinsters.

189? Bevington, L[ouisa] S[arah]. *Common-Sense Country.* Liberty Pamphlets. London: James Tochatti, Liberty Press.

This anarchist socialist view of humanity as essentially good asserts that if society were run according to obvious natural laws, people would live in perfect freedom and revert to the basic decency of human nature.

1890   Curtis, Pauline Carsten. "In the Year '26." *Overland Monthly* 15 (June): 640–59.

As the year 2025 draws to a close, Juliana West (the orphaned daughter of Edith Leete and Julian West of Bellamy's *Looking Backward*) goes to live with her relatives, the Davenports. Roger Davenport, apparently an example of the Nationalist ideal, shows her the weaknesses inherent in Bellamy's scheme: laws forbidding the accumulation of private property are far too easily circumvented; lazy people readily manage to dodge their fair share of work; human nature inexorably draws people toward competition and the satisfaction of their baser appetites (Davenport eventually abandons his family and absconds to Europe with a mistress). Crushed by these revelations, Juliana nonetheless vows to continue to uphold her idealistic Nationalistic principles.

Dixie, Florence, Lady [Caroline Douglas]. *Gloriana; or, The Revolution of 1900*. London: Henry; New York: Standard.

Young Gloriana de Lara, realizing the disadvantages of womanhood, masquerades as Hector D'Estrange. She outperforms her male comrades at everything: gives a sound "drubbing" to a "big, overgrown monster" of a bully, takes high honors at Eton and Oxford, and rides all six winners in a race meet. After gaining a seat in Parliament, she is instrumental in enfranchising women and establishes an enormous Hall of Liberty, where women are trained to achieve physical and mental excellence. Murder and a melodramatic romance follow; Gloriana is triumphant.

[Knox], Adeline Trafton. *Dorothy's Experience*. Boston: Lee and Shepard.

Dorothy Drake, a teacher plagued by religious doubts, resolves them through practical Christianity. She establishes a cooperative home for young working women, where they can receive physical and spiritual comfort.

Pittock, M. A. [Weeks], Mrs. *The God of Civilization: A Romance*. Chicago: Eureka.

This romantic adventure tale describes a South Seas utopia, free of the customs and inhibitions of civilization, inhabited by physically attractive, sensual children of nature. A group of shipwrecked Californians is stranded on the island of Kaahlanai, and several are won over to its natural beauty and uncomplicated way of life. They intermarry and adopt native customs: several choose to remain on the island even when the opportunity to go home arises; others go back to San Francisco briefly but eventually return. Of particular interest are the natives' marital customs: women choose their husbands, and the men are put to death if they refuse; marital vows must be renewed yearly or the union is dissolved. The royal line is matrilineal; the religion is "sincerity, purity and love."

Schreiner, Olive. "Three Dreams in the Desert." In *Dreams*, 65–85. London: Unwin.

In three allegorical dream visions, the narrator first portrays man and woman as two great beasts of burden yoked together and stretched on the sand, then explores the sacrifices women must make to reach the Land of Freedom, and finally describes a future heaven on earth peopled by "brave women and brave men, hand in hand."

Stone, C. H., Mrs. *One of "Berrian's" Novels*. New York: Welch, Fracker.

In Edward Bellamy's *Looking Backward* (1888), Dr. Leete mentions in passing the work of Berrian, a twentieth-century novelist. Stone's romance, set in St. Louis in 1997, purports to be an example of Berrian's work. The plot loosely follows Bellamy's own: a most Victorian young man, hopelessly out of step with his age, attempts to win a modern young woman—although Berrian's heroine, like Bellamy's Edith Leete, accepts traditional gender roles and seems rather Victorian in her own right. In this novel, however, the heroine rejects her anachronistic suitor in favor of a more modern mate, who champions the Nationalistic principles of the Industrial Army.

1891   [Bartlett, Alice Elinor Bowen] Birch Arnold [pseud.]. *A New Aristocracy*. New York: Bartlett.

Three orphans, armed with little more than pluck, good cheer, and Christian values, support themselves and found several small inner-city organizations devoted to self-improvement. Their noble works (and the charms of one of the sisters) draw the attention of a wealthy young man, who finances Idlewild, a model factory. The "new aristocracy" is one of "heart and brain": the protagonists are not only intelligent and aesthetically sensitive, but also unflaggingly loyal, cheerful, brave, and honest—and bound to traditional gender roles.

Fitch, Thomas, and Anna M. Fitch. *Better Days; or, A Millionaire of To-morrow*. San Francisco: Better Days.

David Morning discovers an incredibly rich gold mine and uses the profits to increase the supply of money, develop peace-keeping weapons, and purchase lower Manhattan, where he establishes a community for the "relief of married men." The modernized housing includes such technological innovations as electricity, air conditioning, and pneumatic tubes, as well as improved kitchens for the "relief of women." Anti-Semitic, anti–Native American, and antifeminist, the text's portrayal of women is especially unflattering: Ellen Thornton, the heroine, is a foolish girl who rejects Morning, marries a German baron, and spends most of the novel regretting it; Murella Gonzales, Ellen's rival, is a passionate, stupid, spiteful young woman given to hysterical fits of jealous passion.

Freeman, Ruth Ellis. "Tales of a Great-Grandmother." *New Nation* 1 (15 August, 5 September, 3 October): 458–60, 505–7, 569–77.

This response to Bellamy's *Looking Backward* (1888) provides a fictional twentieth-century retrospective of the nineteenth, focusing on how the changes brought about by Nationalism have particularly benefited women, and anticipates technological and social change that will continue to improve their situation.

Henley, Carra Depuy. *A Man from Mars*. Los Angeles: B. R. Baumgardt.

Professor William Darlington suffers a head injury that enables him to make a series of out-of-body excursions, culminating in a passage to Mars. An arcadian paradise devoted to learning and philosophy, Mars is populated by the souls of deceased terrestrials. No mention is made of gender roles (although it is "the knowledge of men" that is enlarged), and the only references to supernatural forces are passing allusions to "the gods of music" and Daphne's groves.

Larcom, Lucy. *As It Is in Heaven*. Boston: Houghton, Mifflin.

If humanity would only accept the teachings of Christ completely—if people would realize that God's will must be done on Earth, as it is in heaven—then Earth could become a paradise in its own right.

McGlasson [Brodhead], Eva Wilder. *Diana's Livery*. New York: Harper and Brothers.

Despite the lofty ideals of its well-intentioned members, a Kentucky Shaker community is doomed to failure by its harsh restrictions on love and sexual activity. The novel, presented through the eyes of a "worldling" outsider in love with a Shaker girl, details the gradual breakdown of the commune as members react to their enforced celibacy: some turn to alcohol, others to suicide. The most fortunate leave the community and return to traditional marital and family relationships.

Yourell, Agnes Bond. *A Manless World*. New York: G. W. Dillingham.

This nasty little novelette seasons the "doomed humanity" theme of Mary Wollstonecraft Shelley's *The Last Man* (1826) with an unhealthy dollop of racism. A nightmare vision, it portrays nature as mankind's enemy, emitting poisonous gases that render humans unable to procreate. The last generation of mankind sinks gradually into anarchy, mass starvation, and suicide. The central section of the text is a chilling preholocaust vision: a vicious anti-Semitic diatribe that attempts to justify the mass slaughter of the Jewish people on the grounds that they are somehow responsible for the catastrophe. Eventually, the last human being, a selfish, spiteful Jewess who has escaped the pogroms, commits suicide. Traditional gender roles are upheld throughout, although a few men and women transcend gender and, once "animal desire" is eliminated, find "true spiritual affinity" in a "union of souls."

1892   Harbert, Elizabeth Boynton. "*Amore*." Chicago: New Era. Also published as by Lizzie Boynton Harbert; New York: Lovell, Gestefeld.

Led by the precocious and strong-minded (but always impeccably womanly and spiritual) Theodora Dwight, three young women form the Triangle Club, an organization devoted to the idea that God's love is in all things, and that "evil" is nothing more than a human failure to perceive the positive aspects of a given situation. When, for example, an innocent young woman is raped, the apparent catastrophe changes her from a superficial, flighty novel reader into a devoted and loving mother; her attacker undergoes a similar transformation. Home, and the implied "triangle" of mother, father, and child, is presented as the place wherein such ideas can be best taught.

[Hearn, Mary Ann]. Marianne Farningham [pseud.]. *Nineteen Hundred? A Forecast and a Story.* London: James Clarke.

Headed by the emblematically named Arthur Knight, a group of young Christian activists form a model factory community in Wales and work for ameliorated living conditions for the poor. Aided by "young Crusader" movements throughout Britain, the group acquires enough support to head a majority in Parliament. England is gradually re-formed into a perfect Christian state, free of sects and faction, and leads the world into a new age of justice and peace. Traditional gender roles prevail.

[Moore, M. Louise] An Untrammeled Freethinker [pseud.]. *Al-Modad; or, Life Scenes beyond the Polar Circumflex, a Religio-Scientific Solution of the Problems of Present and Future Life.* Shell Bank, Cameron Parish, La.: M. L. Moore and M. Beauchamp.

The fictional 1879 diary of Al-Modad Moetaend details his experiences at the earth's core, deep beneath the North Pole. He encounters an Edenic world, inhabited by a communal, technologically advanced society stressing education, sexual equality, and sexual freedom. The citizens worship the androgynous deity Lo, a being who inspires goodness, simplicity, and vegetarianism.

Tincker, Mary Agnes. *San Salvador.* Boston: Houghton Mifflin.

The orphan Tacita discovers, hidden in a remote, mountainous area of Italy, San Salvador, "the long-lost garden of Eden," a multilingual Christian community whose educated, intelligent, and humane populace sends out missionaries to seek the spiritually and physically needy. Christ is worshiped as the ultimate king, and the Dylar (a hereditary prince) governs the community, aided by a council of elders. Women have a minor role in government and are well educated, but gender roles remain conservative: most women remain home and tend their children, for "the mother of children is the mother of the state"; Iona, a particularly gifted astronomer, has traveled and studied so extensively that she teaches "even in the boys' school."

1893   Bramston, M[ary]. "The Island of Progress." In *The Wild Lass of Estmere and Other Stories,* 227–74. London: Seeley.

While in a coma resulting from a train accident, Dorothea Hollis has a nightmare vision of a twenty-fifth-century island whose inhabitants are devoted to science and technology. It seems a pleasant enough spot at first: there is no disease, poverty, or overwork; education is available to all; and high-tech inventions free the inhabitants of any discomfort. Yet the island is a prison for those with imagination and faith: art, literature, and history are forbidden pursuits; scientific principles have replaced religion. "Extinguishers" eliminate the old and weak, and rebels who believe in the immortality of the soul face imprisonment and torture. Traditional gender roles prevail.

[Jones, Alice Ilgenfritz, and Ella Merchant] Two Women of the West [pseud.]. *Unveiling a Parallel: A Romance*. Boston: Arena. Reprint, New York: Gregg, 1975. Reprint, ed. Carol Kolmerten, Syracuse University Press, 1992.

In a satirical utopia pointing out women's unequal status, an Earth man visits two "Marsian" societies—one secular, one spiritual. In the first, he meets the beautiful, intelligent Elodia, a typical denizen of her single-standard society. Elodia drinks, smokes, and enjoys her bachelor status; active politically, economically, and sexually, she votes, works as a financier, and has affairs (not to mention an illegitimate daughter). Members of the second society are far more spiritual, although likewise egalitarian. They live high in the mountains and devote themselves to the promotion of the good in human nature. Since generosity and mutual respect reign, no laws are needed, and no one is left to live in poverty. Of particular interest is the Marsian creation myth, which eliminates the complications of ribs, apples, and serpents in favor of simple equality: two beautiful and innocent animals, "male and female, sprang simultaneously from an enchanted lake . . . God breathed a soul into them and they were Man and Woman, equals in all things."

Winslow, Helen M[aria]. *Salome Shepard, Reformer*. Boston: Arena.

Faced with factory strikes and distressed by the living conditions of millworkers, Salome Shepard, an idealistic young heiress, defies convention and takes control of the cotton mill she has inherited. Guided by her Christian principles, she initiates dramatic improvements in her employees' living, working, and economic conditions: modern homes are constructed; factory lighting, ventilation, and technology are brought up to date; profit-sharing programs are established. The company flourishes, but the novel ends traditionally: Salome marries her assistant, John Villard, and relinquishes ownership and control of the mill to him.

1894   Knapp, Adeline. "One Thousand Dollars a Day: A Financial Experiment." In *One Thousand Dollars a Day: Studies in Practical Economics*, 11–41. Boston: Arena.

When the profits from the incredibly rich Golconda silver mines are distributed to every adult in America, everyone is wealthy enough to quit working—and does. Shortages are immediate, and money becomes worthless. The resulting crisis is overcome by a barter system, a voluntary labor exchange that provides desperately needed services. Capitalists and politicians are in a bit of a bind until they acquire some useful skills, but the story ends happily, as labor is recognized as the true wealth of the country.

Waisbrooker, Lois [Nichols]. *A Sex Revolution*. Topeka, Kan.: Independent. Reprint, ed. Pam McAllister; Philadelphia: New Society, 1985.

A young widow, whose husband was killed in the Civil War, falls asleep after having read George Noyes Miller's *The Strike of a Sex* (1891), a short novel that details how women achieve total control over their own persons. She has a pacifist dream vision in which women first threaten to die on the battlefield with their husbands unless war is abolished and then assume control of the government. Through eugenic breeding and prenatal influence, they strive to alleviate physical hunger, "heart hunger, soul hunger," and "spiritual starvation."

Waisbrooker, Lois [Nichols]. *The Wherefore Investigating Company*. Topeka, Kan.: Independent.

After suffering the inequities of the American legal system in a variety of forms—slavery, government betrayal of homesteaders, inheritance law, and so forth—a group of people found a community where no individual is permitted to own more than forty acres. Homeless people from around the country are drawn to the society, which centers around a school devoted to teaching principles of justice.

1895   Mears, A[melia] Garland. *Mercia, the Astronomer Royal: A Romance*. London: Simpkin, Marshall, Hamilton, Kent.

In this romance set in the year 2002, the world is a relatively peaceful place, divided into a few monarchies; war has been abolished; education, art, and industry thrive; women have achieved both social and political equality. The astronomer Mercia is loved by three men: the lecherous king who employs her; the loyal scientist who assists her in her work; and a mysterious mystical swami. After a great deal of melodramatic adventure, culminating in a courtroom battle, the novel ends rather ambiguously, from a feminist standpoint: Mercia abandons her profession to marry the swami and help him rule India.

[Sherwood, Margaret Pollack] Elizabeth Hastings [pseud.]. *An Experiment in Altruism*. New York: Macmillan.

A female narrator explores the politics of charity—the "machinery of clubs and organizations" that seeks mechanically to ameliorate (while distancing themselves from) the lives of the poor. Two women, a gifted female physician and a "rescue worker" who seeks to reclaim prostitutes, are presented especially sympathetically: both advocate and practice a "closer sympathy" in human relations.

Von Swartwout, Janet. *Heads; or, The City of Gods: A Narrative of Olombia in the Wilderness*. New York: Olombia.

Aurora Om writes a journal detailing her experiences in the Olombia camp, a militantly peaceful community in the Adirondacks that opposes the "infernal laws, systems, customs, policies and money competition of the Nineteenth Century." The text, supported by a liberal use of biblical quotations (they compose nearly half the book), asserts that God is a dual being, "the Father and Mother lost in androgynous oneness."

1896   [Ames, Eleanor Maria Easterbrook] Eleanor Kirk [pseud.]. *Libra: An Astrological Romance*. Brooklyn: E. Kirk.

This rather quirky blend of astrology, Christianity, spiritualism, and feminism traces the rocky engagement of Elizabeth "Libra" Eastman and Richard "Capricorn" Winterhead. Libra is a strong-willed young woman who questions the subordinate role she must assume if she marries. Ultimately, she refuses not only Mr. Winterhead but the entire marital state and finds herself "free, FREE, FREE, mistress of myself forever and ever. Amen." While not really a utopian novel, *Libra* nonetheless presents a free-spirited, independent heroine who shares the values of many nineteenth-century utopiennes.

Burnham, Elcy. *Modern Fairyland*. Boston: Arena.

In this children's fantasy, a benevolent, socially conscious but rather overbearing princess decides to modernize a community of carefree fairies. She institutes a series of forward-looking programs: the reluctant sprites are clothed, given worthwhile employment, and provided with the latest in modern technology. Eventually, the fairies come to see the advantages of progress and accept its benefits.

Glyn, [Alice] Coralie. *A Woman of Tomorrow: A Tale of the Twentieth Century*. [London]: Women's Printing Society.

Although this text went through two editions, Lyman Tower Sargent has been able to locate only a single copy in a private London collection. As far as I can determine, the narrative relates the history of a young woman who is buried in 1896 and awakens a century later in a eutopia ruled by women.

1897   [Colburn], Mrs. Frona Eunice Wait [Smith]. *Yermah the Dorado: The Story of a Lost Race*. San Francisco: William Doxey. Reprint, London: B. F. Stevens and Brown, 1913.

Yermah, "the Ideal Man of all time," is a blond, blue-eyed Aryan who must leave his home in Atlantis to do a year-long service in a California colony. A considerable portion of the book is a detailed explication of the beliefs of his highly religious society, an amalgam of Brahminism, Buddhism, alchemy, paganism, astrology, and Christianity. Man is seen as evolving to a higher level through study and reincarnation; eventually, the sexes will unite into spiritually perfect beings. "The first Tree of Life was . . . [a] symbol of reproduction—the Universal Mother," and "Adam driven from Paradise typifies the newly separated race—our own—which has abused and degraded the mystery of physical life into a degree of brutality lower than [that of] the animal kingdom." Traditional gender roles predominate, although both sexes study art, music, and oratory, and women serve as priestesses.

Graul, Rosa. *Hilda's Home*. Serialized in *Lucifer, the Light Bearer*, 1897–1903, nos. 641–86.[2] Reprint, retitled *Hilda's Home: A Story of Woman's Emancipation*, Chicago: M. Harmon, ca. 1899. Reprint, Westport, Conn.: Greenwood, n.d.

A young woman's dream of a society devoted to love, liberty, and learning becomes a reality when financed by a millionaire. The Hunter Co-operative Home houses a socialist community that gives women complete equality and frees them from the constrictions of marriage and "enforced motherhood."

Orpen, [Adela Elizabeth Rogers], Mrs. *Perfection City*. New York: D. Appleton; London: Hutchinson.

In this racist attack on communism and feminism, a dainty Eastern newlywed, Olive Weston, comes to the socialist commune of Perfection City, Kansas, with her husband, Ezra. The small community, set in a harsh, bleak, prairie landscape, is the creation of the domineering, manipulative Mme. Morozoff-Smith. It is doomed to failure by the pettiness and jealousies of such inhabitants as Sister Mary Winkle, a lazy, irresponsible, harebrained radical feminist, who sports exaggerated Zouave trousers (which are forever getting in her way) and rears an awkward, androgynous daughter.

1898   [Clarke, Frances H.] Zebina Forbush [pseud.]. *The Co-opolitan: A Story of the Co-operative Commonwealth of Idaho.* Chicago: Charles H. Kerr. Reprint (facsimile ed.), New York: AMS, 1980.

These memoirs of "Senator Braden" detail the establishment of Co-opolis, a cooperative utopia in Idaho. Over a twenty-year period, the society assumes first political, then economic, control of the state. There is some protest by the local non-Co-opolitans: "humanity," after all, "when once it accepts a system, whether good or bad, is loath to abandon it." Capitalists ruined by the utopian community's highly efficient production techniques are among the noisiest protesters. Eventually, however, the Co-opolitans gain control of several western states, extend their interests throughout America, and ship propaganda (in the form of a utopian novel written by the narrator's wife) throughout the world. The society, largely based on Bellamy's *Looking Backward*, enfranchises women and offers them some limited roles in government; however, most "women's work" remains confined to the domestic sphere.

Mason, Eveleen Laura [Knaggs]. *An Episode in the Doings of the Dualized.* Boston: Press of Fish and Libby; Brookline, Mass.: E. L. Mason.

This sequel to Mason's 1889 *Hiero-Salem* describes God as an androgynous being, the "self-unioned one," and predicts a coming "Woman Age" when "men will scale Alpine heights of purity, wisdom and wealth, for the love of the womanhood there, the eternal feminine in Deity."

Springer, Rebecca Ruter. *Intra Muros.* Elgin, Ill.: David C. Cook. 2d [?] expanded ed., bound with David C. Cook's "Jesus the Resurrection Now; or, Our Loved Ones Given Back to Us Here"; Elgin, Ill.: David C. Cook, n.d.

At times, Mrs. Springer's account of her dream visit to heaven reads more like an *Architectural Digest* article than a religious tract: "within the walls" of paradise there are indeed many mansions—all relentlessly decorated and described in minute detail. Most of the remaining text is given over to the author's reunions with myriad deceased relatives and friends. The text is elitist and racist; only upper-middle-class Anglo-Saxons seem to go directly to heaven; those with "dusky faces," whose "poor," "unenlightened" minds "have much to learn" must wait on the fringes of New Jerusalem until the soul of a late (Anglo-Saxon) missionary "leads them higher and higher into the blessed life." Education is stressed: every house has its own extensive library, and well-filled lecture halls feature speakers such as Martin Luther and John Wesley.

1899   Adolph, Anna, Mrs. *Arqtiq: A Study of the Marvels at the North Pole.* Hanford, Calif.: The author.

In a rather surrealistic dream vision, a California woman invents a balloonship-coach and voyages to the North Pole. There, she discovers Arc, a high-tech utopia inhabited by ideal people who enjoy complete gender equality. As in prelapsarian Eden, birth, marriage, and death do not exist. Education is stressed.

Morgan, Harriet. *The Island Impossible*. Boston: Little, Brown.

In this rather episodic juvenile fantasy, young Jack O'Nory dreams of a wonderful island, on which he and his friends engage in a series of daring exploits. The boys and girls enjoy considerable sexual equality as they jointly conquer evil and overcome boring and foolish adults. Finally, however, their approaching adulthood requires that they leave the island. Although more adventure story than utopia, the tale does offer an enlightened view of young women: the girls are as brave and active as the boys throughout and, even after leaving the island, successfully pursue academic, artistic, and medical careers.

Roberts, Evelyn Harvey. *The Pure Causeway*. Chicago: Charles H. Kerr.

Led by a visionary, devout young woman, a group of young people explore the various aspects of society—anthropology, politics, home and family life, industry, organized religion, and education—and find them all sadly lacking in Christian concern for one's fellow. Using Christ's Sermon on the Mount as a blueprint, they form a communal, cooperative society modeled on that of the early Christians: "we wrong no man, we corrupt no man, we take advantage of no man." The community lives simply, producing only what the members need, which results in short hours and abundant time for educational pursuits and religious observances. Disagreeable work is done on a rotating basis, although women are confined to the domestic sphere.

1900   Mason, Caroline A[twater]. *A Woman of Yesterday*. New York: Doubleday, Page.

Anna Benigna Mallison, a would-be missionary to India, is trapped in a loveless marriage to Keith Burgess, an invalid, and is dominated by her strict mother-in-law. After meeting the evangelical social reformer John Gregory, Anna decides to join Fraternia, his egalitarian Christian commune in North Carolina. The harsh living conditions and Gregory's zealous passions doom the community to failure, and after her husband dies, Anna leaves to teach in India.

Richberg, Eloise O. Randall. *Reinstern*. Cincinnati: The Editor Publishing.

In a dream vision, a woman travels by train (of thought?) to an extraterrestrial society characterized by equality, gentleness, humanity, and education. Particular attention is given to child rearing: adults of both sexes are carefully trained to care for children, and employment does not separate the parents from their children. There is no poverty, no servant class, no private property, and no death—just a "change to the next higher plane of materiality."

1901   Reed, Carmen. *Earth's Empress and Victoria: A Romance of Two Queenly Souls and of a Revolt in Africa against a Benign Government*. Detroit: Ruskin Guild.

Adrian Dreux falls into the ocean and is rescued by the impossibly noble, reasonable, and moral Athanasians, an underwater race of immortals. After undergoing surgery, which makes him immortal as well (the society is technologically advanced), he and the beautiful Empress Esmera promptly fall in love. A series of adventures follow, most notably the revolt of a group of ungrateful Americans who were saved by the sea folk. Dreux (now styled Prince Adrian) returns to England and enlists the aid of the British Army. As the story ends, the revolt is overthrown, Prince Adrian and Esmera are wed, and diplomatic relations are established between the empress and Queen Victoria.

1902   Cooley, Winifred Harper. "A Dream of the Twenty-First Century." *Arena* 28 (November): 511–16.

On the evening of 1 January 1900, a woman dreams of 1 January 2000, when women have been instrumental in reforming the "corrupt, subsidized government" of the nineteenth century. Thanks to the changes brought about by women's suffrage, America's healthy, vigorous population enjoys advanced (although unspecified) technology, five-hour workdays, uncrowded cities, and increased longevity. Since the government owns and controls basic resources and utilities, the slums, sweatshops, and monopolies have been abolished. An emphasis on education has led to complete religious tolerance: the "Religion of Humanity" is Christian, but it "does not fear to inculcate the best that has been worked out by every people that has struggled and suffered and aspired beneath the sun."

Hawkins, May Anderson. *A Wee Lassie; or, A Unique Republic.* Richmond, Va.: Presbyterian Committee of Publication.

Inspired by the deathbed vision of an orphaned girl, and horrified by the condition of delinquent boys interred in prison camps, three young people (two men and a woman) establish the Linwood Miniature Republic, which provides young men with a home, education, and extensive vocational training in the trade of their choice. The institution promotes Christian principles and teaches the boys to avoid the evils of alcohol and tobacco. Students of all ages, from kindergarten up, earn their education by working; even the youngest perform chores suited to their age. A student legislature establishes and enforces the laws of the republic.

1902–3   Dixie, Florence, Lady [Caroline Douglas]. "Isola; or, The Disinherited." *Young Oxford* (September–March). Reprint, London: Leadenhall, n.d.

Dixie's verse play details the unhappy adventures of Isola, queen consort of the planet Erth. The lustful king has killed her beloved and put aside Merani, his own rightful wife, and their son, Vergli. Isola escapes from the king and, masquerading as a man, begins a revolution in Vergli's behalf. Through treachery, she is captured, imprisoned, and sentenced to die. The king, on discovering her true identity, attempts to save her, but his reprieve comes to late, and she dies a martyr to true love and freedom. Repentant, the king restores Merani and Vergli to their rightful positions and enacts laws ensuring equal rights for women. Originally written in 1877, the play contains many of the themes that would be developed more fully in Dixie's *Gloriana; or, The Revolution of 1900* (1895).

1903   Kinkaid, Mary Holland [McNeish]. *Walda: A Novel.* New York: Harper and Brothers.

This revision of Genesis might be subtitled "Paradise Rejected," for it offers a disenchanted review of the patriarchal Eden. In Zanah, a secluded American religious commune that smugly considers itself a prelapsarian paradise, the sexually repressed inhabitants worship a misogynistic Old Testament God, believing that "sin came into the world through a woman, and ever since then the man who would reach heaven hath to guard against the wiles of the temptress." The new Adam is a confused young man who has forgone a career as an artist for the less sinful pursuit of schoolteacher; the new Eve is Walda, a beautiful, intelligent young woman who gradually rejects her society and finally leaves it—ironically, seeking happiness with the new snake, a visiting "man of the world" whom she has come to love.

Weiss, Sara. *Journeys to the Planet Mars.* New York: Bradford.

Guided by spirits, a female medium embarks on a series of out-of-body voyages to Ento, or Mars. Entoan civilization is marked by advanced technology and an enlightened approach to social institutions. There is no poverty, since class privilege has been abolished and everyone works; there is no drunkenness, no jail, no official corruption. Chastity is universal; education is compulsory and available to all. Weiss's detailed descriptions (including an extensive glossary of the language and meticulous sketches of the local flora) indicate that Entoan life is very similar to that of Earth—right down to rather Victorian living rooms crammed with furniture, and women devoted to cooking, housekeeping, and child rearing.

1904   [De Bury, F. Blaze, Mme.] F. Dickbury [pseud.]. *The Storm of London: A Social Rhapsody.* London: John Long.

The unhappy Lord Somerville dreams that all clothing, fabric, and books mysteriously disappear from Britain. Fig leaves seem to have disappeared as well, and England suddenly becomes an enormous nudist colony. Lacking the customary signs of social standing as guidelines, people must judge each other on the basis of individual human worth. There is a gradual return to a pastoral way of life, and, in spite of a few diehard traditionalists, England becomes a prelapsarian Eden.

Gilman, Charlotte Perkins. "The Beauty of a Block." *Independent* 57 (14 July): 67–72.

Gilman's nonfiction essay analyzes the organization of New York city blocks and shows how existing arrangements contribute to the city's "grinding monotony, unbroken ugliness, and crowding." She proposes rearranging them into apartment/hotel complexes (with food and laundry services) surrounding an open recreational space. Such a grouping, she argues, would turn city "pigeon-holes" into airy, well-lighted residences with abundant roof playgrounds, recreational facilities, and attractive parklike courtyards. Residents would benefit physically and intellectually, since amenities such as libraries, music rooms, and lecture halls could also be included in the design.

1905   Crow, Martha Foote. *The World Above: A Dualogue.* Chicago: Blue Sky.

This allegorical view of earth and heaven takes the form of a dialogue between two young lovers who live in the Darker Realm, a dystopian underworld. Their faith and courage enable them to discover a passageway to a "light-crowned city" in the World Above.

Evans, Anna D. *It Beats the Shakers; or, A New Tune.* London and New York: Anglo-American.

In a future society where unwanted female children have simply ceased to be born, the lonely and despairing men convince female Venusians to come live on Earth. The men marry them but then subject them to typical terrestrial abuses and cruelties. The unhappy females' patience is at last exhausted, and they return to Venus with their female children, leaving life on Earth to die out. Eventually, however, the planet renews itself and becomes an earthly paradise, which loving men and women share equally.

Fry, Lena Jane. *Other Worlds: A Story Concerning the Wealth Earned by American Citizens and Showing How It Can Be Secured to Them Instead Of to the Trusts.* Chicago: L. J. Fry.

This "prophecy" is set on the planet Herschel (indistinguishable from turn-of-the-century Earth). Tom Vivian establishes the Colony, a cooperative community that sees labor as the true wealth of a society. Women enjoy financial independence and some participation in government, although their duties are generally limited to the domestic sphere. The community is a meritocracy: industrious and generous men and women are awarded the title "Honorable"; the exceptionally praiseworthy are styled "Prince" or "Princess."

Rogers, Bessie Story. *As It May Be: A Story of the Future.* London: John Long; Boston: Richard G. Badger, Gorham Press.

Young Mary Tillman dies in 1905 and revives ten centuries later. She meets Helen Linden, who introduces her to a heaven on earth. The difficulties of human existence have been overcome: no death, accidents, poverty, illness, violence, bad weather, alcohol, or mosquitoes trouble this world of perfect harmony. Children are now born good, and docile "wild" animals wander the streets in peace. Religion is based on the golden rule rather than the Bible, which was "written by men who expressed their opinions." People communicate through mental telepathy and travel by motorized hang gliders. Women are freed of household drudgery by technology, but traditional gender roles still predominate.

Young, F[lorence] E[thel Mills]. *The War of the Sexes.* London: John Long.

An uneven blend of pacifism, feminism, and sexism, this novel relates the dream of misogynist Geoffrey Sterndale, about to leave England to fight in the Boer War. He dreams of a world centuries in the future, in which men, because of advances in military and parthenogenetic technology, have become nearly extinct: he is the only surviving male in the United Kingdom. While seeking to avoid the hordes of women who pursue him, he is protected by the brilliant young Bertranda Harwood, a man-hating fellow scientist with whom he falls in love. He wakes to find that his dream has been an omen, presaging his actual meeting with and attraction to the real Bertranda Harwood. Love prevails; Sterndale gives up his martial mission in favor of a marital one.

1906   Gale, Zona. *Romance Island.* Indianapolis: Bobbs-Merrill.

This rather silly mystery romance features the requisite stolen jewels, missing persons, evil prince, and plucky heroine. The mysterious island of Yaque shelters a technologically advanced society that has mastered perpetual motion and moves at will from the third to the fourth dimension. The plot hinges on a potion that can age or rejuvenate. Traditional gender roles predominate.

Nesbit [Bland], E[dith]. "The Sorry-Present and the Expelled Little Boy." In *The Story of the Amulet,* 288–318. London: T. Fisher Unwin. Reprint, Harmondsworth, England: Puffin Books, 1959, pp. 217–38.[3] Reprint, in *Five Children and It; The Phoenix and the Carpet; The Story of the Amulet,* 572–90. London: Octopus Books, 1979.

Searching for the missing half of a magic amulet, three children (a girl and two boys) transport themselves to the future. London has become an enormous garden, filled with happy, unworried people who stroll through impeccably clean streets and fish in the crystal-clear Thames. Poverty and homelessness are unknown, since all people contribute their fair share (although women continue to remain in the domestic sphere). Children's lives are particularly altered: their homes are padded and heated by hot-air pipes, so tots can romp without hurting themselves on furniture or burning themselves in a fire; schools allow students to pursue individual interests (naughty children unfortunate enough to be suspended mope about miserably until they are permitted to return).

Wheeler, Mary Sparkes. *As It Is in Heaven.* Philadelphia: Universal Book and Bible House. Also published as by One of the Redeemed [pseud.]; Philadelphia: P. W. Ziegler, 1906.

A chatty, anecdotal presentation of heaven as utopia, the text is full of deathbed scenes and casual racism (those African Americans fortunate enough to ascend to heaven shed both their pigmentation and "colored" dialect). Heaven (at least this branch of heaven—each solar system has its own) is a bustling, middle-class environment: the inhabitants dedicate themselves to education, spiritual improvement (and the resulting heightened social status), and employment. Mental telepathy enables people of all nations and ages to communicate; nineteenth-century folk have long conversations with Neanderthals, who seem to disprove Darwin's theories: prehistoric men and women, the narrator asserts, are "not mere animals, capable of development," but are people created "in the likeness and image of God" who have "intellects just as keen" and "perceptions just as clear, and vivid, as ours."

1907   Gilman, Charlotte Perkins. *A Woman's Utopia*. Chaps. 1–4 serialized in the *Times Magazine* 1 (January–March): 215–20, 369–76, 498–504. Published tearsheets of chap. 4 ("Some Beginnings," 498–504) and proofs of chap. 5 ("City Living," 591–96) are on microfilm (Collection 177, Charlotte Perkins Gilman Papers (1860–1935), box 21, folder 260, "Stories") in the Arthur and Elizabeth Schlesinger Library at Radcliffe College.

   A millionaire with an extremely dim view of humanity makes an unusual wager: irritated by the optimism of a group of would-be reformers, he gives them twenty million dollars and twenty years to see if they can improve society. He then travels throughout Asia and Africa for the next two decades. When he returns, he discovers tremendous changes, the result of not only a new religion based on ethical behavior but also the positioning of women at the center of political activity. New York, for example, has been transformed: the harbor and skies are crystal clear; the slums have been wiped out by urban renewal. Parks and rooftop gardens abound; child care, cooking, and laundry services relieve women of household drudgery and free them to participate fully in society. The narrative raises many issues that Gilman will examine more closely in *Moving the Mountain* (1916): compulsory education for foreign immigrants, for example, and women's power to improve the race by marrying only the best of men. Indeed, given the similarities of focus and plot (a man disappears from the United States for several decades and returns to find wonderful changes), *A Woman's Utopia* may well have been an early version of the later novel.

1908   Gilman, Charlotte Perkins. "Aunt Mary's Pie Plant." *Woman's Home Companion* 6 (June): 14, 48–49.

   A newspaperwoman returns to her hometown—which she remembers as "a rambling, disorderly little town," "narrow-minded," "quiet," "poor," and "slow"—to write an article on the horrors of small-town life. To her amazement, she discovers a modern, bustling, "prancing young Utopia." The change has come about because women recognized that their domestic work had monetary value; by specializing in what they do best and marketing their talents in an organized fashion, they have all increased their personal wealth and self-respect.

[Kingscote, Adelina Georgina Isabel Wolff]. Lucas Cleeve [pseud.]. *A Woman's Aye and Nay*. London: John Long.

   This antifeminist, antisuffrage novel presents women as poorly fitted by nature for the exercise of political power. The well-meaning heroine, blinded by feminine emotion, falls victim to a charming political opportunist. She supports his campaign for a parliamentary seat over that of her admirable (but less charismatic) husband, who loses by one vote.

Martin, Nettie Parrish. *A Pilgrim's Progress in Other Worlds, Recounting the Wonderful Adventures of Ulysum Storries and His Discovery of the Lost Star "Eden."* Boston: Mayhew.

John Bunyan meets sci-fi in this moral allegory/space travel adventure. After inventing a balloon cycle, ne'er-do-well Ulysum Storries thoughtlessly abandons his wife and travels throughout the solar system. Accompanied by such allegorical figures as Reliable and Trust, Storries visits the moon and planets, finding most of them far more advanced than Earth in terms of spiritual development and relations between the sexes. His unsuccessful flirtations with a variety of extraterrestrial females open his eyes to his own failings; he finally returns to Earth, rejoins his ever-patient spouse, and lives as a good Christian and loyal husband.

Nichol, C. A. Scrymsour, Mrs. *The Mystery of the North Pole.* London: Francis Griffiths.

Three young Cambridge men, Messrs. Faith, Hope and Chariton, discover a Christian utopia at the North Pole, peopled by a lost tribe of Israel. The hierarchical, highly organized Polar Church is the central focus of the community. There is an emphasis on the religious education of children, and traditional gender roles prevail.

1909   Bachman [Brokaw], Estella. *The Soul of the World.* Pasadena, Calif.: Equitist.

Utopia frequently makes strange bedfellows, as this novel illustrates. The book champions Henry George's "single tax" crusade, balanced land tenure, interracial marriage, reincarnation and Buddhism, language reform (replacing the indefinite pronoun "he" with "va" [pronounced "vey"]), and the key to all mythologies (based on the "fact" that Earth once had Saturn-like rings). In chapter 5, Glen Harding (a beautiful single-tax proponent and mystic) remembers in some detail her life in a prehistoric "divine world of prismatic glory," a time when the "White Brotherhood" of gods taught humanity all arts, crafts, and language. If humankind would only see the benefit of the single tax and balanced land tenure, Bachman argues, humankind could return to this blessed state of "universal equity, harmony, and friendship."

Clyde, Irene. *Beatrice the Sixteenth.* London: G. Bell and Sons.

A time-traveling female scientist discovers the Amazonian society of Armeria. The members, fierce warriors, skillful hunters, and fine agriculturalists, live in chaste marriages. The community is perpetuated by the adoption of unwanted female children from neighboring barbarian tribes.

Everett, Frances. *John Bull: Socialist.* London: Swan, Sonnenschein.

In this antisocialist dystopia, rather preminiscent of Orwell's *1984,* England has become a socialist state and a very bleak place indeed. Majority rule has become mob rule, and in spite of a hardworking minority, crops fail and epidemics rage. People are the property of the state: at age six children are taken from their parents and placed in Training Homes, where they are prepared to labor at work for which they are frequently temperamentally and physically unsuited. Religion, history, and newspapers are abolished. State officials constantly patrol against would-be emigrants. Women's position is deplorable: little more than state brood mares, they are terrorized by bullying males and relegated to traditional gender roles.

Gilman, Charlotte Perkins. "A Garden of Babies." *Success Magazine* 12 (June): 370–71, 410–11.

When her husband and baby die, Jessie—a women whose maternal instincts are exceptionally strong—is devastated. She turns her attention to other people's children: first her sister's twins, then the children of neighboring friends. The project soon turns into a highly successful full-time child-care facility. The babies are happy and healthy: crying is a rarity, sickness and infant mortality all but unknown. Eventually, Jessie trains other young women to found similar establishments in other towns. One imagines that these will be managed in a similarly genteel fashion, given Gilman's rather elitist and xenophobic tone: the baby garden is "not for working women, of course, but for women we all knew, and who knew us," that is, middle-class women who might otherwise have to leave their children with "a low-class foreigner."

Hamilton, Cicely [Mary], and [Christabel Marshall] Christopher St. John [pseud.]. *How the Vote Was Won.* First performed at the Royalty Theatre, London, 13 April. Chicago: Dramatic Publishing, 1910. Reprint, London: E. Craig, 1913.

This one-act comedy, an economic *Lysistrata,* relates how women, tired of "the foolish superstition that all women are supported by men" and resentful of their status as unrepresented taxpayers, leave their jobs and demand support from their male relations until female suffrage is granted and the importance of women workers acknowledged. The strike is successful.

Wiggin, Kate Douglas [Smith]. *Susanna and Sue.* Boston: Houghton Mifflin.

A Shaker community in Maine becomes a refuge for Susanna Hathaway and her daughter, Sue, who flee Susanna's carousing, womanizing husband. The community is presented sympathetically, although Susanna is uncomfortable with its insistence on celibate relationships, "seemingly outside of and superior to sex." Eventually she realizes her own worth (and needs) and returns home to her husband, who, chastened by her absence, has reformed.

1910   Gilman, Charlotte Perkins. "What Diantha Did." *Forerunner* 1 (November 1909–October 1910). Reprint, New York: Charlton, 1910. Excerpted in *Charlotte Perkins Gilman Reader,* ed. Ann J. Lane, 123–40; New York: Pantheon, 1980.

What Diantha Bell does is establish a House Worker's Union and operate several businesses based on scientific housekeeping. Her cooked food delivery service, restaurant, cafeteria, hotel, and housecleaning service are beneficial in various ways: not only are they highly profitable, they also give the union members pride in their own professionalism and demonstrate that cooperative effort can free women from the monotony of domestic drudgery.

1911   Gilman, Charlotte Perkins. *Moving the Mountain.* Serialized in *Forerunner* 2. Reprint, New York: Charlton, 1911. Reprint, Westport, Conn.: Greenwood, 1968.

Lost in Tibet for thirty years, John Robertson is rescued in 1940 by his sister. He returns to America and discovers a socialist, high-tech society free of sexual discrimination, poverty, disease, and crime. There is an emphasis on education, ecology, and cooperation: children are raised in gardens; the air and water have been cleansed; work is done for communal good. The "old tribal deity of the Hebrews," based on the traditional concept of sin, has been rejected; its replacement is the church of Life and Living, which promotes ethical behavior. Creation is seen as an earthly process of eugenics and environmental control: "we make better people now" is a constant refrain.

Minnett, Cora. *The Day after Tomorrow.* London: F. V. White.

This rather convoluted, melodramatic romance is set in the high-tech, egalitarian society of London in 1975. War, poverty, and unemployment have been abolished: Britannia quite literally rules the world and does so primarily to benefit her own citizens. Spiritualism is the new religion; orthodox Christianity has died out. Traditional gender roles predominate.

1912   Gilman, Charlotte Perkins. "Her Memories." *Forerunner* 3, no. 8 (August): 197–201.

A woman looks back on her happy half century at Home Court, a cooperative apartment community featuring amenities such as communal child care, dining halls and cooked food delivery, lecture halls, recreational facilities, and luxurious rooftop gardens.

Gilman, Charlotte Perkins. "Maidstone Comfort." *Forerunner* 3, no. 9 (September): 225–29.

A wealthy young heiress invests in women—providing funds for girls to attend college and supporting female business ventures. Maidstone Comfort is a summer resort that frees women from domestic drudgery: hot meals are delivered to one's home, and skilled professional housekeepers do the cleaning. The community features colorful, cozy little houses (rather than overwhelming, impersonal hotels), which are fitted neatly into the landscape, rather than imposed upon it.

1913   Gillmore, Inez Haynes. *Angel Island.* New York: Phillips. Reprint, New York: Holt, 1914. Reprint, New York: New American Library, 1988.

In this feminist parable, women quite literally learn the value of standing on their own feet. Five men are shipwrecked on an island inhabited by five elusive flying women. Through a cruel trick, the men capture the women and brutally cut off their wings. Since the women have never used their legs, they are virtually helpless. Marriages take place, and children are born, including a daughter whose wings the men plan to clip when she comes of age. To protect her, the women learn to walk—and run—and then threaten to desert their husbands. Finally, the men accept the women as equals. As the novel ends, a winged male child is born.

Gilman, Charlotte Perkins. "Bee Wise." *Forerunner* 4, no. 7 (July): 169–73.

Margery, the "manager" of a college group of highly intelligent women, inherits ten million dollars and founds two "rational paradise[s]" in California. "Beewise" and "Herways" emphasize craftswomanship and ecology (for instance, electrical and solar power; forestry and land management), universal employment with pleasant working conditions ("small mills, pretty and healthful, with bright-clad women singing at their looms"), health care, and education.

Gilman, Charlotte Perkins. "A Council of War." *Forerunner* 4, no. 8 (August): 197–201.

A group of London women, all veterans of the battle for suffrage, propose an organization that will not only train women to run businesses in key areas (for example, paper mills, printing houses, public lecture halls) but will also financially support the enterprises. Such establishments would be operated humanely, with "proper hours, proper wages," and would be staffed exclusively by women and the "right kind" of men.

1915   Gilman, Charlotte Perkins. *Herland*. Serialized in *Forerunner* 6:12–17, 38–44, 65–72, 94–100, 123–29, 150–55, 181–87, 207–13, 237–43, 265–70, 287–93, 319–25. Reprint, ed. Ann Lane; New York: Pantheon, 1979.

Three American men—a macho chauvinist, a chivalrous romantic, and a reasonable narrator—discover Herland, an all-female, parthenogenic community that worships motherhood. Communal, cooperative, and highly matriotic, the society stresses education and ecological concerns. There is little mention of sex: the macho man unsuccessfully attempts to rape his wife, who thrashes him soundly and turns him over to her sisters for justice; the romantic's wife becomes pregnant, but whether by parthenogenesis or more traditional methods is never made clear; the narrator and his wife share a chaste, brother-sister relationship. The story continues in Gilman's "With Her in Ourland" (1916).

Harrison, Eva. *Wireless Messages from Other Worlds*. London: L. N. Fowler.

A record of the author's communications with other worlds, this text depicts an evolving Earth, whose natural and man-made catastrophes (including World War I) are simply by-products of its evolution away from darkness into spiritual enlightenment.

1916   Albertson, Augusta. *Through Gates of Pearl: A Vision of the Heaven-Life*. New York: Fleming H. Revell.

Albertson's dream vision presents a sort of celestial world's fair. Those who would enter do so in an orderly fashion, proceeding through their appropriate gates: children (including those who were aborted—and presumably unbaptized) through the Children's Gate; martyrs (including women who have sacrificed themselves in unhappy marriages) through the Martyrs' Gate; missionaries through the Ambassadors' Gate, and so forth. Once inside, visitors and residents are free to visit numerous monuments and pavilions, many of which feature educational exhibits, such as the "panorama of history," in which every event since Genesis is shown in a wide-screen, full-color format, or the "Plan of Everyday Life," which explains God's purpose to the curious. Heaven is a feast for sense and soul: wonderful food and drink, exquisite music, and beautiful scents surround the joyous, pure spirits who reside there.

Fisher, Mary A[nn]. *Among the Immortals, in the Land of Desire: a Glimpse of the Beyond.* New York: Shakespeare Press.

Paradise, according to this account, is very much like earth, with its laws, banks, employment, marriage, and division according to nationality and race. The divine Law of Compensation prevails, however, and those who were pockmarked on earth now have the best complexions, the deaf have the best hearing, and so forth. The populace is obsessively concerned with earthly activity and politics; they peer at the world through high-powered telescopes and send thought messages via celestial telephones. Women are rewarded for what they have suffered on earth (a spurned wife receives her husband's eternal devotion), but traditional gender roles survive.

Gilman, Charlotte Perkins. "With Her in Ourland." Serialized in *Forerunner* 7:6–11, 38–44, 67–73, 93–98, 123–28, 152–57, 179–85, 208–13, 237–43, 263–69, 291–97, 318–25. Reprint, Westport, Conn.: Greenwood, 1968.

In this sequel to Gilman's *Herland* (1915), Herlander Ellador travels around the world with her American husband, Vandyck Jennings. She is astonished by the havoc wreaked by patriarchal competition and longs for her own matriarchal, communal society. Finally, the couple returns to live in Herland and eventually produces a son—presumably by conventional methods.

Jones, Lillian B. *Five Generations Hence.* Fort Worth, Tex.: Dotson-Jones.

Since blacks and whites cannot coexist, blacks return to Africa and build a new society with skills learned from white culture. In this utopian vision of a prosperous black African civilization, five generations hence, traditional gender roles predominate.

Shapiro, Anna Ratner. *The Birth of Universal Brotherhood.* Kansas City, Mo.: Burton.

Faced with the spiritual, moral, and financial bankruptcy of their country after a devastating world war, devout young Americans from various walks of life find themselves drawn to the spiritual and physical betterment of their less fortunate countrymen. When one of their number becomes president, he appoints the others to spread peace throughout the world. A foundling boy they have nurtured gradually assumes the role of a latter-day Moses and founds a Christian community of love on a South Seas island. Using various methods, including telepathy, they spread their message throughout the world: all men are brothers. Women are to promote "the best of man's possibilities" and to "[encourage] and [inspire] him to bring this into expression." Women are "not called into the fields of material labor" but to "labor for love."

1917   [Snedeker, Caroline] Caroline Dale Owen [pseud.]. *Seth Way: A Romance of the New Harmony Community.* Boston: Houghton, Mifflin. Excerpted in *Daring to Dream: Utopian Stories by United States Women, 1836–1919,* ed. Carol Farley Kessler. Boston: Pandora, 1984.

Written by the great-granddaughter of socialist Robert Owen, this historical novel provides a sympathetic glimpse of the early New Harmony community, its inhabitants (the celebrated/notorious Frances Wright is a featured character), and its institutions. Of particular interest is the manner in which the book explores gender conflicts and provides resolution: a marriage contract, based on an actual contract written by Robert Dale Owen, enables the husband to renounce "the *unjust rights* which, in virtue of [the wedding] ceremony, an iniquitous law tacitly gives [him] over the person and property of another."

1918   [Bennett, Gertrude Barrows] Francis Stevens [pseud.]. "Friend Island." *All-Story Weekly,* 7 September, pp. 217–23. Reprint, in *Under the Moons of Mars,* ed. Sam Moskowitz, 125–36; New York: Holt Rinehart Winston, 1970.

Set in a future time, after "the stronger sex came into its own, and ousted man from his historic pedestal," this short story details the adventures of a retired female sea captain marooned on what seems to be a precursor of the modern Gaea theory: a living island, which the seawoman names Anita. The two female beings coexist in harmony, but an intruding male upsets the balance.

Bruère, Martha [S.] Bensley. "Mildred Carver, U.S.A.: A Romance of the American Girl of To-Morrow." *Ladies Home Journal* 35–36 (June 1918–February 1919) [each issue paged individually]. Reprint, New York: MacMillan, 1919. Excerpted in *Daring to Dream: Utopian Stories by United States Women, 1836–1919,* ed. Carol Farley Kessler. Boston: Pandora Press, 1984.

In post–World War I America, industries have been nationalized, and all eighteen-year-olds must perform a year-long tour of duty in the National Service. Young men and women of nearly all social and cultural backgrounds (no African Americans appear) are brought together, resulting in a generation that values hard work and eschews the artificial barriers of class and nationality. Mildred Carver, the well-bred daughter of a steel baron, and her equally aristocratic fiancé, Nick Van Arsdale, find their values completely altered during their term of service. Ignoring the objections of their families, who expect the pair to live in a constant whirl of frivolous social engagements, the couple chooses instead useful, rewarding careers: he becomes a road construction engineer, she a worker in her father's mill. Their attitude reflects that of their entire generation of young Americans who eagerly anticipate a new world order.

1919   [Bennett, Gertrude Barrows] Francis Stevens [pseud.]. *The Heads of Cerberus.*
        N.p.: Street and Smith. Reprint, Reading, Pa.: Polaris, 1952.

In this antipacifist, anti-isolationist narrative, four unwilling time travelers from Philadelphia find themselves trapped in a dystopian parallel universe. The alternative Pennsylvania, an isolated city-state, exists in an eternal here and now; no news of outside worlds is permitted to enter, and all history books are locked up and heavily guarded. The punishment for reading forbidden texts (and for virtually any other crime) is death. The rulers are a handful of corrupt and parasitic officials who live in luxury while the populace (anonymous beings identified only by numbers) struggle for survival.

1920   Gilman, Charlotte Perkins. "Applepieville." *Independent* 103 (25 September): 365, 393–95.

Gilman's nonfiction essay proposes a new model for farm village organization: a wheel with a community center (featuring such amenities as parks, playgrounds, bandstands, and swimming pools) at the hub. Surrounding this would be a ring of community buildings: libraries, lecture halls, shops, and hotels. The next ring would be composed of homes, behind which would stretch farms (vegetables and fruits first, then larger crops, then forests). Such an arrangement, she asserts, would help reduce the isolation of farmers—and, more crucially, farmer's wives, who are all too frequently driven by stress and loneliness "from home to grave or insane asylum."

Johnston, Mary [Ann]. *Sweet Rocket.* New York: Harper and Brothers.

Anna Darcy, a "Teacher for long years," visits her ex-pupil Marget Land at Sweet Rocket, a Virginia estate. There, through a series of visions, Darcy learns that all division is an illusion: heaven and earth, past and present, life and death, animal and human are all aspects of a greater consciousness. One need only recognize this to travel freely throughout time and space.

1. DREAM REVISIONARIES

1. "Antifeminist" here does not necessarily mean "antiwoman." Although many antifeminist utopian narratives are indeed misogynistic, the majority argue that political and legal equality for women would drag them *down* into the public world of men, corrupting and contaminating the finer, purer, more spiritual female nature.

2. Guillory (1993, 7), for example, considers the canon an essentially political construct and views such criteria as instruments designed expressly to exclude "female, black, ethnic, or working-class authors." Tompkins (1985, 38) suggests that "instead of asking whether a work is unified or discontinuous, subtle, complex, or profound," one might better inquire "whether it was successful in achieving its aims" and "whether those aims were good or bad."

3. Aside from Anne Mary Louisa Montpensier's *La Relation de L'Isle Imaginaire, et l'histoire de la Princesse de Paphlagonie* (1659) and Stéphanie de Genlis's *Les Battuécas* (1816), the first non-English utopian text written by a woman is Hanna Leuchs Radamacher's *Utopia: Ein heiteres Spiel in drei Aufzügen* (1920), as far as I have been able to identify. The only working-class author is Betsey Chamberlain (1841), a Lowell, Massachusetts, millworker.

4. They have thus failed to meet Dr. Johnson's (1765, 329) primary requirement for literary worth: "length of duration and continuance of esteem." Yet, Tompkins argues, one should recognize that such a requirement is ultimately mutable, historically constructed, and profoundly limiting. Tompkins (1985, 3–4) questions "the accepted view that a classic work does not depend for its status on the circumstances in which it is read," arguing instead that "a literary classic is a product of all those circumstances of which it has traditionally been supposed to be independent."

5. Even microfilms are frequently difficult to acquire: the British Library, for example, will send microfilmed texts only if the author has been dead for fifty years. In the case of forgotten writers such as Mrs. C. A. Scrymsour Nichol (1908), Irene Clyde (1909), and Cora Minnett (1911), proof of a death date is hard to come by; they do not surface in any biographies, nor do they appear in the London *Times* obituaries. One text, Coralie Glyn's *A Woman of Tomorrow* (1896), is all but lost to the public; Sargent (1988) has traced a single copy to a private collection in London.

6. The "famous paper" to which they allude is Freud's "Psycho-Analytic Notes on an Autobiographical Account of a Case of Paranoia" (1911).

7. Quissell (1981, 149) asserts that "women utopists revealed an impatience with narrow objectives such as those of the suffragists," seeking instead "the complete transformation characteristic of the genre."

8. Also useful is the work of critics who have examined twentieth-century utopias by women. Mellor's "On Feminist Utopias" (1982) argues that the concept of gender equality is "inherently utopian" because such equality "has never existed in the historical past" (243). She then examines three paradigms for an egalitarian society—

all-female, androgynous, and genuinely egalitarian—and determines "to what extent they are 'abstract' (in Ernst Bloch's terminology) . . . [i.e.,] merely wish-fulfillment fantasies, and to what extent 'concrete' and thus viable blue-prints for future political and social organization" (241). Khanna's "Frontiers of Imagination: Feminist Worlds" (1984, 97) argues that contemporary utopian fiction by women tends to blur oppositions such as "male and female, matter and spirit, public and private rights, ends and means, even technology and ecology." In 1987, Keinhorst defined feminist "critical utopias" as those that not only "offer possible historical alternatives to the present" but also "seek solutions primarily within the public, political sphere" (91). Utopian confrontation with a strange world, she points out, "provokes alienation from inequality which hitherto has been familiar—and socially acceptable" (98). Barr's *Alien to Femininity* (1987) examines ways in which women's speculative fiction can inform contemporary feminist theory.

9. And, of course, vice versa. Many of my students, to my mingled horror and amusement, have considered Huxley's *Brave New World* (1932) a very pleasant place indeed and have seemed as confused as any Fordian about the Savage's negative response to the society.

10. However, I must confess a personal fondness for Khanna's (1984, 273) assertion that utopia "is not, finally, any one place or time, but the capacity to see afresh—an enlarged, even transformed vision."

11. Only one of those (Kingscote 1908) is a utopia, however. Writers tend to create a single ideal society and then move on to other things. There are of course exceptions, among them H. G. Wells, Jules Verne, and, in this study, Eveleen Mason, Charlotte Perkins Gilman, and Elizabeth Stuart Phelps.

12. These rooms are situated in Paleveria, a highly materialistic Martian state. When the terrestrial visitor tours the neighboring province of Caskia, he encounters a spiritually enlightened culture that lives far more simply and is devoted to two other staples of Victorian women's utopian fiction: study and self-improvement. In a typical Caskian home, for example, family activities center around an observatory/library/music room, dominated by "a very fine telescope that must have cost a fortune" (Jones and Merchant 1893, 209).

13. Utopian literature is a slippery genre, and just when we are most certain that we are reading about alien landscapes, we frequently discover that we've really never left home.

14. Spender (1984, 17) points out that "in neither the theatre nor the world of letters had it been possible to impose formal entry requirements (as in medicine and law) and this was one of the reasons that women who had few if any educational qualifications were to be found acting or writing." Acting, however, lacked the privacy, and hence the respectability, associated with authorship.

15. Tuchman (1989, 8) identifies three stages in this process of occupational gender transformation: 1840–79, *"the period of invasion,"* when "most novelists were women, but men began to value the novel as a cultural form"; 1880–99, *"the period of redefinition,"* when "men submitted more novels . . . than women did, but women and men were equally likely to have their fiction accepted"; and 1901–17, *"the period of institutionalization,"* when men's hold on the novel . . . coalesced."

16. In his introduction to *Looking Backward* (New York: Signet, 1962, v), Erich Fromm points out that "after *Uncle Tom's Cabin* and *Ben Hur*, it was the most popular book at the turn of the century."

17. One might argue, however, that a number of utopian narratives by women anticipated Bellamy in both form and content: Mary Griffith's "Three Hundred Years Hence" (1836) tells of a young man who fancies himself buried alive by an avalanche in 1835 and awakened three hundred years later; Marie Howland's *Papa's Own Girl* (1874) is considered by many (including Bellamy's biographer, Arthur Morgan) to have been a prototype for *Looking Backward*.

18. Its twentieth-century counterpart probably would be the Harlequin romance novel.

19. The development of this formula is particularly evident when one contrasts Genesis with John Milton's *Paradise Lost* (1667). In the original myth, God must double as guide and policeman, and conversation is minimal. In books 5–8 of Milton's tale, however, Raphael assumes the role of mentor and, in the best utopian fashion, converses with the newcomer, explaining the history, geography, and regulations of the cosmos.

20. Indeed, utopian elements can be found even in the work of such a down-to-earth author as Jane Austen. In *Persuasion* (1818), Austen's Anne Elliot travels to Lyme Regis and discovers what Gilbert and Gubar (1984, 180) term "an egalitarian society in which men participate in domestic life, while women contribute to public events, a complementary ideal that presages the emergence of an egalitarian sexual ideology." Similarly, Goodwin (1990, 9–10) detects "elements of a feminist utopian vision" in *Pride and Prejudice* (1813), pointing out that a "belief in the pursuit of happiness, and an ability to change and value people for intrinsic reasons rather than economic ones, are part of the novel's expectant view of a better world."

21. They were even alienated from women who did not form part of the competitive pool. As Murray (1982, 12) notes, "The rigid class structure of nineteenth-century English society did much to prevent women from identifying with one another along class lines. Opposing interests, as between servants and mistresses, often proved to be insurmountable obstacles."

22. Although in Bellamy's sequel, *Equality* (1897), Edith is far more visible and active.

2. GENDER AND GENRE IN CANONICAL UTOPIAN FICTION

1. According to a number of historians, the Creator had replaced a kinder, gentler Creatrix: Eisler (1987, xvii) argues that after the "fundamental social shift" from Neolithic agrarian societies based on male-female partnership to nomadic societies based on male domination, the worship of the nurturing Mother-Goddess gave way to the glorification of wrathful male deities such as Jehovah and Zeus; Phillips (1984, 3) asserts that "the story of Eve is also the story of the displacing of the Goddess whose name is taken from a form of the Hebrew verb 'to be' by the masculine God, Yaweh, whose name has the same derivation." This is disputed history, however; many anthropologists and archaeologists argue that proof for such a shift is weak or nonexistent.

2. Thucydides, after all, did call Herodotus "the father of lies."

3. The classical period did, however, see the continuance of the "Cokaygne utopia," a lighthearted escapist fantasy of superabundance: examples include Aristophanes's land of plenty in *Ecclesia*?*usae* (392 B.C.E.) and Lucian's Island of the Blessed in his *A True Story* (200 C.E.). Modern Cokaygne utopias exist in children's dreams of a land of chocolate rivers, lollipop trees, and ice cream mountains, or in texts such as

Stanislaw Lem's drug-based pharmotopia, *The Futurological Congress* (1974). Such fantasies are only tangentially utopian according to the criteria of this study, however: it is not really an alternative society, but merely a description of wonders (fish leaping into fishermen's hands, for example); neither is it a true exemplar, since it lacks any didactic purpose whatsoever. Indeed, such tales reject nature's gifts and moderation, championing instead the dubious cause of excess in all its forms.

4. Even Plato's own student Dionysius II, trained as the prototypical philosopher-king, proved to be a disappointment. Dionysius was an incompetent general, whose campaigns were invariably failures; he also was a poor judge of character, who, consumed by jealousy, dismissed his ablest ministers because of their popularity with the citizens of Syracuse.

5. Except for such fortunates as the divine favorite, Mary, who was allegedly born without original sin and assumed into heaven while still alive.

6. Augustine (1945, 2:389) dearly loved to enumerate the evils that befall humankind, and his lists of mundane calamities often read like some overzealous insurance policy: "loss of children, of goods or of credit, the false dealing of others, false suspicion, open violence, and all other mischiefs inflicted by others . . . poverty, imprisonment, bonds, banishments, tortures, loss of limbs or senses, prostitution to beastly lust."

7. One might even return to the Garden; many medieval Christians, after all, believed that Eden still existed on earth. Kumar (1987, 12) asserts that the legend persisted until the beginning of the sixteenth century: Columbus, for example, was convinced that "he had found the Garden of Eden at the mouth of the Orinoco River with its four tributaries."

8. One particularly gullible reader of Thomas More's *Utopia* was so taken with the place that he publicly volunteered to become its first bishop.

9. The most well known of these was the transcendentalist community of Brook Farm, on which Nathaniel Hawthorne based the setting of *The Blithedale Romance* (1852).

10. See Sargent (1988).

11. On Sunday, 13 November 1887, there were massive political demonstrations in Trafalgar Square, with protests regarding unemployment and governmental infringements on rights of free speech. The protest was crushed with brutal efficiency; a mounted police force charged the assembled mass, trampling demonstrators underfoot. Many were wounded; two died.

12. As opposed to polygamy, in which either sex may have a plurality of mates.

13. Indeed, many supposedly non-gender-specific rituals seem directed exclusively toward women and their presumed frailties: in "An Ambiguous Legacy: The Role and Position of Women in the English Utopia," Sargent (1975, 138) points out that "although in More's famous premarital ritual each potential partner is shown nude to the other, *all* the reasons given for the practice relate to the possible deformity of the woman."

14. I have modernized the spelling.

15. "Estans plus soigneuses de l'honneur de leurs maris que de toute autre chose, elles cherchent en mettent leur solicitude à avoir le plus de compaignes qu'elles peuvent, d'autant que c'est un tesmoignage de la vertu du mary."

16. I have modernized the spelling.

17. The royal dinghy is not the only vessel to prove inadequate; Voluptuaria has been eagerly awaiting a visit from "the great poet of Twickenham," but "it would be Madness

in him to attempt a voyage hither in the leaky Condition his Cockboat is in" (Cock 1741, 30).

18. These pornographic utopias—and their associations with the imperial project—are discussed in "Nudes from Nowhere: Pornography, Empire, and Utopia" (Lewes 1993).

19. Ironically, Bellamy does seem to have predicted one twentieth-century "type": the mall rat.

20. Bellamy himself seems to have reconsidered this point. In *Equality*, the 1897 sequel to *Looking Backward*, Edith Leete explains to Julian that clothing (including shoes and hats), carpets, curtains, and dishware are all fashioned from paper or other cheap and easily recycled materials. Breakfast and lunch are sent in via pneumatic tube.

21. Cf. Ira Levin's *The Stepford Wives*.

22. The narrator enjoys a brief romantic encounter with a beautiful seventeen-year-old girl who finds him tremendously attractive and follows him through England—this despite the fact that he is in his midfifties and remarks that he appears to be "a man of eighty" (Morris [1890] 1920, 27) to his youthful-looking hosts.

23. It had even less to say to working-class women, who generally had the added handicap of illiteracy, which might further explain why the identifiable women in this study are, with one exception (Betsey Chamberlain, a factory worker), all members of the middle or upper class.

24. Some critics consider Cavendish's "The Inventory of Judgements Common-wealth" in *The World's Olio* (1655) to be her earliest work of utopian fiction. Her brief schematic for an ideal commonwealth asserts that a loving monarch should contract with his people to rule justly, eschewing favoritism and greed, giving wit precedence over beauty, and honoring poets. Since it is, however, more a work of political philosophy than fiction (drawing perhaps from texts such as Machiavelli's *The Prince*, which first appeared in English in 1640), it technically lies outside the boundaries of this study.

25. Eliza Fowler Haywood's *Memoirs of a Certain Island Adjacent to Utopia* (1725) employs a similar inversion. Her "certain island" is once again England, and the "memoirs" a series of satirical anecdotes. A young traveler arrives in England and encounters a mournful Cupid, who leads him to an Enchanted Well, where the foibles of the famous and infamous are revealed. Although the visitor and guide are male, the tale details how the female figures of Astraea and Reason help two other females, Beauty and Virtue, regain their authority over the isle.

26. Rohrlich (1984) relates Ann Lee's ghastly experiences with childbirth to her linking of sexual intercourse and sin.

27. Some attempts were made, however, to render woman's work a bit less onerous: the celebrated Shaker chair, for example, was designed to be hung from pegs on the wall, in part to facilitate cleaning (and in part to provide more room for religious ceremonial dancing—"shaking").

28. A number of similar attacks on experimental communitarian societies emerge later in the century: Louisa May Alcott's "Transcendental Wild Oats" (1873) pokes fun at the pretensions of Bronson Alcott's socialistic Fruitlands community; Eva Wilder McGlasson's *Diana's Livery* (1891) depicts a Shaker community doomed by its harsh restrictions on love and sexual activity; and Elizabeth Orpen's *Perfection City* (1897) attacks communism and feminism in her tale of a small experimental community that fails because of the pettiness and jealousies of its radical inhabitants.

3. NINETEENTH-CENTURY UTOPIAN FICTION IN CONTEXT

1. Sachs and Wilson (1978, 25) note that one of the judges "said he hoped the case would forever exorcise and lay the ghost of a doubt which ought never to have made its appearance."

2. England's First Reform Bill (1832) had much the same effect on British women; before the act, Lisa Tickner (1988, 4) points out, "women had not voted, but then neither had most men." The bill's use of the words "male person," however, made women's exclusion legal rather than merely traditional.

3. As Bartowski (1989, 5) points out, "Writing from the margins and coming into speech in full knowledge of power *over*, feminists have tended to imagine instead about power *to*."

4. "A drawing-room looks now like a camp," complained a contemporary author. "You see a number of bell-tents of different colours, the poles sustaining them appearing at the summit. These are the signs of habitation. . . . Is there not power of repression under the Building Act?" (Cunnington [1937] 1990, 186).

5. In 1865, an English newspaper reported that "not a year passes but in this country alone hundreds suffer death by burning through crinoline" (Cunnington [1937] 1990, 221).

6. One mixed blessing of the industrial age was the invention of standardized shoe sizes. Previously, women's shoes had been made to fit the individual foot comfortably; numbered sizes, however, imposed an empirical standard on women's feet (a size two was "daintier" than a size five), and women felt it a matter of pride to force their feet into the lowest-numbered size possible. A midcentury newspaper commented that "there scarcely exists an Englishwoman whose toes are not folded one over the other, each of these crooked, and their nails almost destroyed. From childhood, the rage for tight shoes and small feet exists" (Cunnington [1937] 1990, 168).

7. Oddly enough, many women seemed to enjoy wearing corsets. In an 1870 letter to the *Englishwoman's Domestic Magazine,* one female reader commented on the "delicious sensation of perfect compression" afforded by the stays and was confident that, "when once accustomed to it," women would undergo tight lacing even "if appearance were no consideration at all" (cited in Murray 1982, 67).

8. Indeed, one text forgoes clothing altogether. Freedom from the confinement of fashion is carried to an extreme in Blaze De Bury's *The Storm of London* (1904). When all clothes and fabric mysteriously disappear from Britain, the island suddenly becomes an enormous nudist colony. De Bury damns fashion as the root of class distinction; she argues that nudity is not only a great equalizer but also forces one to keep oneself in better shape, since one has no clothes to hide an ungraceful or overweight figure.

9. Attempts to popularize the garment sometimes proved disastrous: in 1851, a "Grand Bloomer Ball" was held in London, and "only ladies dressed in correct Bloomer attire were admitted—unfortunately these, in the main, turned out to be ladies of the town, and a fantastic orgiastic brawl brought the evening to an end" (Crow 1972, 128).

10. Such garments were also considered to help prevent disease: in her memoir, *Leaves from a Life* (1908), Jane Ellen Panton notes that Mrs. Bloomer's clothing-reform movement was known as the "doctrine of hygienic clothing," in part because it enabled women to avoid dragging "yards of skirts after them through the muddy germ-laden streets" (cited in Murray 1982, 68).

11. Physical labor was not perceived as a particular threat to women's health; intellectual exertion was the culprit. In 1874, Dr. Edward Clarke argued that factory girls who labored in sweatshops were generally healthier because "they work their brains less" (cited in Rothman 1978, 46).

12. Some women, however, took exception to this domestically biased view. Barbara Bodichon argued that "women want work both for the health of their minds and bodies. They want it often because they must eat and because they have children and others dependent on them—for all the reasons that men want work" (cited in Helsinger, Sheets, and Veeder 1983, 149). Margaret Fuller asserted that women are fit to fill "any" position: "let them be sea-captains, if you will" (174).

13. Although, as Donnelly (1986, 100) notes, "at first it was feared that dealing with such things as urinals would be too shocking for female nurses."

14. Rendall (1984, 126) notes that Oberlin, for example, "took a . . . restricted view of the purposes of education for women, seeing their students very much as future ministers' wives." Rothman (1978, 27, n.) points out that "even after admission, a woman had to demonstrate her individual ability to enroll in courses that were routinely open to a man. Women were admitted only in the Ladies Course; after completing one term, they could request permission to take courses in other branches. So too, until 1874, female graduates were not allowed to read their essays at Commencement Day as the men did."

15. Even the most hardened adults, however, can benefit from education. "*Educate your criminals,*" the residents of Saturn warn the Recorder of Eva Harrison's *Wireless Messages from Other Worlds* (1915, 91, original emphasis), "That is the way to save them."

4. CONTRASTS IN BRITISH AND AMERICAN TEXTS

1. The British perception of empire, that is. In reality, Ronald Hyam (1976, 15) notes, with the possible exception of India, the so-called empire was "a ragbag of territorial bits and pieces, some remaindered remnants, some pre-empted luxury items, some cheap samples. All that red on the map represented in truth at best only a dominion of opinion and a grand anomaly, and at worst a temptation to illusions of grandeur and a gross abuse."

2. Anna Evans's *It Beats the Shakers; or, A New Tune* (1905) offers a not-too-subtle warning to would-be brides. She describes a world populated entirely by lonely and despairing men, who convince female Venusians to come to Earth and marry them. After the mass nuptials are conducted, however, the women are subjected to a full spectrum of terrestrial abuses and cruelties: they are cut off from their friends, treated like slaves, and given killing amounts of physical labor to perform by their brutal, drunken, profligate husbands. Eventually, the unhappy women flee back to Venus with their female children, leaving life on Earth eventually to die out. Although Evans was an American, her novel was published in both England and America; the vulnerability of mail-order brides was yet another issue that seemed to interest women on both sides of the Atlantic.

3. As Elizabeth Waterhouse points out in *The Island of Anarchy* (1887), an island of misfits and outcasts has a decided dystopian potential. In her depressing parable, dangerous anarchists and revolutionaries are transported from London to an island where

they can do no harm to anyone but themselves. Although a few of the deportees find salvation through their conversion to Christianity, the majority enthusiastically dedicate themselves to vice, dispute, and pugnacity.

4. In the few British women's utopian narratives that are set in distant lands, the place must be civilized, brought into line with imperial social order. In Harriet Martineau's *Dawn Island* (1845), for example, a tropical island is inhabited by lazy men and servile women who live in filthy dwellings and practice human sacrifice, cannibalism, and infanticide. Civilization arrives in the form of a European ship, and the natives are eventually won over to commerce and Christianity—the twin emblems of imperialism. The natives of Millicent Garrett Fawcett's *Tales in Political Economy* (1874) are less fierce but are equally primitive and far more obstinate: they live miserably, slaves to foolish tribal customs and superstitions. The efforts of a visiting group of British sailors to enlighten the tribe are completely unsuccessful. In the present study, the only positive British utopia to be set in an exotic land is Mrs. C. A. Scrymsour Nichol's *Mystery of the North Pole* (1908). Nichol's polar community is not a true frontier, however, but an imaginary world based on her conception of an ideal London. The North Pole is no arctic wasteland, but a technologically advanced, urban society—the accommodations are reminiscent of "a first-class hotel in London" (78). Its inhabitants and their values are equally Victorian: the blond, fair-skinned natives are highly religious, physically healthy, well educated, and politically conservative (traditional class and gender hierarchies are firmly in place).

5. Trollope cites Oscar Wilde's "Ave Imperatrix," which asserts that "the steep road of wide empire" was climbed with "bare and bloody feet" and mourned "the brave, the strong, the fleet . . . loved ones lying far away, / What words of love can dead lips send! / O wasted dust! O senseless clay! / Is this the end! Is this the end!"

6. In 1892, Prime Minister Asquith avowed that "as to the great mass of the sex, the only thing that can be asserted with truth is that they are watching with languid and imperturbable indifference the struggle for their own emancipation" (Tickner 1988, 55).

7. Sachs and Wilson (1978, 34) note that "in every [pre-1918] case heard by the Scottish and English judges in which a decision had to be given on whether women were debarred merely by sex from exercising public functions or entering a profession, that decision went against the women."

8. Similarly, modern antifeminists reproach working women for disregarding their maternal responsibilities.

9. Many American authors, however, were westerners themselves, and some even visited and lived in alternative communities: Marie Howland, for example, spent some time in Fourier's French phalanstery, and Lois Waisbrooker lived in the anarchist communities of Pacific City and Home.

10. Rosa Graul's *Hilda's Home* (ca. 1897) is set somewhere in the unspecified "west"; Louisa May Alcott's "Transcendental Wild Oats" (1873) in rural New England; Lillie Blake's "A Divided Republic" (1887) in Washington territory; Eveleen Mason's *Hiero-Salem* (1889) and *An Episode in the Doings of the Dualized* (1898) in Wisconsin; Mrs. M. A. Pittock's *The God of Civilization* (1890) in Hawaii; Adeline Knapp's "One Thousand Dollars A Day" (1894) in rural Illinois; Janet Von Swartwout's *Heads; or, The City of Gods* (1895) in the Adirondacks; Frances Clarke's *The Co-opolitan* (1898) in Idaho; Caroline Mason's *A Woman of Yesterday* (1900) in rural North Carolina; Kate Douglas Wiggin's *Susanna and Sue* (1909) in a Maine Shaker community; Charlotte Gilman's

"Bee Wise" (1913) in California; and Caroline Snedeker's *Seth Way* (1917) in the Indiana community of New Harmony.

11. In England, this anachronism was noted when women assumed traditionally male roles during the First World War; enfranchisement followed soon after.

12. Actually, Utah had enfranchised women in 1870, but female suffrage there was revoked in 1887 as a result of anti-Mormon sentiment in Congress. Suffrage came with statehood in 1896.

13. In Amanda Douglas's *Hope Mills; or, Between Friend and Sweetheart* (1879), a mill-worker creates an industrial commune; in Elizabeth Stuart Phelps's *An Old Maid's Paradise* (1879) and *Burglars in Paradise* (1886), a group of single women share a free existence in a summer cottage; in Helen Stuart Campbell's *Miss Melinda's Opportunity* (1886), working women form a cooperative household; in Mary Cruger's *How She Did It; or, Comfort on $150 a Year* (1888), a young woman establishes a household loosely based on Owenite principles; in Alice Bartlett's *A New Aristocracy* (1891), three orphans found several small inner-city organizations devoted to self-improvement and help to create Idlewild, a model factory community; in Helen Winslow's *Salome Shepard, Reformer* (1893), an heiress/millowner reforms her mill into a model factory community; in Rosa Graul's *Hilda's Home* (ca. 1897), a free-love community develops into a cooperative business emporium; and in Frances H. Clarke's *The Co-opolitan* (1898), a group of people establish a cooperative commonwealth in Idaho.

14. In Charlotte Perkins Gilman's "With Her in Ourland" (1916), a sequel to *Herland* (1915), the utopienne Ellador agrees to visit Europe with her American husband. After witnessing the havoc wreaked by high-tech weaponry and patriarchal competition, however, she is heartbroken, homesick, and insistent on returning to her own pastoral, communal society.

15. This highly intellectual, highly political protagonist probably owes a great deal to her author's literary foremothers and the British social structure: "bluestockings" such as Mary Wortley Montagu, Hannah More, and Elizabeth Carter offered models of women valued for their wit, intelligence, and political savvy, while female members of the English aristocratic classes had long been encouraged to develop a modicum of intellect and self-assertion. American women tended to reject the bluestocking tradition as unwomanly: Conrad (1978, 41) notes that "the 'blue's' intellectual and sexual credentials were constantly called into question" by American promoters of true womanhood. In addition, the American bourgeois tradition, with its emphasis on domestic values, discouraged female independence and argued that woman's highest calling was to be a wife and mother. Conrad cites Harriet Martineau's conviction that "the intellect of [American] women is confined" and adds that, "judging America by its treatment of women, [Martineau] could hardly call it a civilization" (41). Alexis de Tocqueville's observations were similar: in *Democracy in America* ([1840] 1953, 2:214) he noted (with some approval) that "the women of the United States are confined within the narrow circle of domestic life, and their situation is in some respects one of extreme dependence."

16. Albinski, citing anthropologist Shirley Ortner's "Is Female to Male As Nature Is to Culture," suggests that the British distrust of the domestic sphere is related to the late nineteenth-century European assumption that the female's reproductive physiology and childlike, emotional temperament linked women to nature, while man's freedom from childbearing and logical, rational temperament linked him to culture. In Britain, wom-

anliness was thus perceived as fundamentally nonintellectual, and the domestic was seen as the only appropriate sphere. American narratives reflect a less divisive " 'culture' defined in terms of aesthetics and morality rather than the wider sense of thought and technology" (Albinski 1988, 4), in which women might participate fully.

17. They are called "aunts" by a male narrator who likens his marriage to a Herlander to "set[ting] up housekeeping with a female ant in a highly developed anthill" (Gilman [1915] 1979, 123).

18. Although several texts—most notably, Anna Evans's *It Beats the Shakers; or, A New Tune* (1905)—present dystopian all-male societies, I have been unable to locate any utopian text in which men reproduce themselves without women.

19. Indeed, Albinski (1988, 31) points out that "much of *Gloriana* reads like an uncanny forecast of the militant suffrage movement." The leader of Dixie's female military corps, for example, is Flora Desmond, nicknamed the Captain; the Women's Social and Political Union's Flora Drummond bore a similar descriptive epithet, the General.

20. Yet while women as a whole might be politically weak, a few wield enormous economic power, and Gloriana's school is funded by "lavish subscriptions of the women of Great Britain, Ireland, and the world at large" (Dixie 1890, 83).

21. It should be noted that in American novels, powerful women frequently step down once their missions have been accomplished and permit their husbands to continue in their places. In *Gloriana,* however, the situation is reversed: Evelyn Ravensdale, Gloriana's beloved, assumes the ministry during the revolution, but he immediately relinquishes the position to Gloriana upon her triumphant return.

22. Given the relatively abbreviated life span of a prolific American wife in 1894, Lovella's fifty-year-plan would involve up to three generations of women, ample time for old ways to be forgotten.

23. Clapperton's utopia is one of the few British texts situated in contemporary London. Her protagonist, however, is typical of the public, take-charge English utopian heroines in this study. While she establishes a communal home in which married couples can live together as equals, she is curiously distanced from domestic bliss and always in control: an orphaned, only child who remains happily unmarried throughout the novel, she is free of any familial or romantic entanglements; wealthy and well educated, she is the tacit ruler of the establishment.

5. RATIONALISM, EVANGELICALISM, AND VATICISM

1. "Rationalist" is an important qualifier here, for it helps distinguish between vatic feminism and "apocalyptic" feminism. Apocalyptic feminism is described by Helsinger, Sheets, and Veeder (1983, 2:xv) as "a radical version of the angelic ideal which combines a belief in woman's distinctive nature with claims for a leadership role in the world—a female savior leading the way to a fuller humanity and ushering in a new era of community and love." The key word here is "angelic": apocalyptic feminism, which emphasizes female superiority, is an extreme form of the evangelical impulse and an almost exclusively American phenomenon. Vatic feminism, which emphasizes female equality, is grounded in rationalism and is common to both English and American narratives.

2. The original reads: "alle the feyer werkyng and all the swete kyndly officis of dereworthy motherhed" (Julian of Norwich 1978, 2:593).

3. A moral role with classical precedents: Strabo (1924, 3:183), for example, writes of the Scythian women, who are "the founders of religion . . . who provoke the men to

the more attentive worship of the gods, to festivals, and supplications; it is a rare thing for a man living who lives by himself to be found addicted to these things."

4. One should keep in mind, however, that in Locke's First Treatise ([1690] 1969, 37) a divine and natural hierarchy is assumed: although God "gives not . . . any authority to Adam over Eve, or to men over their wives, but only foretells what should be the woman's lot, [He] would order it so that she should be subject to her husband, as we see that generally the laws of mankind and customs of nations have ordered it so, and there is, I grant, a foundation in nature for it." Locke (or, for that matter, Hobbes) could actually be cited on both sides of the question of women's natural rights.

5. Cavendish never reveals her heroine's name; the young woman does, however, gain a title—empress—granted her by a man.

6. Cavendish was perhaps responding to the decline of formal education for women, which had begun in the sixteenth century. As Fraser (1984, 123–24) points out, Henry VIII's crusade against Catholicism destroyed not only the monasteries but the convents as well. This "deprived English girls not only of convenient places of local learning, but also of a pool of women teachers in the shape of the nuns themselves."

7. Her focus is clearly rationalist/egalitarian, for although her empress-heroine is a model of moral decorum, she is never actually called on to demonstrate her moral superiority through the active rejection or condemnation of vice. The details of the kidnapping, for example, occupy only a page, and the heroine's reaction to the outrage is never specifically detailed. The particulars of the heroine's education, however, occupy nearly one-half of the text, and the remainder is devoted to her exploits in such highly public arenas as courts of law and battlefields.

8. Later, the empress is even more explicit, wondering "whether it was an evil Spirit that tempted Eve, and brought all the mischiefs upon Mankind: or, Whether it was the Serpent?" (Cavendish 1666, 81). Eve is no longer even one of the usual suspects.

9. It is not until this point that the empress, who has so far appeared the very model of an English gentlewoman, is revealed as an alien from yet another world. The world she left, the world connected at the North Pole, is not Earth, nor is it linked to Earth in any way other than spiritually.

10. Only nonpotent males—very young schoolboys and very old or disabled menials—are permitted to reside at the hall for any extended period of time.

11. Similar domestic corruption can be found in Samuel Richardson's *Clarissa* (1747–48): the tragic events of the plot are set in motion by the heroine's greedy father, envious sister, and spiteful brother, who insist that she wed the odious but wealthy Mr. Soames.

12. The superabundance of cads in Scott's world might be due in part to the alarming mortality rate of the few honorable men in the novel. Of the ten "good" men who manage to refrain from excessively immoral behavior while living in the worldly sector, nine predecease their wives and daughters (the tenth man may not even count, since he is unmarried, too old to pose any physical or amatory threat, and dead before the book is over). A good man, it seems, is not only hard to find but is also almost impossible to keep alive.

13. "Les incommodités particulières à la femme . . . c'est une raison suffisante pour l'exclure de cette primauté" (Rousseau [1755] 1959, 3.242).

14. As Landes (1988, 3) points out, "A public man is one who acts in and for the universal good," while "a public woman is a prostitute, a commoner, a common woman."

15. Certainly, French feminism was not forwarded by champions such as the notori-

ous Marquis de Sade, who asserted in *La Philosophie dans la boudoir* (1795) that "the right can never be given to one sex to take possession of the other; and never can one of the sexes or classes have an arbitrary right over the other" (cited in Rover 1970, 9).

16. These qualities were also seen as natural aptitudes for reform activity, particularly the religious instruction of the poor. Women's benevolent societies were active throughout the 1830s and 1840s (especially in America), seeking to ameliorate the living conditions of the poor and to reclaim "fallen" women. Although these moral crusaders were frequently forced to venture into the public sphere, they did not do so as public figures; instead, they acted as benevolent missionaries—analogous, perhaps, to nuns who travel away from the convent to perform charitable acts yet never surrender its protection. The churches and clubs under whose auspices the moral crusaders operated were similar extensions of the domestic sphere.

17. I have modernized the spelling.

18. In short, to reconcile the poor to their condition and prevent future radical outbreaks.

19. Hale's own utopia, *Liberia, or Mr. Peyton's Experiments* (1853), promotes the abolition of slavery and the emigration of African Americans to a free African state—two major concerns of evangelical thinkers. Traditional gender roles are firmly in place: women are relegated to the private sphere and function as spiritual exemplars.

20. Beecher also argued that slavery should be ended by a process of gradual elimination, which infuriated staunch abolitionists such as Angela Grimké (Spender [1982] 1988, 226).

6. VATICISM AND WOMEN'S UTOPIAN FICTION

1. Banks (1981, 56) points out that feminists such as Lucy Stone "believed that a loveless marriage was immoral, but thought it a dangerous topic to introduce into a women's rights discussion."

2. Literally, "woman's rock."

3. Jackson (1989) argues that "the male gaze is one of the means by which men subdue women; looking *at* women, making women the object of the look rather than subjects who see in their own right, is part of the mechanism of sexual control and the subjugation of women" (xxiii); she notes that "one of the identifying features of the Byronic hero in Romantic literature was his mesmerizing gaze, the power of the eye to fix and transfix women" (n., xxxiv). See also Mulvey 1975.

4. In addition, Jones and Merchant avoid the practical considerations necessitated by a realistic setting: in both *Papa's Own Girl* (Howland 1874) and *Margaret Dunmore* (Clapperton 1888), for example, money must somehow be acquired to fund the socialistic projects, and the disapproval of the communities' neighbors must be overcome. Martian society, already in place, frees the author from practicality and prejudice.

5. This is in line with nineteenth-century views of gender difference; as Murray (1982, 9–10) points out, "Womanliness was as much defined by the absence of male qualities as by the presence of the conventionally feminine graces and virtues . . . to be womanly required a total ignorance of male concerns, from politics to higher mathematics to sexuality."

6. The counterpart of Mother Earth is Father Mars, who, despite his bellicose name, seems equally nurturing and solicitous of his children.

7. The incurably promiscuous are castrated or sterilized; the incurably insane are executed.

7. POST-1920 WOMEN'S UTOPIAN FICTION

1. Fussell (1977, 22) notes the high diction used to sustain these romantic ideas: instead of men going to war, fighting, and being killed by the enemy, "staunch comrades" (or "lads") were "summoned" to "join the colors," "gallantly assail the foe," and "fall" before the opposing "host."

2. An officer might breakfast in the trenches and dine at his club in London (Fussell 1977, 64).

3. The single exception that seems to prove the rule is Agnes Bond Yourell's uncomfortably prescient *A Manless World* (1891). This nasty little novelette seasons the "doomed humanity" theme of Mary Wollstonecraft Shelley's *The Last Man* (1826) with an unhealthy dollop of racism. A nightmare vision, it portrays nature as mankind's enemy, emitting poisonous gases that render human beings unable to procreate. The last generation of mankind sinks gradually into anarchy, mass starvation, and suicide. The central section of the text is a chilling preholocaust vision, a vicious anti-Semitic diatribe that attempts to justify the mass slaughter of the Jewish people on the grounds that they are somehow responsible for the catastrophe.

4. Some British women suspected that their "triumph" was not as grand as it seemed: Millicent Garrett Fawcett, for example, suggested that "the vote was not granted to women as recognition of their war contribution or even because their case was strong enough to warrant legislation, but because there had to be a new franchise bill to include the returning service men who had lost their residence qualification for voting; and some women were included in this bill—designed primarily for men—almost as an afterthought" (Spender 1984, 30).

5. Even servants were new and improved. Carol Dyhouse (1981, 108–9) cites postwar organizations such as the League of Skilled Housecraft, which awarded "certificates of competency in domestic subjects." Such "schemes" attempted to "raise the social prestige of domestic service as a skilled occupation."

6. Jensen and Scharf (1983, 5) describe a "flapper" as "most often, a single young working woman whose consumer tastes exceeded her meager income."

7. Separatist texts such as Gilman's *Herland* or Clyde's *Beatrice the Sixteenth* would have been particularly ironic to many Englishwomen, for such depictions of all-female societies was oddly parallel to their own postwar society. Fussell (1977, 316) notes that "after the war women dramatically outnumbered men, and a common sight in the thirties . . . was the standard middle-aged Lesbian couple in tweeds, who had come together as girls after each had lost a fiancé, lover, or husband."

8. Albinski (1990, 78) cites only six optimistic English utopias written between 1920 and 1960; of these, only one, Elsie Kay Gresswell's *When Yvonne Was Dictator* (1935), is characterized as "directly in the tradition of the Victorian novels."

9. Hamilton's coauthor was Christabel Marshall, a suffrage advocate, translator, and biographer, whose only other experience with playwriting was a rather strained one-acter, *Coronation*, cowritten with Charles Thursby in 1911. Although *How the Vote Was Won* reflects the feminist sentiments and optimism of both women, its polish, easy wit, and crackling dialogue are probably the product of the far more experienced Hamilton.

10. In reality, such unity would have been highly unlikely, since egalitarian feminists such as Hamilton represented a decided minority; most women's views of themselves and their place in the world were far more conservative.

11. Although the reference is obviously comic, it does provide the modern reader with a nostalgic glimpse of an age when beds simply were expected to be made, no matter what.

12. Social Darwinists could argue that women such as Phillida are indirectly responsible for war, since, by withholding their favors from all but the most warlike, they help perpetuate humankind's aggressive tendencies.

13. Ada seems to prefigure Aldous Huxley's (1932) Linda (the "civilized" mother of *Brave New World*'s John Savage, who is inadvertently abandoned on an Indian reservation). Both are urban creatures, absolutely helpless in a primitive setting, who devote the majority of their energies to lamenting their fate; both are flirtatious and promiscuous and are physically attacked by resentful tribal women.

14. Fussell (1977, 317) points out that "from 1914 to 1918 [Britain's] gold reserve diminished dramatically. The beneficiary was the United States, which emerged an undisputed 'Great Power' by virtue of manufacturing and shipping matériel." Fussell also cites Marc Ferro's observation that the United States "could rightly be considered the only victor of the war, since their territory was intact, and they became creditor to all the other belligerents."

15. These three "candles" are Sarah Norcliffe Cleghorn's "Utopia Interpreted" (1924), Claire Myers Spotswood's *The Unpredictable Adventure: A Comedy of Woman's Independence* (1935), and Gertrude Short's *A Visitor from Venus* (1949).

16. The house, which seems to have been designed by Frank Lloyd Wright (or perhaps Howard Roark), has "two stories and a strange roof flat as a floor. There was more window than wall upon its walls, and the windows went on straight around the corners" (Rand 1938, 89).

17. Liberty, in the tradition of utopian heroines created by male writers, is virtually silent throughout the book. What dialogue she manages, information regarding her virginity, her devotion, and her willingness to submit to Equality's will in all things, invariably points out her own submissive state. Her body language is equally deferential: "The head of the Golden One bowed slowly, and they stood before us, their arms at their sides, the palms of their hands turned to us, as if their body were delivered in submission to our eyes" (Rand 1938, 57).

18. Not unlike Julia in Orwell's *1984* (1949), who sleeps while Winston reads a supposedly forbidden treatise.

19. In 1927, Cicely Hamilton had predicted such a situation, which she saw as a reaction against female emancipation. She predicted that an antifeminist backlash (to borrow Susan Faludi's term) would be marked by a return to restrictive female clothing. The result of such atavistic garb would be horrifyingly familiar: "by hampering the movements of its wearers and disinclining them to exercise, [such clothing] will make them to a certain extent dependent of the good offices of the sex whose muscles and breathing apparatus are not hampered by the fashion of their clothes" (cited in Spender 1984, 79). Clothing reform remains a hotly contested issue even today. Faludi (1991) has pointed out that in 1988, "Pierre Cardin produced capelike wraps that fit so tightly that even the New York Times fashion page found it 'fairly alarming because the models wearing them cannot move their arms' " (186). Romeo Gigli's "skirts were so tight the models could only hobble down the runway" (186–87). And Bob Mackie pointed out

that "a lot of women took the tailored look too far and it became unattractive. . . . Probably, psychologically, it hurt their femininity" (173). Presumably, tasteful frocks such as the chain mail and leather ensembles Mr. Mackie has designed for Cher will solve the problem.

20. Conversely, the lack of battlefield coverage during the Gulf War of 1991 probably contributed to its relatively wide public acceptance.

21. Reproduction still requires the fertilizing gamete of a male animal to trigger the process, although none of the male traits are retained. The women of the Motherline use the semen of stallions for this purpose.

22. Indeed, sisterhood proved such a powerful strategy that it was adopted by corporate America, albeit under the more acceptable label of "networking."

23. One of two future worlds visited by Connie Ramos, Piercy's twentieth-century protagonist.

24. Firestone (1970, 35) argues that "feminism is the inevitable female response to the development of a technology capable of freeing women from the tyranny of their sexual-reproductive roles—both the fundamental biological condition itself, and the sexual class system built upon, and reinforcing, this biological condition."

25. Many women were also outraged by Stokely Carmichael's assertion that "the only position for women in SNCC [the Student Nonviolent Coordinating Committee] is prone" (Eisenstein 1983, 126).

APPENDIX

1. This bibliography draws heavily on several others, especially those of Albinski 1988; Kessler 1985, 1990; Patai 1981; Roemer 1976; and Sargent 1988.

2. I am relying on Carol Farley Kessler's research here. The only microfilm copy of *Lucifer, the Light Bearer* I have been able to locate begins with chap. 30 and is missing numbers 103–648, 650–52, 656, 659–80, and 681–872. A monograph copy of the text is kept in the University of Texas's special collections but is unavailable through interlibrary loan.

3. Lyman Tower Sargent states that the Puffin book edition has a copyright of 1901 but that there is no indication of such in the 1906 edition. The 1979 Octopus Books edition lists a 1906 copyright.

WORKS CITED

Adolph, Anna. 1899. *Arqtiq: A Study of the Marvels at the North Pole*. Hanford, Calif.: The author.

Albinski, Nan Bowman. 1988. "Utopia Reconsidered: Women Novelists and Nineteenth-Century Utopian Visions." *Signs* 13, no.4:830–41.

———. 1988. *Women's Utopias in British and American Fiction*. London: Routledge.

———. 1990. "The Laws of Justice, of Nature, and of Right: Victorian Feminist Utopias." In *Feminism, Utopia, and Narrative*, ed. Libby Falk Jones and Sarah Webster Goodwin, 50–68. Knoxville: University of Tennessee Press.

Alcott, Louisa May. [1873] 1975, 1981. "Transcendental Wild Oats: A Chapter from an Unwritten Romance." Ed. William Henry Harrison. Reprint, Harvard, Mass.: Harvard Common.

Andreadis, A. Harriette. [1968] 1984. "The Woman's Commonwealth: Utopia in Nineteenth-Century Texas." In *Women in Search of Utopia: Mavericks and Mythmakers*, ed. Ruby Rohrlich and Elaine Hoffman Baruch, 86–96. New York: Schocken.

Anthony, Susan B., and Ida Husted Harper, eds. 1902. *The History of Woman Suffrage*. 6 vols. Indianapolis: Hollenbeck.

Appleton, Jane Sophia. [1848] 1971. "Sequel to 'The Vision of Bangor in the Twentieth Century.'" In *American Utopias*, ed. Arthur O. Lewis, Jr., 243–65. New York: Arno Press and the New York Times.

Aristophanes. 1923. *Ecclesiazusae*. Trans. Benjamin Bickley Rogers. London: G. Bell.

Arnold, Matthew. [1868–69] 1964. "Hebraism and Hellenism." In *Matthew Arnold: Selected Poetry and Prose*, ed. Frederick L. Mulhauser, 266–78. New York: Holt Rinehart and Winston.

Augustine, Saint. 1945. *The City of God*. Trans. John Healey. London: J. M. Dent and Sons.

Austen, Jane. [1813] 1966. *Pride and Prejudice*. Norton Critical Edition. Reprint, New York: Norton.

———. [1818] 1971. *Persuasion*. Reprint, Oxford, England: Oxford University Press.

Bacon, Francis. [1627] 1966. *The New Atlantis*. In *The Advancement of Learning; and, New Atlantis*. London: Oxford University Press.

Bailey, Susan F. 1983. *Women and the British Empire: An Annotated Guide to Sources*. New York: Garland.

Banks, Olive. 1981. *Faces of Feminism*. New York: Saint Martin's.

Barr, Marleen. 1987. *Alien to Femininity: Speculative Fiction and Feminist Theory*. New York: Greenwood.

Bartlett, Alice Elinor Bowen [Birch Arnold, pseud.]. 1891. *A New Aristocracy*. New York: Bartlett.

Bartowski, Frances. 1989. *Feminist Utopias*. Lincoln: University of Nebraska Press.

Baruch, Elaine Hoffman. 1984. "Women in Men's Utopias." In *Women in Search of Utopia: Mavericks and Mythmakers*, ed. Ruby Rohrlich and Elaine Hoffman Baruch, 209–18. New York: Schocken.

Beecher, Catherine E. [ca. 1855] 1972. *Letters to the People on Health and Happiness*. Reprint, New York: Arno Press.

Behn, Aphra Amis. 1687. *The Emperor of the Moon: A Farce*. London: R. Holt, for J. Knight and F. Saunders.

———. [1688] 1967. *The History of Oroonoko; or, The Royal Slave*. In *Shorter Novels: Seventeenth Century*, ed. Phillip Henderson, 145–224. London: J. M. Dent.

Bellamy, Edward. [1888] 1966. *Looking Backward, 2000–1887*. Ed. Robert C. Elliot. Boston: Houghton Mifflin.

———. 1897. *Equality*. New York: D. Appleton.

Black, Clementina, ed. 1915. *Married Women's Work: Being the Report of an Inquiry Undertaken by the Women's Industrial Council*. London: Bell.

Blake, Lillie Devereux. [1887] 1892. "A Divided Republic: An Allegory of the Future." In *A Daring Experiment and Other Stories*, 346–60. New York: Lovell, Coryell.

Brome, Richard. 1640. *The Antipodes: A Comedie*. London: J. Okes, for Francis Constable.

Brown, Dee. 1958. *The Gentle Tamers: Women of the Old Wild West*. New York: G. P. Putnam's Sons.

Browning, Elizabeth Barrett. [1838] 1900. "An Island." In *Complete Works of Elizabeth Barrett Browning*, 6 vols., ed. Charlotte Porter and Helen A. Clarke, 2:37–44. New York: Thomas Y. Crowell.

Burke, Edmund. [1790] 1973. "Reflections on the Revolution in France." In *Reflections on the Revolution in France; and, The Rights of Man*, 13–266. Garden City, N.Y.: Doubleday.

Butler, Samuel. 1872. *Erewhon; or, Over the Range*. London: Trubner.

Campanella, Thomas. [1623] 1981. *The City of the Sun: A Poetical Dialogue*. Trans. Daniel J. Donno. Reprint, Berkeley: University of California Press.

Campbell, Helen Stuart. 1886. *Miss Melinda's Opportunity*. Boston: Roberts.

Cavendish, Margaret Lucas, Duchess of Newcastle. 1655. "The Inventory of Judgements Commonwealth, the Author Cares Not in What World It Is Established." In *The World's Olio*, 205–12. London: J. Martin and J. Allestrye.

———. [1662] 1985. "Female Orations." In *The Norton Anthology of Literature by Women*, 73–76. New York: Norton.

———. 1666. "The Description of a New World, Called the Blazing World." Pt. 4 of *Observations upon Experimental Philosophy*. London: A. Maxwell.

Chamberlain, Betsey [Tabitha, pseud.]. [1841] 1977. "A New Society." In *The Lowell Offering: Writings by New England Mill Women (1840–1845)*, ed. Benita Eisler, 208–10. Philadelphia: J. B. Lippincott.

Charnas, Suzy McKee. 1978. *Motherlines*. New York: Berkley.

Cixous, Hélène. 1976. "The Laugh of the Medusa." Trans. Keith Cohen and Paula Cohen. *Signs* 1, no. 4:875–93.

Clapperton, Jane Hume. 1888. *Margaret Dunmore; or, A Socialist Home*. London: Swan, Sonnenschein, Lowrey.

Clark, Kenneth. 1964. *Ruskin Today*. Middlesex, England: Penguin.

Clarke, Frances H. [Zebina Forbush, pseud.]. [1898] 1980. *The Co-opolitan: A Story of the Co-operative Commonwealth of Idaho*. Reprint, New York: AMS.

Cleghorn, Sarah. 1924. "Utopia Interpreted." *Atlantic Monthly* 128, no. 56:216–24.

Clyde, Irene. 1909. *Beatrice the Sixteenth*. London: G. Bell and Sons.

Cock, Samuel [pseud.]. 1741. *A Voyage to Lethe, by Captain Samuel Cock, Sometime Com-*

mander of the Good Ship the Charming Sally, Dedicated to the Right Worshipful Adam Cock, Esq., of Black-Mary's-Hole, Coney-Skin Merchant. London: J. Conybeare.

Conrad, Susan P. 1978. *Perish the Thought: Intellectual Women in Romantic America, 1830–1860.* Secaucus, N.J.: Citadel Press.

Cooley, Winifred Harper. 1902. "A Dream of the Twenty-First Century." *Arena* 28 (November): 511–16.

Corbett, Elizabeth Burgoyne [Mrs. George Corbett]. 1889. *New Amazonia: A Foretaste of the Future.* London: Tower.

Corbett, Elizabeth T. 1869. "My Visit to Utopia." *Harper's New Monthly Magazine* 38:200–204.

Coultrap-McQuin, Susan. 1990. *Doing Literary Business: American Women Writers in the Nineteenth Century.* Chapel Hill: University of North Carolina Press.

Cridge, Annie Denton. 1870. *Man's Rights; or, How Would You Like It? Comprising Dreams.* Boston: William Denton.

Crow, Duncan. 1972. *The Victorian Woman.* New York: Stein and Day.

Cruger, Mary. 1888. *How She Did It; or, Comfort on $150 a Year.* New York: D. Appleton.

Cunnington, C. Willett. [1937] 1990. *English Women's Clothing in the Nineteenth Century.* Reprint, New York: Dover.

Curtis, Pauline Carsten. 1890. "In the Year '26." *Overland Monthly* 15 (June): 640–59.

Davidhoff, Lenore, and Catherine Hall. 1987. *Family Fortunes: Men and Women of the Middle Class, 1780–1850.* Chicago: University of Chicago Press.

Davis, Rebecca Harding. 1866. "The Harmonists." *Atlantic Monthly* 17:529–38.

De Bury, F. Blaze, Mme. [F. Dickbury, pseud.]. 1904. *The Storm of London: A Social Rhapsody.* London: John Long.

de Genlis, Stéphanie. 1816. *Les Battuécas.* Paris: Maradan.

Dixie, Florence, Lady Caroline Douglas. 1890. *Gloriana; or, The Revolution of 1900.* London: Henry; New York: Standard.

Donnelly, Mabel Collins. 1986. *The American Victorian Woman: The Myth and the Reality.* Westport, Conn.: Greenwood.

Douglas, Amanda Minnie. [1879] 1880. *Hope Mills; or, Between Friend and Sweetheart.* Reprint, New York: Charles T. Dillingham.

Drane, Augusta Theodosia, Mother Frances Raphael. [1877] 1898. *The New Utopia.* Reprint, London: Catholic Truth Society.

DuBois, Ellen. 1987. "The Radicalism of the Woman Suffrage Movement: Notes toward the Reconstruction of Nineteenth-Century Feminism." In *Feminism and Equality,* ed. Anne Phillips, 127–38. New York: New York University Press.

D'Urfey, Thomas. 1686. *A Common-Wealth of Women.* London: R. Bentley and J. Hindmarsh.

Dyhouse, Carol. 1981. *Girls Growing Up in Late Victorian and Edwardian England.* London: Routledge and Kegan Paul.

Edgeworth, Maria. 1795. *Letters to Literary Ladies.* London: J. Johnson.

Ehrenreich, Barbara, and Deirdre English. 1979. *For Her Own Good: 150 Years of the Experts' Advice to Women.* Garden City, N.Y.: Anchor.

Eisenstein, Hester, ed. 1983. *Contemporary Feminist Thought.* Boston: G. K. Hall.

Eisler, Riane. 1987. *The Chalice and the Blade.* San Francisco: Harper and Row.

Eliot, George. [1871] 1977. *Middlemarch.* Norton Critical Edition. Reprint, New York: Norton.

Ellis, Sarah. 1843. *Wives of England.* London: Fisher.

Evans, Anna D. 1905. *It Beats the Shakers; or, A New Tune.* London and New York: Anglo-American.

Faludi, Susan. 1991. *Backlash: The Undeclared War against American Women.* New York: Crown.

Farnham, Eliza. 1864. *Woman and Her Era.* 2 vols. New York: A. J. Davis.

Fawcett, Millicent Garrett. 1874. *Tales in Political Economy.* London: Macmillan.

Firestone, Shulamith. 1970. *The Dialectic of Sex: The Case for Feminist Revolution.* New York: William Morrow.

Fisher, Mary Ann. 1916. *Among the Immortals, in the Land of Desire: A Glimpse of the Beyond.* New York: Shakespeare.

Flexner, Eleanor. 1971. *Century of Struggle.* New York: Atheneum.

Ford, Mary H. 1889. "A Feminine Iconoclast." *Nationalist,* November, 252–57.

Foucault, Michel. 1970. *The Order of Things: An Archeology of Human Sciences.* New York: Pantheon.

Franklin, Penelope, ed. 1986. *Private Pages: Diaries of American Women, 1830s–1970s.* New York: Ballantine.

Fraser, Antonia. 1984. *The Weaker Vessel: Women's Lot in Seventeenth Century England.* London: Weidenfield and Nicolson.

Fraser, Flora. 1987. *The English Gentlewoman.* London: Barrie and Jenkins.

Freeman, Ruth Ellis. 1891. "Tales of a Great-Grandmother." *New Nation* 1 (15 August, 5 September, 3 October): 458–60, 505–7, 569–77.

Friebert, Lucy. 1983. "World Views in Utopian Novels by Women." *Journal of Popular Culture* 17:49–60.

Fromm, Erich. 1962. Introduction to *Looking Backward, 2000–1887,* by Edward Bellamy, v–xxii. New York: Signet.

Fulford, Robert. 1957. *Votes for Women: The Story of a Struggle.* London: Faber and Faber.

Fuller, Margaret. [1855] 1971. *Woman in the Nineteenth Century.* Reprint, New York: Norton.

Fussell, Paul. 1977. *The Great War and Modern Memory.* Oxford, England: Oxford University Press.

Gilbert, Sandra M., and Susan Gubar. 1984. *The Madwoman in the Attic.* New Haven, Conn.: Yale University Press.

Gilman, Charlotte Perkins. [1911] 1968. *Moving the Mountain.* Reprint, Westport, Conn.: Greenwood.

———. 1913. "Bee Wise." *Forerunner* 4, no. 7:169–73.

———. [1915] 1979. *Herland.* Ed. Ann Lane. Reprint, New York: Pantheon.

———. [1916] 1968. "With Her in Ourland." Reprint, Westport, Conn.: Greenwood.

Glyn, Alice Coralie. 1896. *A Woman of Tomorrow: A Tale of the Twentieth Century.* [London]: Women's Printing Society.

Godwin, Francis [Domingo Gonzales, pseud.]. 1638. *The Man in the Moone; or, A Discourse of a Voyage Thither.* London: John Norton.

Goodwin, Sarah Webster. 1990. "Knowing Better: Feminism and Utopian Discourse in *Pride and Prejudice, Villette,* and *Babette's Feast.*" In *Feminism, Utopia, and Narrative,* ed. Libby Falk Jones and Sarah Webster Goodwin, 1–20. Knoxville: University of Tennessee Press.

Graul, Rosa. [ca. 1897] ca. 1899. *Hilda's Home: A Story of Woman's Emancipation.* Reprint, Chicago: M. Harmon. Originally serialized in *Lucifer, the Light Bearer* 649:78–79 (chap. 30); 654:118–19, 655:126–27; 657:141–43; 658:150–51: 681:334.

Green, Harvey. 1983. *The Light of the Home.* New York: Pantheon.

Gresswell, Elsie Kay. 1935. *When Yvonne Was Dictator*. London: John Heritage.

Griffith, Mary. 1836. "Three Hundred Years Hence." In *Camperdown; or, News from Our Neighborhood: Being Sketches by the Author of "Our Neighborhood,"* 9–92. Philadelphia: Carey, Lea and Blanchard.

Gronlund, Lawrence. 1884. *The Coöperative Commonwealth in Its Outlines: An Exposition of Modern Socialism*. Boston: Lee and Shepard.

Guillory, John. 1993. *Cultural Capital: The Problem of Literary Canon Formation*. Chicago: University of Chicago Press.

Habermas, Jürgen. 1989. *The Structural Transformation of the Public Sphere: An Inquiry into a Category of Bourgeois Society*. Trans. Thomas Burger and Frederick Lawrence. Cambridge, Mass.: MIT Press.

Hale, Sarah Josepha Buell. 1853. *Liberia: or, Mr. Peyton's Experiments*. New York: Harper and Brothers.

Hall, Joseph. [1605] 1937. *The Discovery of a New World*. Reprint, Cambridge, Mass.: Harvard University Press.

Hamilton, Cicely Mary. [1922] 1928. *Theodore Savage: A Story of the Past or Future*. Reprint, New York: Charles Scribner's Sons. Originally titled *Lest Ye Die*.

————, and Christabel Marshall [Christopher Saint John, pseud.]. 1909. *How the Vote Was Won*. First performed at the Royal Theatre, London, 13 April. Chicago: Dramatic Publishing, 1910.

Hammerton, A. James. 1979. *Emigrant Gentlewomen: Genteel Poverty and Female Emigration, 1830–1914*. London: Croom Helm.

Harris, Barbara J. 1978. *Beyond Her Sphere: Women and the Professions in American History*. Westport, Conn.: Greenwood.

Harrison, Brian. 1978. *Separate Spheres: The Opposition to Women's Suffrage in Britain*. New York: Holmes and Meier.

Harrison, Eva. 1915. *Wireless Messages from Other Worlds*. London: L. N. Fowler.

Harsin, Jill. 1968. "Housework and Utopia: Women and the Owenite Socialist Communities." In *Women in Search of Utopia: Mavericks and Mythmakers*, ed. Ruby Rohrlich and Elaine Hoffman Baruch, 73–84. New York: Schocken.

Hawthorne, Nathaniel. 1852. *The Blithedale Romance*. Boston: Ticknor, Reed and Fields.

Haywood, Eliza Fowler. [1725] 1972. *Memoirs of a Certain Island Adjacent to Utopia, by a Celebrated Author of That Country*. Reprint, New York: Garland.

Hearn, Mary Ann [Marianne Farningham, pseud.]. 1892. *Nineteen Hundred? A Forecast and a Story*. London: James Clarke.

Helsinger, Elizabeth, Robin Lauterbach Sheets, and William Veeder. 1983. *The Woman Question*. 3 vols. New York: Garland.

Henley, Carra Depuy. 1891. *A Man from Mars*. Los Angeles: B. R. Baumgardt.

Herodotus. 1942. *The Persian Wars*. Trans. George Rawlinson. New York: Modern Library.

Hesiod. 1959. *The Works and Days. Theogony. The Shield of Herakles*. Trans. Richard Lattimore. Ann Arbor: University of Michigan Press.

Hobbes, Thomas. [1651] 1983. "De Cive." In *The Clarendon Edition of the Philosophical Works of Thomas Hobbes*, 3 vols., ed. Howard Warrender. Oxford, England: Clarendon.

Howells, William Dean. 1894. *The Traveler from Altruria*. New York: Harper and Brothers.

Howland, Marie Stevens Case. [1874] 1975. *Papa's Own Girl*. Reprint, Philadelphia: Porcupine.

Huxley, Aldous. 1932. *Brave New World*. New York: Doubleday.

Hyam, Ronald. 1976. *Britain's Imperial Century, 1815–1914: A Study of Empire and Expansion*. New York: Barnes and Noble.

Jackson, Rosemary. 1989. Introduction to *What Did Miss Darrington See? An Anthology of Feminist Supernatural Fiction*, xv–xxxv. New York: Feminist Press (CUNY).

Jensen, Joan, and Lois Scharf. 1983. *Decades of Discontent: The Women's Movement, 1920–1940*. Westport, Conn.: Greenwood.

Johnson, J. W. 1968. "Prehistoric Myths." In *Utopian Literature: A Selection*, ed. J. W. Johnson, 3–5. New York: Modern Library.

Johnson, Samuel. [1759] 1977. *The History of Rasselas, Prince of Abyssinia*. In *Samuel Johnson: Selected Poetry and Prose*, ed. Frank Brady and W. K. Wimsatt, 73–153. Berkeley: University of California Press.

———. [1765] 1977. "Preface to Shakespeare." In *Critical Theory since Plato*, ed. Hazard Adams, 329–36. New York: Harcourt Brace Jovanovich.

Jones, Alice Ilgenfritz, and Ella Merchant [Two Women of the West, pseud.]. 1893. *Unveiling a Parallel: A Romance*. Boston: Arena.

Julian of Norwich. 1978. *A Book of Showings to the Anchoress Julian of Norwich*. 2 vols. Ed. Edmund Colledge and James Walsh. Toronto: Pontifical Institute of Mediæval Studies.

Keinhorst, Annette. 1987. "Emancipatory Projection: An Introduction to Women's Critical Utopias." *Women's Studies* 14:91–99.

Kent, Edward. [1848] 1971. "The Vision of Bangor in the Twentieth Century." In *American Utopias*, ed. Arthur O. Lewis, Jr., 61–73. New York: Arno Press and the New York Times.

Kessler, Carol Farley. 1984. *Daring to Dream: Utopian Stories by United States Women, 1836–1919*. Boston: Pandora.

———. 1985. "Notes toward a Bibliography: Women's Utopian Writing, 1836–1899." *Legacy* 2, no. 2:67–71.

———. 1990. "Bibliography of Utopian Fiction by United States Women, 1836–1988." *Utopian Studies* 1, no. 1:1–58.

Khanna, Lee Cullen. 1968. "Change and Art in Women's Worlds: Doris Lessing's *Canopus in Argos: Archives*." In *Women in Search of Utopia: Mavericks and Mythmakers*, ed. Ruby Rohrlich and Elaine Hoffman Baruch, 269–79. New York: Schocken.

———. 1984. "Frontiers of Imagination: Feminist Worlds." *Women's Studies International Forum* 7, no. 2:97–102.

Kingscote, Adelina Georgina Isabel Wolff [Lucas Cleeve, pseud.]. 1908. *A Woman's Aye and Nay*. London: John Long.

Kinnard, Cynthia D. 1986. *Antifeminism in American Thought: An Annotated Bibliography*. Boston: G. K. Hall.

Knapp, Adeline. 1894. "One Thousand Dollars a Day: A Financial Experiment." In *One Thousand Dollars a Day: Studies in Practical Economics*, 11–41. Boston: Arena.

Knight, Anne. [1847] 1902. "Women's Suffrage." In *Women's Suffrage*, ed. Helen Blackburn, 19. London: Williams and Norgate.

Knight, Ellis Cornelia. [1790] 1993. *Dinarbas: A Tale, Being a Continuation of Rasselas, Prince of Abyssinia*. Ed. Ann Messenger. Reprint, East Lansing, Mich.: Colleagues Press.

Kolmerten, Carol A. 1990. *Women in Utopia: The Ideology of Gender in the American Owenite Communities*. Bloomington: Indiana University Press.

————, ed. 1990. *Unveiling a Parallel: A Romance,* by Alice Ilgenfritz Jones and Ella Merchant. Syracuse, N.Y.: Syracuse University Press.

Kolodny, Annette. 1975. *The Lay of the Land.* Chapel Hill: University of North Carolina Press.

Kumar, Krishan. 1987. *Utopia and Anti-Utopia in Modern Times.* Oxford, England: Basil Blackwell.

Landes, Joan B. 1988. *Women and the Public Sphere in the Age of the French Revolution.* Ithaca, N.Y.: Cornell University Press.

Lane, Mary E. Bradley. [1880–81] 1889. *Mizora: A Prophecy: A Mss. Found among the Private Papers of the Princess Vera Zarovitch, Being a true and faithful account of her journey to the interior of the earth, with a careful description of the country and its inhabitants, their customs, manners and government.* Reprint, New York: G. W. Dillingham.

Lee, John D. 1955. *A Mormon Chronicle: The Diaries of John D. Lee, 1848–1876.* 2 vols. Ed. Robert Cleland and Juanita Brooks. San Marino, Calif.: Huntington Library.

Lem, Stanislaw. 1974. *The Futurological Congress.* New York: Harcourt Brace Jovanovich.

Levin, Ira. 1978. *The Stepford Wives.* London: Signet.

Lewes, Darby. 1989. "Gynotopia: A Checklist of Nineteenth-Century Utopias by American Women." *Legacy* 6, no. 2:29–41.

————. 1993. "Nudes from Nowhere: Pornography, Empire, and Utopia." *Utopian Studies* 4, no. 2:66–73.

Locke, John. [1690] 1969. "The Second Treatise of Civil Government." In *Two Treatises of Government,* ed. Thomas I. Cook, 121–247. New York: Hafner.

Loudon, Jane Webb. 1827. *The Mummy! A Tale of the Twenty-Second Century.* London: Henry Colburn.

Lucian of Samosata. 1953. *A True Story.* In *Lucian,* 8 vols., trans. A. M. Harmon, 1:247–357. Cambridge, Mass.: Harvard University Press.

Lupton, Thomas. 1580. *Siuqila. Too good, to be true: omen. Though so at a vewe, yet all that I tolde you, is true, I upholde you: now cease to aske why for I can not lye. Herein is shewed by waye of dialogue, the wonderfull maners of the people of Mauqsun, with other talke not frivolous.* London: Henrie Bynneman.

Luria, Gina. 1974. *The Feminist Controversy in England, 1788–1810.* New York: Garland.

Lyttelton, George, Baron. 1776. "Advice to a Lady." In *The Works of George Lord Lyttelton.* 3 vols. London: J. Dodsley.

Manley, Mary de la Rivière. 1709. *Secret Memoirs and Morals of Several Persons of Quality of Both Sexes, from the New Atalantis, an Isle in the Mediterranean.* London: John Morphew and J. Woodward.

Manuel, Frank E., and Fritzie P. 1979. *Utopian Thought in the Western World.* Cambridge, Mass.: Harvard University Press.

Marshall, Christabel [Christopher St. John, pseud.], and Charles Thursby. 1911. *Coronation.* London: International Suffrage Shop.

Martin, Nettie Parrish. 1908. *A Pilgrim's Progress in Other Worlds: Recounting the Wonderful Adventures of Ulysum Storries and His Discovery of the Lost Star "Eden."* Boston: Mayhew.

Martineau, Harriet. [1837] 1966. *Society in America.* 2 vols. New York: AMS.

————. 1845. *Dawn Island: A Tale.* Manchester, England: J. Gadsby.

Mason, Caroline Atwater. 1900. *A Woman of Yesterday.* New York: Doubleday, Page.

Mason, Eveleen Laura Knaggs. 1889. *Hiero-Salem: The Vision of Peace.* Boston: J. G. Cupples.

————. 1898. *An Episode in the Doings of the Dualized.* Boston: Press of Fish and Libby; Brookline, Mass.: E. L. Mason.

McGlasson [Brodhead], Eva Wilder. 1891. *Diana's Livery.* New York: Harper and Brothers.

Mead, Lucia True Ames. 1889. *Memoirs of a Millionaire.* Boston: Houghton Mifflin.

Mears, Amelia Garland. 1895. *Mercia, the Astronomer Royal: A Romance.* London: Simpkin, Marshall, Hamilton, Kent.

Mellor, Anne K. 1982. "On Feminist Utopias." *Women's Studies* 9:241–62.

Mill, John Stuart. [1869] 1985. "The Subjection of Women." In *John Stuart Mill: Three Essays,* 427–548. Oxford, England: Oxford University Press.

Milton, John. [1667] 1983. *Paradise Lost.* In *John Milton: Complete Poems and Major Prose,* ed. Merritt Y. Hughes, 207–469. Indianapolis: Bobbs-Merrill.

Minnett, Cora. 1911. *The Day after Tomorrow.* London: F. V. White.

Montaigne, Michel de. [1580] 1965. "Des Cannibales." In *Les Essais de Michel de Montaigne,* 202–17. Paris: Presses Universitaires de France.

Montpensier, Anne Mary Louisa d'Orleans, Duchesse de. 1659. *La Relation de L'Isle Imaginaire, et l'histoire de la Princesse de Paphlagonie.* Bordeaux: [Jean Regnauld Segrais].

Moore, M. Louise [An Untrammeled Freethinker, pseud.]. 1892. *Al-Modad; or, Life Scenes beyond the Polar Circumflex, a Religio-scientific Solution of the Problems of Present and Future Life.* Shell Bank, Cameron Parish, La.: M. L. Moore and M. Beauchamp.

More, Hannah. 1799. *Strictures on the Modern System of Female Education.* 2 vols. London: T. Cadell, Jr., and W. Davies.

More, Thomas. [1516] 1975. *Concerning the Best State of a Commonwealth and the New Island of Utopia.* Ed. Robert M. Adams. Norton Critical Edition. Reprint, New York: Norton.

Morris, William. [1890] 1920. *News from Nowhere; or, An Epoch of Rest.* Reprint, London: Longmans, Green.

Morson, Gary Saul. 1981. *The Boundaries of Utopia.* Austin: University of Texas Press.

Mulvey, Laura. 1975. "Visual Pleasure and Narrative Cinema." *Screen* 16, no. 3:6–18.

Mumford, Lewis. 1941. *The Story of Utopias.* New York: Peter Smith.

Murray, Janet Horowitz. 1982. *Strong-Minded Women, and Other Lost Voices from Nineteenth-Century England.* New York: Pantheon.

Nichol, C. A. Scrymsour, Mrs. 1908. *The Mystery of the North Pole.* London: Francis Griffiths.

Nordhoff, Charles. 1875. *The Communistic Societies of the United States, from Personal Visit and Observation.* New York: Harper and Brothers.

Orpen, Adela Elizabeth Rogers. 1897. *Perfection City.* New York: D. Appleton; London: Hutchinson.

Orwell, George. 1949. *1984.* London: Secker and Warburg.

Owen, Robert. 1831. *Outline of the Rational System of Society, Founded on Demonstrable Facts Developing the Constitution and Laws of Human Nature. Being the only effectual remedy for the evils experienced by the population of the world: the immediate adoption of which would tranquilize the present agitated state of society, and relieve it from moral and physical evil, by removing the causes which produce them.* London: Bradbury and Evans.

Patai, Daphne. 1981. "British and American Utopias by Women (1836–1979)." *Alternative Futures: The Journal of Utopian Studies* 2–3:184–206.

Pearson, Carol. [1977] 1981. "Coming Home: Four Feminist Utopias and Patriarchal Experience." Reprint, in *Future Females: A Critical Anthology,* ed. Marleen Barr. Bowling Green, Ohio: Bowling Green University Press.

Perkins, A. J. G., and Theresa Wolfson. 1939. *Frances Wright, Free Enquirer.* New York: Harper and Brothers.

Pfaelzer, Jean. 1983. "A State of One's Own: Feminism as Ideology in American Utopias, 1880–1915." *Extrapolation* 24, no. 4:311–28.

Phelps [Ward], Elizabeth Stuart. 1879. *An Old Maid's Paradise.* Boston: Houghton, Osgood; London: James Clarke.

———. 1886. *Burglars in Paradise.* Boston: Houghton Mifflin.

Phillips, John. 1984. *Eve: The History of an Idea.* San Francisco: Harper and Row.

Piercy, Marge. 1976. *Woman on the Edge of Time.* New York: Ballantine.

Pittock, M. A. Weeks, Mrs. 1890. *The God of Civilization: A Romance.* Chicago: Eureka.

Plato. 1955. *The Republic.* Trans. Benjamin Jowett. New York: Vintage Books.

Pope, Alexander. [1714] 1967. "The Rape of the Lock: An Heroi-Comical Poem." In *Pope: Poetical Works,* ed. Herbert Davis, 88–109. London: Oxford University Press.

Quennell, Peter. 1949. *John Ruskin: The Portrait of a Prophet.* London: Collins.

Quissell, Barbara. 1981. "The New World That Eve Made." In *America As Utopia,* ed. Kenneth M. Roemer, 148–74. New York: Franklin.

Radamacher, Hanna Leuchs. 1920. *Utopia: Ein heiteres Spiel in drei Aufzügen.* Dresden and Dusseldorf.

Rand, Ayn. 1938. *Anthem.* London: Cassell.

Rendall, Jane. 1984. *The Origins of Modern Feminism: Women in Britain, France, and the United States, 1780–1860.* New York: Schocken.

Richardson, Samuel. [1747–48] 1985. *Clarissa; or, The History of a Young Lady.* Reprint, Middlesex, England: Penguin.

Riley, Glenda. 1981. *Frontierswomen: The Iowa Experience.* Ames: Iowa State University Press.

———. 1988. *The Female Frontier: A Comparative View of Women on the Prairie and the Plains.* Lawrence: University Press of Kansas.

Roemer, Kenneth M. 1976. *The Obsolete Necessity: America in Utopian Writings, 1888–1900.* Kent, Ohio: Kent State University Press.

Rogers, Bessie Story. 1905. *As It May Be: A Story of the Future.* London: John Long; Boston: Richard G. Badger, Gorham Press.

Rohrlich, Ruby. 1984. "The Shakers: Gender Equality in Hierarchy." In *Women in Search of Utopia: Mavericks and Mythmakers,* ed. Ruby Rohrlich and Elaine Hoffman Baruch, 54–61. New York: Schocken.

Rosenberg, John D. 1985. *Carlyle and the Burden of History.* Cambridge, Mass.: Harvard University Press.

Rossi, Alice, ed. 1971. *The Feminist Papers: From Adams to De Beauvoir.* New York: Bantam.

Rothman, Sheila. 1978. *Women's Proper Place: A History of Changing Ideals and Practices, 1870 to the Present.* New York: Basic Books.

Rousseau, Jean Jacques. [1755] 1959. "Discours sur l'économie politique." In *Oeuvres Complètes de Jean-Jacques Rousseau,* 3:239–78. Paris: Gallimard.

———. [1762] 1966. *Émile.* Trans. William Boyd. Reprint, New York: Teacher's College Press.

Rover, Constance. 1967. *Women's Suffrage and Party Politics in Britain, 1866–1914.* London: Routledge and Kegan Paul.

————. 1970. *Love, Morals and the Feminists*. London: Routledge and Kegan Paul.

Sachs, Albie, and Joan Hoff Wilson. 1978. *Sexism and the Law*. New York: Macmillan.

Sargent, Lyman Tower. 1975. "An Ambiguous Legacy: The Role and Position of Women in the English Utopia." *Extrapolation* 16:137–48.

————. 1988. *British and American Utopian Literature, 1516–1985: An Annotated, Chronological Bibliography*. New York: Garland.

Schreiner, Olive. 1890. "Three Dreams in the Desert." In *Dreams*, 65–85. London: Unwin.

Scott, Sarah Robinson. [1762] 1986. *A Description of Millenium Hall, and the Country Adjacent*. Reprint, New York: Virago.

Shelhamer, Mary Theresa. 1885. *Life and Labor in the Spirit World, Being a Description of the Localities, Employments, Surroundings, and Conditions in the Spheres*. Boston: Colby and Rich.

Shelley, Mary Wollstonecraft. [1826] 1965. *The Last Man*. Reprint, Lincoln: University of Nebraska Press.

Short, Gertrude. 1949. *A Visitor from Venus*. New York: William Frederick.

Sidney, Sir Philip. [1590]. *The Countesse of Pembrokes Arcadia*. London: William Ponsonbie.

Snedeker, Caroline [Caroline Dale Owen, pseud.]. 1917. *Seth Way: A Romance of the New Harmony Community*. Boston: Houghton, Mifflin.

Spender, Dale. [1982] 1988. *Women of Ideas and What Men Have Done to Them*. Reprint, London: Pandora.

————. 1984. *Time and Tide Wait for No Man*. London: Pandora.

————, ed. 1987. *The Education Papers: Women's Quest for Equality in Britain, 1850–1912*. London: Routledge and Kegan Paul.

Spenser, Edmund. 1590, 1596. *The Faerie Queene*. London: William Ponsonbie.

Spotswood, Claire Myers. 1935. *The Unpredictable Adventure: A Comedy of Woman's Independence*. New York: Doubleday.

Stanton, Theodore, and Harriot Stanton Blatch, eds. 1922. *Elizabeth Cady Stanton, As Revealed in Her Letters, Diary and Reminiscences*. New York: Harper and Brothers.

Stone, C. H., Mrs. 1890. *One of "Berrian's" Novels*. New York: Welch, Fracker.

Strabo. 1924. *The Geography of Strabo*. 8 vols. Trans. Horace Leonard Jones. London: William Heinemann.

Stretzer, Thomas [Roger Pheuquewell, pseud.]. 1741. *A New Description of Merryland, Containing a Topographical, Geographical, and Natural History of That Country*. Bath, England: J. Leak and E. Curll.

Swift, Jonathan [Lemuel Gulliver, pseud.]. [1726] 1970. *Gulliver's Travels*. Ed. Robert A. Greenberg. Norton Critical Edition. Reprint, New York: Norton.

————. [1731] 1973. "A Beautiful Young Nymph Going to Bed." In *The Writings of Jonathan Swift*, ed. Robert A. Greenberg and William Bowman Piper, 538–40. Norton Critical Edition. New York: Norton.

Thomas, Bertha. 1873. "A Vision of Communism: A Grotesque." *Cornhill Magazine* 28 (September): 300–310.

Thompson, Paul. 1967. *The Work of William Morris*. New York: Viking.

Thompson, William. [1825] 1983. *Appeal of One Half the Human Race, Women, against the Pretensions of the Other Half, Men, to Retain Them in Political, and Thence in Civil and Domestic Slavery*. Reprint, London: Virago.

Thornton, A. P. 1965. *Doctrines of Imperialism*. New York: John Wiley and Sons.

Tickner, Lisa. 1988. *The Spectacle of Women*. Chicago: University of Chicago Press.

Trollope, Joanna. 1983. *Britannia's Daughters: Women of the British Empire*. London: Hutchinson.

Tocqueville, Alexis de. [1840] 1953. *Democracy in America*. 2 vols. Trans. Henry Reeve. Ed. Phillips Bradley. Reprint, New York: Alfred A Knopf.

Tompkins, Jane. 1985. *Sensational Designs: The Cultural Work of American Fiction, 1790–1860*. New York: Oxford University Press.

Tuchman, Gaye. 1989. *Edging Women Out*. New Haven, Conn.: Yale University Press.

Von Swartwout, Janet. 1895. *Heads; or, The City of Gods: A Narrative of Olombia in the Wilderness*. New York: Olombia.

Waisbrooker, Lois Nichols. [1894] 1985. *A Sex Revolution*. Ed. Pam McAllister. Reprint, Philadelphia: New Society.

Waterhouse, Elizabeth. 1887. *The Island of Anarchy: A Fragment of History in the 20th Century*. Reading, England: Miss Langley, Lovejoy's Library.

Weiss, Sara. 1903. *Journeys to the Planet Mars*. New York: Bradford.

Weisstein, Naomi. 1971. "Psychology Constructs the Female; or, The Fantasy Life of the Male Psychologist." In *From Feminism to Liberation*, ed. Edith Hoshino Altbach, 143–59. Cambridge, Mass.: Schenkman.

Wiggin, Kate Douglas Smith. 1909. *Susanna and Sue*. Boston: Houghton Mifflin.

Wilson, Abba Gould. 1874. *Dress-Reform*. Boston: Roberts.

Winslow, Helen Maria. 1893. *Salome Shepard, Reformer*. Boston: Arena.

Wollstonecraft, Mary. [1792] 1975. *A Vindication of the Rights of Woman*. Ed. Carol Poston. Norton Critical Edition. Reprint, New York: Norton.

Wood, J., Mrs. 1882. *Pantaletta: A Romance of Sheheland*. New York: American News.

Wright, Frances, Mme. D'Arusment. 1822. *A Few Days in Athens, Being the Translation of a Greek Manuscript Discovered in Herculaneum*. London: Longman, Hurst, Rees, Orme and Brown.

Wro[a]th, Mary Sidney, Lady. [1621] 1709. *The Countess of Mountgomeries Urania*. London: John Morphew and J. Woodward.

Young, Florence Ethel Mills. 1905. *The War of the Sexes*. London: John Long.

Yourell, Agnes Bond. 1891. *A Manless World*. New York: G. W. Dillingham.

Index

Darby Lewes
is an Assistant Professor of English at
Lycoming College in Williamsport, Pennsylvania.
She received her bachelor's degree from Saint Xavier University
in Chicago, her master's from Northwestern University, and her
doctorate from the University of Chicago.